ENTREPRENEURSHIP

JERRY W. MOORMAN

Assistant Vice President for Academic Affairs
and Associate Professor of Business
Mesa State College
Grand Junction, Colorado

JAMES W. HALLORAN

Director of the Small Business Development Center
Clayton State College
Morrow, Georgia

SOUTH-WESTERN PUBLISHING CO.

Cover Photo/Illustration: © Mike Wilson
Diana Fleming
Courtesy of TCBY
Federated Department Stores, Inc.

Page 41 Photo: Ralph Cowan/Tony Stone Worldwide/Click Chicago, LTD.

Managing Editor: Robert E. Lewis
Senior Developmental Editor: Willis S. Vincent
Editorial Production Manager: Carol Sturzenberger
Production Editor: Mark Cheatham
Senior Designer: Jim DeSollar
Production Artist: Sophia Renieris
Photo Researcher: Kimberly A. Larson
Associate Director/Photography: Diana W. Fleming
Assistant Photographer: Mimi Ostendorf
Marketing Manager: Donald H. Fox

ISBN: 0-538-61675-X

Library of Congress Catalog Card Number: 91-61649

3 4 5 6 7 8 9 D 99 98 97 96 95 94

Printed in the United States of America

PREFACE

What an exciting time to be embarking upon a career in business. At no time in recent history has the world market been in such a state of change. Eastern Europe and the states that once comprised the Soviet Union have made drastic changes in the way they conduct business. They have begun to embrace capitalism with vigor and anticipation. At the heart of that anticipation is the belief that individuals can own and operate their own businesses with success. This interest and belief in entrepreneurship is sweeping the world.

In the course of America's history as a free country, we can trace the country's phenomenal success to the spirit of individual entrepreneurs who were not afraid to strike out on their own in pursuit of business dreams. Large companies such as Xerox and Apple Computers began as dreams of individuals. From those small dreams grew large, successful corporations.

Entrepreneurs will mold the future business success of America, just as they have molded the past. As we race toward the year 2000, entrepreneurs will be blazing the trail through business innovation and creativity.

A BOOK FOR ENTREPRENEURS

Entrepreneurship is a resource designed and written with entrepreneurs in mind. It is written in simple and understandable language. All topics were carefully chosen with an eye toward presenting practical material for use in real entrepreneurial situations.

Both authors have extensive experience as small business consultants. The results of working with and advising hundreds of clients are reflected throughout the book. That experience combined with the latest learning theory has been used to create a text that is both technically accurate and educationally sound.

TEXT ORGANIZATION

Entrepreneurship is divided into six units. The topics are arranged so that readers encounter the steps to entrepreneurship in a logical order.

- Unit 1 serves as an introduction to and overview of entrepreneurship. It deals with the individual as an entrepreneur and presents an overview of the process necessary to plan small businesses.
- Unit 2 starts with getting to know your customers, followed by competition. An examination of location and facilities is followed by a detailed explanation for developing the marketing plan. The unit concludes with a discussion of pricing and sales planning.
- Unit 3 devotes itself to financing small business. Topics include initial capitalization and financial planning, personal finances, and analyzing financial sources.
- Unit 4 moves students into the management area of a new business. Four chapters cover the subjects of forms of ownership, personnel, management control, and sources of assistance for entrepreneurs.
- Unit 5, perhaps the most technical in nature, breaks down the legal requirements of entrepreneurship. Business law information that will be of the most immediate need to entrepreneurs is presented. Topics include special regulations, contracts and agreements, buying and selling, and real property and insurance.
- Unit 6 moves into an examination of career opportunities in entrepreneurship. It examines purchasing existing businesses and franchises. The final chapter of the unit—and the last in the text— discusses current and future trends in entrepreneurial opportunities.

Each chapter in the text opens with chapter objectives followed by a chapter introduction. Following the body of narrative in each chapter is a section called "Jeff Burnett—Entrepreneur." In this section, a fictional entrepreneur named Jeff Burnett applies the knowledge learned from that specific chapter. As you will see, sometimes he is successful and sometimes he makes mistakes. Other end-of-chapter features include the Summary, Vocabulary Builder, Review Questions, Discussion Questions, Critical Thinking exercise, Short Case, and Project Challenge. Project Challenge is designed to allow each student to apply the chapter information toward the completion of a hypothetical entrepreneurial venture of his or her own choosing.

In addition to the text, the authors have developed a *Student Workbook* (stock no. GV02AD) that reinforces the text material. There is also a *Teacher's Manual* (stock no. GV02AX), which includes a teaching outline, a matrix that correlates chapter activities to objectives, teaching suggestions, and transparency masters. The *Teacher's Manual* also includes answers to the textbook, test, and workbook questions. A *Test Bank* (stock no. GVO2AG) is provided, which includes questions for each chapter as well as a pretest and a final exam. And a MicroExam is available, providing another method of checking comprehension.

Jerry W. Moorman
James W. Halloran

CONTENTS

UNIT 3   FINANCING THE SMALL BUSINESS

UNIT 4   MANAGING THE SMALL BUSINESS

UNIT 1

ENTREPRENEURSHIP AND YOU

1

You as an Entrepreneur

After mastering the information contained in this chapter, you should be able to:

1-1 Describe the nature of entrepreneurship.

1-2 Define what it takes to be a successful entrepreneur.

1-3 Explain why individuals decide to become entrepreneurs.

1-4 Explain the importance of choosing the right environment in which to work.

1-5 Describe how to explore possibilities that might lead to becoming an entrepreneur.

entrepreneurship, the act of managing an enterprise that has the potential to make a profit or incur a loss.

entrepreneur, an individual who is willing to take the risk of investing time and money in a business that has the potential to make a profit or incur a loss

WHAT IS AN ENTREPRENEUR?

Did you know that if you operated a lemonade stand as a child you were an entrepreneur? You took the risk that you could sell enough servings to pay for the lemonade, cups, and sugar, and generate additional income to compensate yourself for the time you spent setting up the stand and selling the product. Whether one is selling lemonade or starting a company that will research the cure for the common cold, the act of managing that enterprise is **entrepreneurship** and the individual is acting as an **entrepreneur.**

Illus. 1-1   If you operated a lemonade stand as a child, you were an entrepreneur.

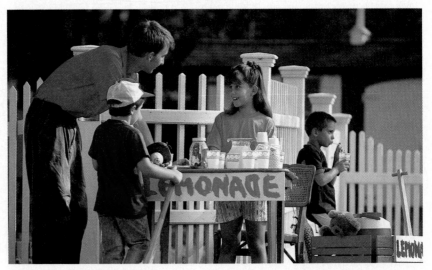

Gabe Palmer/The Stock Market

An entrepreneur is very simply an individual who is willing to risk investing time and money in a business activity that has the potential to make a profit or incur a loss. Entrepreneurs sense the needs of the marketplace and take risks to reach the goals that are important to them. Whether they start a business or create a new direction for a large organization, they are the innovators. Entrepreneurs make things happen.

Contribution to Our Economy

Entrepreneurs come from all types of backgrounds. There are no age barriers or educational requirements. The types of businesses that entrepreneurs create come in all shapes and sizes. They range from craft shops to consulting firms to construction companies.

Entrepreneurs are active in all classifications of business activity. Figure 1-1 illustrates the percentage of small businesses that exist in different categories. Entrepreneurs are the foundation of the small business sector of our country's economy. This sector accounts for more than half of the jobs in America and the majority of new product innovations. These

Figure 1-1 Small Businesses in Different Categories

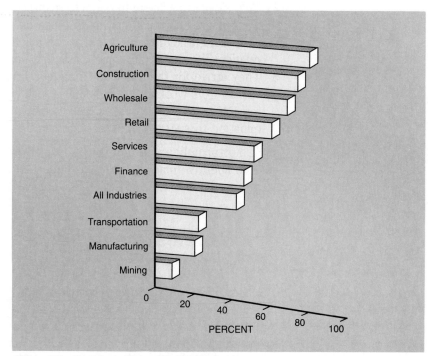

Office of the President, State of Small Business.

small business owners are essential to the economic strength of our country. It is important for us to understand these risk-takers and what makes them successful.

Why Become an Entrepreneur?

Individuals who venture out on their own into the marketplace as entrepreneurs do so for a combination of three reasons:

1. They desire to control their own destinies. This desire brings about the greatest benefits and is often the greatest motivator. As small business owners, individuals control how they wish to run their personal lives. Entrepreneurs plan their own business activities. They schedule their professional responsibilities and duties around their personal priorities. Entrepreneurs are not told when they must go to meetings at the expense of missing important events in their personal lives, such as a child's school play or a family reunion. Entrepreneurs make these types of decisions based on how important they feel a business activity is and not on how important anyone else believes it is. This right is the greatest reward of entrepreneurship.
2. They desire to achieve freedom from direct supervision of a boss. Entrepreneurs still must answer to those on whom they depend, such as bankers, landlords, suppliers, or possibly franchisors; however, these relationships are on an equal basis and not a subordinate one.
3. They strive for the potential to achieve profits greater than a salary earned from working for someone else. This is the hardest objective to achieve and usually takes the longest to accomplish. If the determination to succeed is present, it can be a reachable goal.

Unfortunately, more new small businesses fail than succeed in our very competitive marketplace. It is important for us to understand why some succeed while others fail. (See Figure 1-2.)

CHARACTERISTICS OF SUCCESSFUL ENTREPRENEURS

Small Business Administration, a federal agency created to assist the development of the country's small business sector

The **Small Business Administration** (SBA), a federal agency created to assist the development of the country's small business sector, reports that 24 out of every 100 businesses starting out today will be closed in two years. An additional 27 will close within four years. Within six years, more than 60 will shut down. It is very difficult to succeed as a small

Figure 1-2   *Small Business Start-ups and Failures*

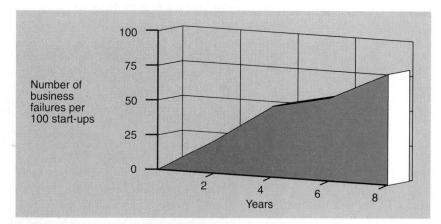

Source: Small Business Administration

business owner. Those who do should be commended for beating the odds. The entrepreneurs who head these businesses will have succeeded because they probably had good business plans, and because they possess the unique individual characteristics needed to overcome the obstacles encountered along the way.

A business plan is a written description of all the steps necessary to ensure success in opening and operating a business. Creating a business plan will be discussed at length as you proceed through the textbook.

Necessary Characteristics

The necessary personal characteristics of successful entrepreneurs are as follows:

1. Entrepreneurs must possess the confidence to make decisions. Small business owners cannot "pass the buck." They make the decisions that will determine success or failure. Decisions are usually made without the advantage of a professional research staff or the numerous committees that are part of large corporations. Decision makers must be confident in their abilities. When a decision turns out to be wrong, entrepreneurs need the confidence to bounce back because they will immediately face another decision to make.
2. Entrepreneurs need to have determination and perseverance. Unfortunately, there will be times when things will look quite bleak. Entrepreneurs must be willing to persist until the objective is achieved. Too many businesses fail prematurely because the owner grows tired

Illus. 1-2   When customers are few, running a business takes perseverance and determination.

Jay Bachemin for SWP

of the struggle. Running a business is not easy and only the determined succeed.

3. Successful entrepreneurs should possess creativity. Why do some businesses selling the same product or service succeed while others do not? The successful entrepreneur is doing something better than the competition. A very competitive marketplace is dominated by those who can think and move quickly to attract customers.

4. Successful entrepreneurs have a need to achieve. They are constantly setting new goals. The challenge of attaining those goals is fun for them. Very wealthy entrepreneurs do not need to continue to expand their businesses or earn more money for financial reasons—they get most of their satisfaction from achieving goals they have set.

Questions to Ponder

To determine if the ingredients previously described are part of his or her character, an aspiring entrepreneur can do a self-analysis by answering the following questions.

1. Do you give up on your favorite football team when it is two touchdowns behind with five minutes left to play? Determined entrepreneurs do not give up easily.

2. If you see a stream, are you curious as to where it started and where it ends? Entrepreneurs are constantly looking for answers and information. Entrepreneurs are curious and ask questions. It is part of the creative process.

3. Do people look to you for leadership in critical times? As a small business owner, the entrepreneur is the captain, leader, and motivator at all times. These responsibilities require self-confidence.

4. Are you constantly resetting your goals in building toward a long-term objective? Always reaching for new heights means achieving goals and striving for others.

5. Do you consult others for most decisions? Successful entrepreneurs must have the confidence to make decisions on their own.

6. Do you tend to be a daydreamer? Entrepreneurs are dreamers. Their dreams motivate them and produce creative energy. However, dreams must be based on a sense of reality.

7. Do routine chores cause you to be restless? Entrepreneurs are action-oriented goal-seekers. Sometimes it is difficult for them to do the necessary, routine aspects of their jobs.

8. Are you stubborn? A certain amount of stubbornness comes from determination. Be stubborn, but also be sensible.

9. Do you like yourself? Confidence comes from within the individual. Good leadership stems from self-assuredness.

10. Is making money your only goal in starting a business? The satisfaction of doing things on your own should rank higher than making money.

WORKING IN THE RIGHT ENVIRONMENT

Success as an entrepreneur requires being committed to a business or an idea. Commitment involves long hours and an abundance of energy. If entrepreneurs work in the wrong field, they will not be able to make the necessary commitment over the long haul. As individuals, we strive to reach our potential. Since self-employed people are working toward their own goals, as opposed to someone else's goals, they are more likely to reach their potential.

Goal-setting in an environment you enjoy is stimulating and exciting. Since the choice of a vocation represents a great commitment on the part of the entrepreneur, it must be in a field of interest and enjoyment. The choice of a vocation should not be made without considering past experiences that were meaningful and fulfilling. An administrator who was restless while working behind a desk, but enjoyed working with people, needs to think about that reality before considering opening a business that would confine his or her activities to an office. Analyzing past experiences gives the entrepreneur an idea of the experiences that will most likely bring personal satisfaction.

Career Anchors

career anchors, essential satisfiers we wish to achieve from our work

Dr. Edgar Schein of M.I.T. University has identified five **career anchors**—technical, managerial, security, creativity, and autonomy. Within these five anchors, he identified vocational choices. Anchors refer to the important motivators within us. These anchors help us to make choices, determine directions, pursue ambitions, and measure success. They help determine business choices and also influence job changes.

technical anchor, trait that allows individuals to derive satisfaction from doing a specific job correctly

An individual with a **technical anchor** gains satisfaction from being able to do a specific job correctly. People with technical anchors might be technicians, surgeons, or any other kind of specialist. Such individuals are not as concerned with titles and promotions as much as with being considered experts in their fields. These people should seek self-employment in areas that allow them to concentrate on a specific mission. Automobile mechanics, computer-repair shop owners, hobby shop owners, and small technology manufacturers are examples of entrepreneurs who work at specific job pursuits.

Illus. 1-3   An individual with a technical anchor gains satisfaction from doing a specific job correctly.

Robert Llewellyn/Superstock

managerial anchor, trait that allows individuals to be satisfied by working with and through people and by assuming many duties and responsibilities

security anchor, trait that allows individuals to be satisfied by working in a large organization with the assurance of long-term employment

creativity anchor, trait that allows individuals to derive satisfaction from coming up with unique ideas

autonomy anchor, trait that allows individuals to be satisfied by being free thinkers and individualists

Individuals with a **managerial anchor** are generalists as opposed to specialists. They enjoy working with people. They are able to handle many duties and responsibilities. As entrepreneurs, they do well in businesses with multiple outlets, or in businesses producing and selling many products. Chain store owners and manufacturers who produce many types of products are examples of entrepreneurs with managerial anchors.

People with a **security anchor** are generally not equipped to handle the risks of self-employment. They are content to work in large organizational environments that offer regular paychecks, company benefit programs, and the assurance of long-term employment. Purchasing and managing a well-established franchise, such as MacDonald's or Pizza Hut, or an existing successful business might appeal to a person with this type of anchor; however, these types of firms are expensive to acquire because they have proven to be successful. The initial risk was taken by someone else who is entitled to additional compensation for successfully developing the franchise or business. When establishing a new business, there is little in the way of security.

Individuals with a **creativity anchor** enjoy coming up with unique ideas. They do not like routine tasks and are constantly looking for new ways of doing things. They are often successful as small business owners because they are able to devise better ways to sell products or services. People with creativity anchors should be wary of business opportunities that depend principally on administrative talents. These types of people excel in promotion-minded businesses, such as advertising agencies, and also in retail merchandising.

People with an **autonomy anchor** are free thinkers and individualists. They are seldom concerned with security. They have a natural aptitude for starting small businesses; however, they sometimes do not have the patience and endurance needed to stick with it. Individuals with autonomy anchors like to do things their own way with little interference from others. Inventors, writers, and artists are examples of this anchor classification.

Sample Career Anchor Questions

To help you determine what your career anchors are, a list of questions follows. Answering these questions truthfully and realistically can help lead you to the work environment that is right for you.

1. What are your greatest career aspirations?
2. What kinds of changes in your work responsibilities do you enjoy the most?

3. When have you particularly enjoyed your work?
4. What do you dislike about your work?
5. Is it important for you to receive recognition?
6. When do you feel the most fulfillment from your work?
7. How would you describe your career ambitions?
8. What is most important to you when you seek your first job after graduation?
9. What strategy will you use in attaining job progression?
10. What characteristics of a career are most important to you?

Values, Attitude, Needs, Expectations

The ultimate goal of all entrepreneurs should be to match their values, attitudes, needs, and expectations with a business opportunity. This process is referred to by the acronym **VANE**, which is derived from the initial letter of each term—values, attitudes, needs, expectations.

VANE, acronym for values, attitudes, needs, expectations

Values are the intangible beliefs and inner convictions that we hold dearly. Attitudes refer to how we feel about something. Needs are the tangibles (the things we see) and intangibles (the things we feel) that we must have to live an acceptable lifestyle. Expectations are the minimum goals that we attempt to achieve.

Aspiring entrepreneurs who have given thoughtful analysis to their values, attitudes, needs, and expectations will feel confident that they are personally prepared for the challenge ahead of them. If equipped with a proper business plan, they have greatly enhanced their chances for a successful business.

SETTING PERSONAL GOALS

Once career values, attitudes, needs, and expectations are determined, aspiring entrepreneurs need to look specifically at what business they should enter. Having acknowledged that goal-oriented individuals make successful entrepreneurs, it is important that the goal-setting starts with stating the priorities in their personal lives.

Making Choices

An aspiring entrepreneur must establish personal goals with respect to income, personal satisfaction, and status.

Income. In setting realistic goals concerning income level, the new business owner must be aware that there is initially a direct correlation between how much money and time is invested and how much potential profit there is. Over a period of time, the experience, perseverance, and creativity of the owner will determine profits. For instance, in most retail and service businesses, the owner will do well to make a profit of 20 percent of total, or gross, sales. To make a profit of $40,000 per year, the business must generate annual sales of $200,000. If $40,000 is the profit goal, enough money must be invested in inventory, fixtures, and equipment to guarantee sales of $200,000. If some of the initial money is borrowed, the interest and principal to be paid back must come from the $40,000 profit.

Quite often you hear that it takes five years to get a business on its feet. Five years is the most commonly used payoff period on a new business loan. Until the initial debt is paid, there is seldom much extra income available for the owner. For example, an entrepreneur starts a business that requires an investment of $100,000. The owner has $50,000 and borrows $50,000 from the bank and promises to pay the loan back over five years. The first year, the business may sell $200,000 in goods and make a profit of $40,000. The owner must pay the bank out of profits earned each year until the loan is paid off. The business's finances look like this after the first year:

Total investment	$100,000
Borrowed funds	50,000
Sales	200,000
Profit	40,000
Less principal and interest	−13,000
Available to owner (before taxes)	27,000

Because the owner is forced to borrow, he or she will not be able to realize the goal of a $40,000 personal profit until there is growth in sales or the debt is paid. In reality, the owner has invested $50,000 cash and given up a salary to make a risky $27,000 per year. Before a business can be declared a success, not only will the original debt have to be paid, but the owner should also have regained the original $50,000 investment. However, once the initial debt is paid and sales have increased, the profits can be generous enough to pay an attractive salary and show healthy retained earnings. **Retained earnings** are profits that remain in the business for either future use for business expansion or for distribution to the owner(s) as an investment payback. The investment payback is termed **return on investment.** In this case, the owner is to be paid back the $50,000 which was initially invested in the business. The same business five years later might look as follows:

retained earnings, profits that remain in a business for future use

return on investment, the payback of the money invested in a business operation

Sales	$350,000
Profit	70,000
Less principal and interest	−0
Available to owner	55,000
Retained earnings	15,000

Goal-setting with respect to income needs and expectations must be realistic concerning amount invested, returned, and future potential return. For example, business owners should not expect a 100 percent payback on their investment within one year. Entrepreneurs must realize they will have to make some financial sacrifices in their own lives and, as a result, may have to adjust their goals because of unexpected changes in the business's earnings.

Personal satisfaction.   When setting goals for personal satisfaction, entrepreneurs must state the goals they wish to attain in addition to making a profit. These goals are usually intangible and include such things as what they wish to contribute to society or family. People need to feel satisfied with what they do in this world. Working in a career that is personally rewarding greatly enhances the ability of a person to achieve satisfaction.

Status.   Declaring a status goal is an important process in determining the best business to enter. In the context of entrepreneurship, status refers to the respect a business owner receives based on how others feel about his or her business or vocation. The noted psychologist Dr. Abraham Maslow includes status, the need for respect from others, as a need we all share. Since businesses require so much personal input from entrepreneurs, it is important that they take great pride in their efforts. Recognition of accomplishments is an important motivation for many individuals.

Type of Work

After declaring personal goals, individuals should match the type of work that really excites them to their goals. These goals might include working with numbers, selling, office work, working with one's hands, working outdoors, or other preferences. A decision about work goals dictates what an individual's main occupation will be for at least eight hours per day, five days per week.

Another consideration is how a person feels about working with people. Would the individual rather work alone? How does the person feel about selling? Profits are generated by the exchange or sale of goods and services; therefore, selling is an important business function. Some

Illus. 1-4   This farmer likely chose his vocation because of a decision about work goals.

Photo Courtesy of New Idea, Coldwater, Ohio

entrepreneurs engage in direct, face-to-face selling with customers. Others assign this responsibility to someone else or choose a business in which selling can be handled in an impersonal manner, such as through the mail or over the telephone. In any selling situation, there will be interaction with employees, suppliers, and customers. Some businesses place more emphasis on one group than another. New business owners must decide on the selling environment in which they feel most comfortable.

The entrepreneur will have to decide the amount of time and involvement required in running a business. Is it to be a full-time endeavor, a part-time project, or possibly a business that will start small with the goal of growing into a full-time business? Small businesses offer all forms of arrangements, ranging from weekend or off-hours involvement to full-time management. Many operate under **absentee management** in which the owner oversees the business but is not present. Sometimes timing and the nature of the situation dictates the decision, as it did for Mary Lawrence.

absentee management, when a business owner oversees the business but is not present at the location

During Mary's maternity leave from her job as a school teacher, she had more time available to work on her favorite hobby, making custom jewelry for friends and acquaintances. Her creations were imaginative and were received very enthusiastically. The husband of one of her friends was a manufacturer's representative for some fashion clothing and accessory companies. After seeing Mary's work, he offered to take some samples with him to the fall fashion show at the Atlanta Apparel Mart to display to retailers. He returned with orders totaling more than $25,000. Mary had the start of a very prosperous full-time business, and eventually hired her husband on a full-time basis as well.

Many successful businesses start as part-time operations until sufficient demand for a product or service requires the owner to quit his or her regular employment.

Life-style

The life-style preferred by the entrepreneur should have a bearing on the type of business to open. Does the owner like to travel, work at night, entertain clients, or be entertained? As stated, small businesses come in all sizes and forms. Their owners can decide how they want to live. To many, the idea of controlling one's life-style is the greatest advantage and appeal of small business ownership. Starting a business is a declaration of independence.

Capabilities

The abilities and characteristics that the entrepreneur has developed are an important part of the decision-making process. Thought needs to be given to both the physical and psychological demands of any venture. A list should be made of the abilities that have been developed through education, career, hobbies, and interests.

Finally, what are the entrepreneur's financial capabilities? This question is usually the toughest to answer and represents the biggest obstacle to entrepreneurs. Care must be taken in determining how much money is available and how much the individual is willing to invest in a business. The degree of confidence in the business idea and how much risk the individual is willing to take will help determine the amountof investment required. Individuals should not risk everything in a new business venture. They also need to consider personal living expenses for themselves and their families. Tables 1-1 and 1-2 can serve as guides for aspiring entrepreneurs in evaluating business opportunities.

Table 1-1

GUIDE FOR SETTING PERSONAL GOALS

GOALS	**Income Needed** $_____ 1st year $_____ 2nd year $_____ 3rd year	**Personal Satisfaction Objective** *(Rank from 1 to 6)* _____ Recognition by others _____ Fame _____ Helping others _____ Expressing creativity _____ Expertness _____ Other	**Status Considerations** *(Rank from 1 to 4)* _____ Status in community _____ Feeling challenged _____ Personal growth potential _____ Expertness _____ Other
TYPE OF WORK DESIRED	**Type of Activity** *(Rank from 1 to 6)* _____ Sales _____ Clerical _____ Working with hands _____ Working outdoors _____ Freedom of movement _____ Technology	**People Contact** *(Rank from 1 to 5)* _____ Direct contact with customers _____ Indirect contact with customers _____ Frequent contact with suppliers _____ Close contact with personnel _____ Work alone	**Business Involvement** *(Rank from 1 to 5)* _____ Part-time _____ 8 hours per day, 5 days per week _____ 10 to 12 hours per day, 5 to 7 days per week _____ Weekends and off-time hours only _____ Absentee management
LIFE-STYLE	**Travel Desired** Example: 1 day a week? 1 week a month? _____ _____ _____	**Amount of Entertaining Involved** _____ _____ _____	**Community Involvement Desired** _____ _____ _____

(Table 1-1 continued)

PHYSICAL AND PSYCHOLOGICAL CAPABILITIES	Example: Age and Stamina _____ _____ _____ _____ _____ _____ _____
LEARNED ABILITIES	Example: Specialist, Generalist _____ _____ _____ _____ _____ _____
FINANCIAL CAPABILITIES	Example: How much money can you invest? Do you need matching funds? _____ _____ _____ _____ _____
RISK FACTOR CONSIDERATIONS	*(Circle One)* 1. High-risk, high-profit potential 2. Moderate risk factor, moderate profit potential 3. Lower risk factor, slower profit growth potential

Table 1-2   Determining Capital Available

ASSETS		LIABILITIES	
Cash on hand and in bank	$_____	Notes payable to bank	$_____
Government securities	$_____	Notes payable to others	$_____
Stocks and/or bonds	$_____	Accounts and bills due	$_____
Accounts and notes receivable	$_____		
Real estate owned		Real estate mortgage	
Home	$_____	Home	$_____
Auto	$_____	Other	$_____
Other	$_____	Other debts	$_____
Cash surrender value	$_____		
Life insurance	$_____		
TOTAL ASSETS	$_____	TOTAL LIABILITIES	$_____

NET WORTH CALCULATIONS

Total assets	$_____
Less total liabilities	$_____
Equals capital surplus	$_____
Amount of capital willing to risk	$_____

JEFF BURNETT—ENTREPRENEUR

To illustrate how a successful business is established, you will follow Jeff Burnett through every chapter in this text. You will learn of his successes and his mistakes in building his retail business.

After six months in the corporate world, Jeff Burnett was already fighting the routine. The thought, "How can people ride the same elevator at the same time, to the same place, day after day, year after year?" raced through his mind every morning and every evening as he went in and out of the corporate headquarters of a large petroleum company. Jeff was a typical recent college graduate out to conquer the world of big business. The only problem was that he didn't like it. He didn't like the routine, the rules, or the boss who would question his arrival time when it was 8:05 A.M. "I can't do it," he told his wife. "I need some independence."

One year later, he was a sales representative for a national distributor of records, tapes, and compact discs (CD's). This was more like it. He was in charge of his time and his schedule. He worked out of his house and saw his boss once a week. It was better, but some things bothered him. Sales meetings were called on short notice at the discretion of his boss. It didn't matter if they conflicted with personal events which had been planned long in advance. If his boss called, Jeff had to go.

The boss was demanding and unrelenting on the sales force, sometimes using unscrupulous methods to make sales quotas. Then, there was the evaluation when Jeff was told he had a poor attitude because he did not applaud after a slide presentation about the company executives. Jeff wondered, "Maybe I don't fit the corporate mold. Maybe instead of worrying about 50 retail accounts, I would be happier worrying about two or three of my own. The problems would be my problems, but the successes would be mine, too. No more routine, no more boss, just me. Yes, I am going to try it. I will own and run my own store. I can do it. I just need to find a way."

There was no doubt he had the right background. In three years of selling to the industry, he had learned a lot. He believed he could deal with the public. He was patient, not afraid to work hard, and possessed a business education. He would have to learn more about merchandising, but he believed that he was creative. He had enough confidence in himself to assume a reasonable risk and make decisions. His age, 29, was a plus because he was not tied into a pension plan and was not yet concerned about sending children through

Illus. 1-5 Entrepreneur Jeff Burnett decided he would like to buy or start a retail store offering records, tapes, and CD's.

Jay Bachemin for SWP

college. Desire, along with support from his wife, led Jeff to investigate retail opportunities. He decided he would buy or start a retail music store selling records, tapes, and CD's.

We will get to know Jeff as he proceeds step by step through his business plan. For now, we have determined Jeff's motivation. He wanted to be able to control his destiny. He was not happy working toward someone else's goals; he wished to work toward his own goals. He has picked the retail environment, which does indeed match his background and his personal characteristics. His career anchors show a strong managerial and creative orientation. The retail industry he is pursuing is of a general nature rather than highly technical. The retailing choice will allow him to use his creative abilities in product display, advertising, and buying. Jeff does not have a security anchor, as evidenced by his career path and ambitions to date. The choice of a well-established industry shows that he has a conservative side, which would not be indicative of people with autonomy anchors.

Jeff has now started down the path of entrepreneurship, and we will catch up with him in the next chapter as he starts to write out his plan of action.

CREATIVE ENTREPRENEURSHIP

To be an entrepreneur, we have learned that there are no requirements of age, education, or certification. So anyone with an idea, self-confidence, determination, creativity, and the need to achieve can be an entrepreneur. Sometimes special hobbies, skills, or talents give people ideas. Have you ever had an idea for a business or an invention that you wish you had investigated? Next time, don't stop with the idea—explore the possibilities as Tim Holton did.

Tim was 16 years old and a baseball card collector. His hobby was sometimes an annoyance to his mother, who often threatened to throw away his cards if he continued to leave them spread out on his bedroom floor. He shuddered to think of this possibility since he owned some cards that he knew would be of great value in the future. So, he took a poster-size sheet of green cardboard, drew a baseball diamond on it, and attached his cards to the positions on the diamond that the players had played. He made a number of these and proudly displayed them on his bedroom walls. Soon his friends were copying his idea. He wondered if he had stumbled upon an idea that, if produced, would sell.

Tim and his father, with the help of a design engineer at his father's plant, produced a thousand units for resale. The first production run cost $1,500. They purchased the necessary materials and proceeded to try to sell them through mail order advertising.

The first advertisement was a small 1-by-3 inch mail order advertisement in a national weekly sports publication, the *Sporting News*. The cost of the advertisement, $480, added to the production cost meant that they had more than $2,000 invested in the idea. Tim very nervously awaited the results. The day after the ad ran, Tim hurried to their rented post office box and was elated to find more than $600 in receipts and orders. More orders followed, and although the receipts were not enough to recover the total initial investment, he earned enough money to proceed with the idea. Other advertising media were used, and ideas such as wholesaling to retail collectors' stores were tried. Tim and his dad even visited a major league team in an unsuccessful effort to sell them on the idea of using the plaque as a promotional item at one of their games. Some ideas were successful and some were not. The product did eventually make some money, but the real value was the excitement it gave Tim. Through his initiative, he was able to conceive, develop, and market a product. His research showed that there were twenty million baseball card collectors in the United States alone. He dreamed of being able to sell to ten percent of that market and make huge profits. A simple idea devised to get Tim out of the doghouse with his mom resulted in a money-making venture. Whether the profits were great or small, Tim Holton experienced the challenge and the excitement of entrepreneurship. You can, too![1]

SUMMARY

Entrepreneurs are risk-takers who are able to sense the needs of the marketplace. They are often small business owners who are willing to invest their money, time, and abilities in pursuit of achieving profits at the risk of incurring losses. Entrepreneurs are also found in large organizations and businesses as the innovators of ideas. They possess the personal characteristics of self-confidence, determination, creativity, and the need to achieve.

It is important that these individuals work in environments that are personally satisfying to them so they work to their utmost potential. Their values, attitudes, needs, and expectations must match the goals they set out to accomplish.

It is mandatory that aspiring entrepreneurs write out a good business plan. The business plan will act as a guide to achieving objectives. The business plan must take into consideration personal goals with respect to income, personal satisfaction, status, work content, and life-style.

Entrepreneurship is available to anyone with the necessary personal characteristics to succeed in building a business.

VOCABULARY BUILDER

On a separate sheet of paper, write a brief definition of each word or phrase based on your reading of the chapter.

1. Entrepreneurship
2. Entrepreneur
3. Small Business Administration
4. Career anchors
5. Technical anchor
6. Managerial anchor
7. Security anchor
8. Creativity anchor
9. Autonomy anchor
10. VANE
11. Retained earnings
12. Return on investment
13. Absentee management

---

[1]Reprinted, with permission, from book #30049 *The Entrepreneur's Guide to Starting a Successful Business* by James W. Halloran. Copyright 1987 by Liberty Hall Press/TAB Books, a division of McGraw-Hill, Blue Ridge Summit, PA 17294 (1-800-233-1128 or 1-717-794-2191).

REVIEW QUESTIONS

1. Define the term *entrepreneur.*
2. Why do individuals become entrepreneurs?
3. What is the purpose of a business plan?
4. Recall the necessary characteristics of successful entrepreneurs.
5. Identify the five career anchors.
6. How does determining an individual's career anchor(s) help in deciding on a business endeavor?
7. Why is a security anchor not a good career anchor for an aspiring entrepreneur?
8. What is meant by values, attitudes, needs, and expectations as applied to entrepreneurship?
9. What personal goals should be addressed by individuals before opening a business?
10. Why does it normally take five years for a business to become successful?
11. Why is it important to calculate the return on investment of a business opportunity?
12. What determines how much money an entrepreneur should invest in a business opportunity?

DISCUSSION QUESTIONS

1. Why are entrepreneurs so vital to the economic well-being of our country?
2. How do the four essential characteristics of successful entrepreneurs relate to the reasons individuals open small businesses?
3. What is the importance of being in the right work environment?
4. Apply VANE analysis to choosing a business.
5. What is the danger of not considering return on investment in deciding on a business opportunity?

CRITICAL THINKING

Using an idea of your own, develop a scenario depicting yourself as an entrepreneur. What are the risks of the enterprise? What needs does the enterprise serve? What contribution to society would it make? What are its economic implications?

SHORT CASE: AIRPLANES VERSUS YOGURT

Woody Harmon had spent his entire career of 22 years as an airline pilot for a major commercial airline. Labor and management problems threatened to close the airline in 1989. He was too old to be a prime candidate for a position with another airline, and too young to retire. Woody knew he must prepare for a new career in case the company collapsed. It didn't take long. One of his friends, Isabel Lopez, was the owner of a local frozen yogurt store chain. "Great business, great profit potential, Woody, as long as you work hard and keep an eye on it." It sounded perfect to Woody. He spent a Saturday helping Isabel at one of the stores and excitedly reported to his wife, Ann, that he had found what he wanted to do. Ann worried about Woody's lack of business experience, but Woody insisted that it was right for him. She kept her fingers crossed that the airline would continue to fly.

It didn't, and Woody signed a three-year lease within two weeks of his final flight. He borrowed $75,000 on his house, and, with Isabel's help and advice, ordered all the equipment and frozen yogurt mix needed to open the store.

He absolutely hated the frozen yogurt business. Working seven days a week, confined to a small store, and supervising sales clerks was far from what he was interested in doing. Business started slowly, which further depressed him. He was making poor business decisions, was irritable at home, and couldn't sleep because he kept thinking of his large, sinking investment. He looked to the sky with every passing airplane. Why, he thought, had he ever thought he could be a retailer? He belonged in an airplane, not in a frozen yogurt store.[2]

Questions

1. What could have been done to prevent this situation?
2. What should Woody do now?

PROJECT CHALLENGE

As you proceed through the textbook you can start to write out a business plan for a hypothetical business of your choice. As you proceed, each chapter will give recommendations on each step. The challenge from this chapter is to determine what type of business you wish to investigate. Once you decide, write a paragraph describing why you have chosen that particular type of business.

---

[2]Case study entitled "Airplanes versus Yogurt" reprinted, with permission, from book #3511 *Why Entrepreneurs Fail: Avoid the 20 Pitfalls of Running Your Own Business* by James W. Halloran. Copyright 1991 by Liberty Hall Press/TAB Books, a division of McGraw-Hill, Blue Ridge Summit, PA 17294 (1-800-233-1128 or 1-717-794-2191).

2
Planning the Small Business

GETTING STARTED

Getting into business is much like going on a long journey. Both undertakings require time, effort, know-how, and a sense of adventure. Both are more enjoyable and rewarding if you know how to go, what to take along, how long it will last, and what to expect along the way. You may still encounter some surprises, but chances are you will be well prepared to deal with them.

Illus. 2-1   Starting a business is much like taking a long journey.

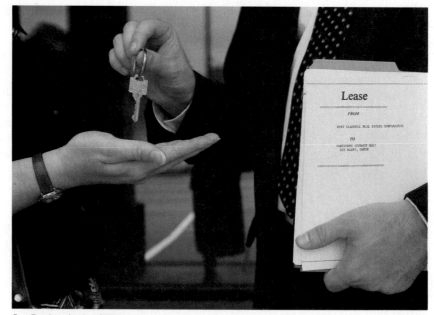

Jay Bachemin for SWP

24

PLANNING

Once aspiring entrepreneurs have identified a business idea that seems promising, they must begin preparing for the journey that will transform the idea into a business success. The key step in the preparations is planning. Planning is the systematic process of developing an outline for the accomplishment of a goal or set of goals. A well-prepared outline serves as a road map that guides the traveler to the desired destination.

Planning is one of the most important skills needed for starting a business. Whether the entrepreneur is going to start a new business, buy an established business, or purchase a franchise, good planning is the key to business success.

THE BUSINESS PLAN

business plan, a written description of all steps necessary to ensure success in opening and operating a business

A **business plan** serves as a manual to help the entrepreneur during the design and start-up phases of the business. It also states the entrepreneur's expectations, which serve as criteria by which business performance can be periodically evaluated. A good business plan is an ever-evolving resource that grows and changes with the business. As such, it should be consulted regularly and updated annually.

Many an entrepreneur has stumbled upon an idea that seems certain to be a success. It is tempting to skip the planning phase and jump right into business. After all, a day spent planning is a day without profit.

The considerations involved in starting and maintaining even the smallest business can be overwhelming. Neglecting even a minor detail may cause unnecessary aggravation and expense. Overlooking a major-detail may ultimately lead to business failure.

Writing a comprehensive business plan ensures that all of the details of the proposed business are addressed. It helps the entrepreneur avoid many of the pitfalls that can delay or prevent business success.

Many entrepreneurs have plenty of ideas but very little capital with which to start a business. Most of them have to go to a bank or other financial institution for a loan.

More than one-third of all banks require a written business plan before they will consider loaning money for a small business. Nine out of ten banks will probably require that the entrepreneur provide some form of written information about the new business venture.[1] A comprehensive

---

[1]Moorman, Jerry, "What Bankers Have to Say About Business Planning," *IDEAS For Marketing Educators,* March 1990, pp. 7–8.

*Illus. 2-2 More than one third of all banks require a written busi-
ness plan.*

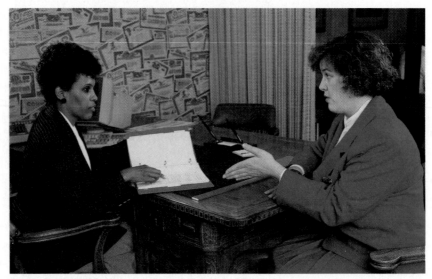

Jay Bachemin for SWP

and detailed business plan shows the bank that the entrepreneur has invested considerable time and effort in planning what will be a successful
business. Such a proposal is more likely to win the bank's support than
one that presents only sketchy details.

FORMULATING A BUSINESS PLAN

Below is an outline of a typical business plan. Several of the headings
on the outline may not be applicable to certain types of businesses. In
these cases the headings may be omitted from the business plan. Also,
the amount of information required under each heading will vary from
business to business.

1. Concept History and Background
    A. Description of Product or Service
    B. Idea History
    C. Summary of Experience
2. Goals and Objectives
3. Marketing Plan
    A. Consumers and Demand
    B. Competition

     C. Geographic Market

     D. Pricing Policy

  4. Legal Requirements

  5. Form of Ownership

  6. Financial Plan

     A. Initial Capitalization Plan

     B. Projected Income Statement

     C. Projected Operating Statement

     D. Cash Flow Projection

  7. Organization, Management, and Staffing Plan

     A. Organization Chart

     B. Employee Requirements

     C. Resumés

     D. Personal Financial Statements

     E. References

  8. Special Considerations

     A. Production and Manufacturing Needs

     B. Facility Needs

     C. Education and Training Needs

     D. Land and Utility Needs

     E. Research and Development

     F. Other

    The individual components of a business plan and how they are developed will be described in greater detail in later chapters. For the purpose of discussing the general principles of business planning, however, a brief description of each component and its importance in the planning process are covered here.

Concept History and Background

The first part of the business plan describes the business concept, how it was developed, and what qualifications the potential entrepreneur has for the intended business.

Description of Product or Service.   In the business plan the potential entrepreneur should describe in very specific terms the product or service that the business is going to offer. The description should point out how the product or service is different from or better than existing products or services. Such description aids in determining the feasibility of the proposed business.

Illus. 2-3 A business plan should describe the business concept, how it was developed, and the potential entrepreneur's qualifications.

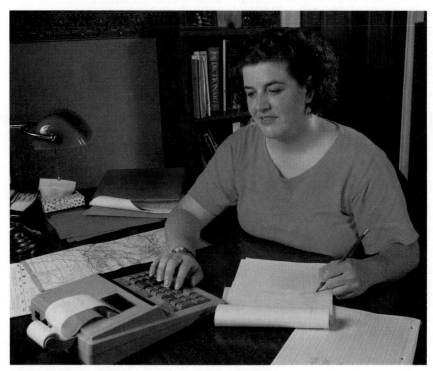

Jay Bachemin for SWP

Idea History. An idea history summarizes when, how, and why the potential entrepreneur developed the idea for the business. This component is important primarily during the loan application process. At least half of all bank loan officers require entrepreneurs to include an idea history in their business plans.[2]

Summary of Experience. Most banks consider a written summary of the entrepreneur's experience an essential component of the business plan. The summary should highlight practical exposure to the intended business. Relevant volunteer work and leisure pursuits, as well as paid employment, may have provided valuable experience that could be

---

[2]Moorman, Jerry, "What Bankers Have to Say About Business Planning," *IDEAS For Marketing Educators*, March 1990, pp. 7–8.

helpful in running the business. Such experience may greatly increase the business owner's chances of success both at the bank and in the marketplace.

Goals and Objectives

A goal can be defined as the overall end toward which one directs one's efforts. An objective is a specific result which is desired. For example, a well-defined goal should answer the question, "What do I want to achieve?" An objective must state what specific results one wishes to accomplish which will ultimately aid in reaching one's goal.

Goals and objectives are important because they provide direction and focus for your activities. How will you know where you are going unless you identify where you want to go? A high school football team might set a goal of becoming divisional champions this season. One of the objectives may be to win eight out of eight games. By setting the goal and several objectives, the team has established the direction it will take.

Goals and objectives work in much the same way for entrepreneurs by keeping business owners focused on what they are trying to achieve. Many entrepreneurial goals deal with profitability. Goals and objectives are also useful to banks because the lender must know the entrepreneur's intentions. More than two thirds of banks require written goals and objectives for at least the first year.[3] For this reason, entrepreneurs should be insightful, realistic, and concise when writing goals and objectives for the business plan.

Short-Term and Long-Term Goals

Entrepreneurs need to set both short- and long-term goals. A short-term goal is one that can be achieved in a short period of time, perhaps within several months or a year. A long-term goal is one that is to be achieved over a long period of time, such as a number of years. The entrepreneur should set short- and long-term goals concerning both financial and personal interests, always focusing on the ultimate goal of the business.

As an example, a short-term personal goal might sound like this: Work part time while planning a new business, then, at the end of one year,

---

[3]Moorman, Jerry, "What Bankers Have to Say About Business Planning," *IDEAS For Marketing Educators,* March 1990, pp. 7–8.

quit my other job and devote all of my efforts to opening and managing the new business. A long-term financial goal might sound like this: Pay back my $20,000 start-up loan within six years.

Using Goals and Objectives to Measure Success

Success can be measured by how close entrepreneurs come to reaching their goals and objectives. Certainly one of the most satisfying feelings for entrepreneurs comes from achieving the goals and objectives they established—personal as well as financial. If they accomplish this, they should consider themselves successful.

If, after some period of time, goals or objectives are not being met, they may have been unrealistic in the first place. The entrepreneur should re-evaluate the business and try to determine what went wrong. The important thing to remember is to review, re-evaluate, and, if appropriate, re-establish goals and objectives at least once a year to make sure that the business venture is on the path to success.

Marketing Plan

Just speculating that many people will want to buy a product or service is not enough. Entrepreneurs need to quantify information about their potential markets.

marketing plan, defines and quantifies consumers, demand, competition, geographic market, and pricing policy for a specific small business

The **marketing plan** defines and quantifies consumers, demand, competition, geographic market, and pricing policy for a specific small business. Most business experts consider the marketing plan a key component of the planning process. Drawing an accurate picture of the potential market for a product or service helps the entrepreneur to set realistic goals and objectives for the business. Successful entrepreneurs will devote considerable attention to the marketing plan, as will bank loan officers.

Consumers and Demand.   The first part of the marketing plan describes the consumers and demand for the product or service. It may profile a typical customer in terms of age, sex, income, occupation, family status, or other characteristics that make that person likely to frequent the business. It may also estimate how often a typical customer will want to buy the product or service and at what price.

Competition.   The second part of the marketing plan deals with competition. Suppose you decide that a shoe store is a good venture. We all know that everybody in town is already wearing shoes. In other words, they are shopping at your competitors' stores. The only way for you to bring customers into your new store is to lure them away from the competition. One way you can do this is by making your store different from others in terms of location, selection, quality, price, or service. But in order to make your store different, you need to know about the competition. In addition you need to consider what the competition's reaction will be to your business. What will you do, then, to counteract their responses?

As you plan your business, you should learn as much as possible about the competition. In particular, you should determine how the competition is different from the business you have in mind. All of this information should be summarized in your marketing plan.

Do banks think you should be concerned with your competition? You bet they do! One of the first questions many loan officers ask is, "What can you tell us about your competition?" If your answer is "Nothing," their next statement may well be "Goodbye!"

Geographic Market. This part of the marketing plan describes the geographic area from which the business will draw its customers. The entrepreneur must project how far people will be willing to travel to frequent the business, and from which areas they will come. Correctly identifying the geographic market makes setting realistic sales goals easier. Thus identifying the geographic market is a crucial step in planning a business.

Pricing Policy. The last part of the marketing plan consists of the pricing policy, which determines how you will set prices for the product or service. The prices set have a direct impact on the number of customers the entrepreneur will have and the profits accumulated. A carefully considered pricing policy can help you achieve your sales and profit goals.

Legal Requirements

As aspiring entrepreneurs consider opening their new businesses, legal problems are the last thing on their minds. But if they do not devote time and attention to the legal aspects of a new business, legal problems may soon be the *only* thing on their minds. Entrepreneurs must consider potential legal problems before they actually go into business.

The legal requirements for conducting almost any business today can be extensive and complicated. The planning phase is the proper time to consider what these requirements are and how they will be met.

Entrepreneurs should determine what patents, copyrights, agreements, contracts, or other legal arrangements will be needed to carry out day-to-day business. All of these items should be included in the business plan. Indeed, 94 percent of the banks doing business with entrepreneurs

Illus. 2-4 Entrepreneurs should determine what patents, copyrights, agreements, contracts, or other legal arrangements will be needed to carry out day-to-day business.

in new small business ventures require that the legal aspects of the ventures be addressed in the planning process.[4]

Form of Ownership

When you seek financial assistance, you must have decided upon a form of ownership for your business. If you are going it alone, this part of the plan is easy. If you are starting the new business with one or more other people, however, choosing the form of ownership becomes a very critical decision. Form of ownership has ramifications for business management, division of profits, division of labor, liability, and many other issues.

The most common forms of ownership are sole proprietorship, partnership, and corporation. Each of these will be discussed in detail in Chapter 11. Entrepreneurs must decide during the planning phase which form of ownership best suits the needs of the business and the people involved.

Financial Plan

financial plan, portion of the business plan that projects start-up costs, income, operating expenses, and cash flow

Along with the marketing plan, the financial section of the business plan is a key component in the overall planning process. A basic **financial plan** contains the entrepreneur's estimates for the following categories:

[4]Moorman, Jerry, "What Bankers Have to Say About Business Planning," *IDEAS For Marketing Educators*, March 1990, pp. 7–8.

1. cost of starting the business and maintaining it for a specified period of time (initial capitalization plan)
2. projected income
3. projected operating expenses
4. projected cash flow

Starting Point?   Some small business experts say that potential entrepreneurs should start their business planning processes with the financial plan. They argue that, until the entrepreneur determines what the proposed venture will cost and whether or not it is feasible, other planning is fruitless.

A Crucial Step.   All experts agree that the financial plan must be developed very carefully. Poor financial planning at the start of a business venture almost inevitably leads to overall business failure. Therefore most bank loan officers carefully scrutinize all four categories in the financial plan.

Organization, Management, and Staffing Plan

Although opening day may be a long way off, the entrepreneur must determine how many employees the business will require and what their responsibilities will be. Such concerns are addressed in the organization, management, and staffing plan section of the business plan.

Organization Chart.   The organization chart deals with the actual management of the business. The chart defines who will be responsible for tasks such as purchasing, advertising, accounting, and hiring personnel. The chart also shows who reports to whom in the organizational hierarchy.

Employee Requirements.   Planning for an appropriate number of employees is essential. If too few employees are hired, there will not be enough people to meet customers' needs. On the other hand, if too many employees are hired, the excessive labor costs will unnecessarily decrease profits. During the business planning phase the entrepreneur should use information such as the organization chart and projected sales figures to estimate how many employees will be needed.

Resumés, Personal Financial Statements, and References.   If opening a new business will require bank financing, each borrower must prepare a resumé, a personal financial statement, and a list of references. The resumé outlines the borrower's education and work experience. Banks use the resumé to help them determine whether the entrepreneur has the necessary background for the proposed business. The personal financial statement describes the borrower's financial condition. In particular, it shows what assets the borrower could use as collateral—something of value pledged as security—for the loan. Banks use the personal financial statement to evaluate the borrower's ability to repay the loan. The list of references contains the names and addresses of people who can supply information concerning the character and habits of the potential borrower.

Special Considerations

The last component of the business plan deals with any special considerations that apply to the entrepreneur's chosen business. Some small businesses will have many special considerations; some will have none.

If the business will be to manufacture a product, the list of special considerations may be quite lengthy. If the entrepreneur's business will consist exclusively of selling a service, however, the only special consideration may be a facility. Other special considerations may include training—either for the entrepreneur or employees—land and utility needs for the operation, and research and development of the proposed product or service. The entrepreneur's goal is to recognize and deal with all of these special considerations during the planning process.

DECIDING WHETHER OR NOT TO GO INTO BUSINESS

Once the business plan is complete, the entrepreneur can make the final decision as to whether or not to go into business. The three most useful pieces of information are the marketing plan, the financial plan, and the personal financial statement. If the entrepreneur has planned carefully, these items should reveal whether there is a market, how much money it will take to reach that market, and whether enough resources are available to pull it all together.

SOURCES FOR PLANNING ASSISTANCE

Many an entrepreneur has a great deal of enthusiasm plus a wealth of technical knowledge in a chosen field. What usually is lacking is management expertise and specific information about the nuts and bolts of starting a business. If that is the case, a variety of resources can offer assistance. Three of the most commonly available resources are described below.

Local Community Colleges

Many community colleges have small business development centers designed to assist local businesses.

Chamber of Commerce

In many communities, the chamber of commerce has a small business development committee that can offer guidance to entrepreneurs.

Small Business Administration

The Small Business Administration (SBA) is an independent federal government agency with offices in most metropolitan areas. The SBA offers a range of services including seminars, counseling, and loans.

Accountants and Attorneys

During the planning process, the entrepreneur should establish a working relationship with an accountant and an attorney who have experience

Illus. 2-5 In many communities, the chamber of commerce has a small business development committee that can offer guidance and assistance to entrepreneurs.

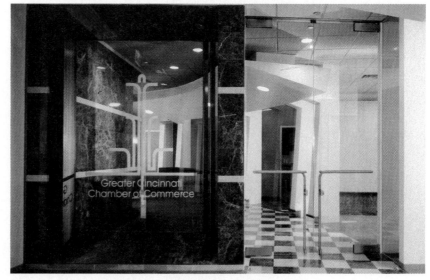

Space Design International, Greg Matulionis, Cincinnati, Ohio

with small businesses. The accountant should review or, in some cases, help to develop the financial plan. The attorney should be consulted to determine the legal requirements of the proposed business.

These professionals are a necessary part of the planning process regardless of whether you are starting a new business, buying an existing business, or purchasing a franchise. Their fees, which usually run $100 an hour and up, must simply be viewed as part of the expense of doing business.

JEFF BURNETT—ENTREPRENEUR

Jeff has decided to pursue his dream of being his own boss. He is ready to begin developing a business plan for a retail music store. He isn't convinced, however, that he has to complete all the items listed in the business plan outline. Surely there must be some shortcuts that a smart guy like him can figure out. If there are, he knows that he can find them.

If the shortcuts work for him, maybe you can use them too. If they don't work out—well, at least you know not to waste your time on them. He does decide, though, that it would be a good idea to develop some basic goals and objectives. He may even spend some time writing his idea history.

As you read about Jeff, you will see that he has many successes along with a few failures. Keep an eye on him! He probably acts much like an average entrepreneur would act.

SUMMARY

Planning is critical to the ultimate success of a small business. At the heart of the process is the business plan, which contains the following components:

1. Concept History and Background
2. Goals and Objectives
3. Marketing Plan
4. Legal Requirements
5. Form of Ownership
6. Financial Plan
7. Organization, Management, and Staffing Plan
8. Special Considerations

The completed business plan contains the information a potential entrepreneur needs to decide whether or not to start the business. Planning assistance is available from community college business development centers, the chamber of commerce, and the Small Business Administration. An entrepreneur should also engage the services of an accountant and an attorney during the planning process.

VOCABULARY BUILDER

On a separate sheet of paper, write a brief definition of each word or phrase based on your reading of the chapter.

1. Business plan
2. Marketing plan
3. Financial plan

REVIEW QUESTIONS

1. Why is careful planning crucial to developing a small business?
2. What are the eight components of a business plan?
3. How can a business plan help an aspiring entrepreneur decide whether or not to go into business?
4. What are three sources of assistance available to entrepreneurs?
5. What services can an accountant and an attorney provide during the business planning phase?

DISCUSSION QUESTIONS

1. What are the two key components of a business plan and why are they so important?
2. Why must entrepreneurs consider the competition when developing a business plan?
3. What is the importance of staffing to business success?
4. What is the importance of the form of ownership to the business operations of a small business?

CRITICAL THINKING

Sue Lee is a young woman who lives in your hometown. Recently she has been thinking about starting her own small business. After a lot of thought and discussion with friends and local store owners, she has decided to open an import shop dealing in original Japanese art and gift items.

Assuming that you are the banker who reviews her business plan, what are the good and bad points of the plan? This exercise should make you think about how the components of the business plan should be written.

1. Choose one of the eight components of the business plan (refer to the outline) and write it as if you were Sue Lee. Create explanations that sound convincing, well researched, and realistic.
2. Next, choose another component and write it so that it is lacking in good thought, development, and practicality. Then trade papers with a classmate and "correct" each other's weak components of the business plan by improving them with your own ideas and words. When you are finished, talk about how the changes you each made improved Sue's business plan.

SHORT CASE: TO LOAN OR NOT TO LOAN

Michael Hardin lives in a small town 50 miles north of Atlanta. Recently he has been thinking about starting his own small business. After a lot of thought and discussion with friends, he has decided to open a video rental store.

Knowing that he needs a loan to get his business started, Michael went to his bank. He had been doing business at First State Bank since he was a teenager. Before going, he called ahead and made an appointment with Bob Swanson, the commercial loan officer. Bob is the banker who talks to all of the people who want business loans.

After Michael explained his idea, Bob's first question was, "How much money do you need?" Michael's answer was that he thought ten or fifteen thousand dollars should be enough.

"There's a lot of difference between ten thousand and fifteen thousand dollars, Michael," said Bob. "Let me see your business plan and I'll help you figure the exact amount you need."

Michael hesitated for a moment, then asked, "What's a business plan?"

Questions

1. Do you think Mr. Swanson will loan Michael the money he needs? Would you? Why or why not?
2. Which part of the business plan will Mr. Swanson probably want to see first? Why?
3. What is the first thing Michael needs to do after leaving the bank if he doesn't want his business dream to die?

PROJECT CHALLENGE

In the last chapter you decided what type of business you were interested in investigating. As the first step in the business planning process, start a business plan notebook. Briefly respond to each of the following:

a. Write a one or two paragraph description of the product or service that your business will market.
b. How did you get the idea for this business?
c. What experience do you have in the intended business?
d. Develop two goals you hope to attain during the first year in business. Develop two goals you hope to attain within five years.

Now, using your responses to the items above, write the first component of your business plan—the concept history and background. Remember that this should include a description of your product or service, an idea history, and a summary of your experience and qualifications. As you proceed through the chapters of this text, you will be adding other components of the business plan to your notebook.

UNIT 2

MARKETING THE SMALL BUSINESS

3
Getting to Know Your Customers

After mastering the information contained in this chapter, you should be able to:

3-1 Describe a market.
3-2 Understand the importance of customers' needs.
3-3 Understand the steps of the research process used to learn about markets.
3-4 Explain how to conduct a demographic study.
3-5 Determine market potential.

customer, an individual who has the means to satisfy his or her needs

market, a group of consumers who have an unsatisfied need for a particular product or service

WHAT ARE CUSTOMERS?

Customers are the most important part of a business. Without customers, there can be no business. To be sure of having customers, entrepreneurs must make an effort to determine the needs of the **market** and identify groups of consumers that are likely to have an unsatisfied need for the product or service to be offered.

Potential customers' perceptions of need differ as a result of many environmental factors. When he formulated his theory on the hierarchy of human needs in 1920, Dr. Abraham Maslow cited five levels of need that we all share. Even though they are common needs, they vary in intensity depending on environmental background. Environmental background includes size of family, cultural orientation, upbringing, family values, and anything else that influences people during childhood and early adulthood.

All of us share physiological needs (basic survival needs such as food and water) in a similar degree of need satisfaction. We also share safety needs (protection needs such as shelter and clothing) in similar degrees of need satisfaction. It is at the love and belonging needs (social needs such as friends, family, and group identification) level of the hierarchy that most people begin to differ. The intensity of our need to be surrounded by people and our reliance on their support largely depends on the environment in which we were raised. Self-esteem needs (individual needs such as achieving status and recognition in the eyes of others and the need for self-respect) also vary widely depending on personality makeup. Many people reach as far as possible to meet their self-actualization needs (feeling accomplishment and achievement, and fulfilling personal capabilities), while others accept personal limitations at a fairly low level.

Illus. 3-1 The buyer of a luxury car is not shopping simply for transportation but may be seeking to fulfill self-esteem and self-actualization needs.

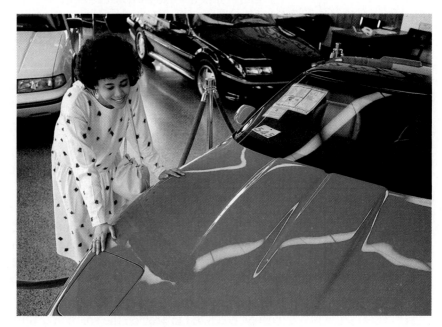

It is important to know that we all have these needs, and that the importance we place on them differs. It is sometimes difficult to recognize the need level. For example, the buyer of a basic, no-frills Chevrolet is shopping for transportation. The need level being addressed is, in all probability, the love and belonging need. By having transportation, the buyer will be able to get to work, go shopping, and visit others. All of these activities relate to social need. The buyer of a Corvette, however, is not shopping for transportation. Purchasing a luxury car will fulfill self-esteem and self-actualization needs. The buyer hopes to receive recognition from others through the car's image. Also, being able to purchase such a car will enhance the buyer's sense of achievement, accomplishment, and fulfillment of personal capabilities.

WHERE ARE THE CUSTOMERS?

The starting place for approaching a market is determining what group of customers has the strongest need and motivation to buy what is being sold. It is essential to learn how many customers there are and where they are located.

Entrepreneurs use **market research** to learn about the characteristics of their market. The more entrepreneurs know about the people or companies they will be serving, the more successful they will be at making wise, well-informed decisions. Since many business decisions will be based on the information found in the research of the market, the information must be accurate and timely. Collecting and properly analyzing information reduces the risk in making a decision.

market research, systematic gathering, recording, and analyzing of information concerning the market for goods and services

Market Research

Properly conducting market research requires completing six steps (see Figure 3-1).

Define the Question.   The first step in the market research process is to define the question. Often, entrepreneurs have concerns or are not sure about certain aspects of their businesses. By putting these concerns into words, they define the question. A typical question entrepreneurs ask themselves is, "Which people are most likely to buy from my business?"

Determine Needed Data.   After the question has been identified, data must be collected to provide the solution. Entrepreneurs must determine what kind of data will help answer the question. Not all data will provide the needed information. For example, data about the number of customers who visit a certain mall each year does not indicate what those customers purchase.

demographic study, a study of the statistics for the population in the proposed market

per capita income, average amount of money made or received, per person, on an annual basis

ethnic ratio, the proportion of a particular ethnic group to total population

gender ratio, the proportion of each gender to total population

economic stability, an economy's ability to withstand changes

psychographics, psychological variables (personality, attitude, beliefs, self-concept) and lifestyle values

Collect Data.   Entrepreneurs determine if there is a market for a product or service by collecting and studying information about the consumers in the desired market. Collecting data begins with a **demographic study** of the market.

Entrepreneurs, in conducting demographic studies for consumer-oriented products or services, should collect data about age, employment status, education, **per capita income, ethnic ratio, gender ratio,** and **economic stability** of the target population. The **psychographics** of the market should also be researched. Are the people socially active or do they keep to themselves? Do they have a lot of leisure time? The answers to these questions will be important in determining if the intended product or service can be sold successfully.

If the product or service is industry oriented, such as selling surgical equipment to hospitals, the entrepreneur should conduct a study of the targeted industry. Data for a study of an industry would include the number

Figure 3-1   The Entrepreneur's Practical Guide to Market Research

of potential customers in the industry, their locations, and the sizes of the companies or organizations in terms of sales revenues and number of employees. It is also necessary to learn the particulars of the industry, such as economic trends and which companies are leaders, to fully understand the needs of the market.

The information collected will include **secondary data** and **primary data.** Secondary data is available at a local chamber of commerce, library, or community college. These institutions provide published information

secondary data, information already published and available

primary data, information collected for the first time for a specific project about the number of people living in a community, average education level, per capita income, and gender ratios. Such data were collected by Alison Nichols, an entrepreneur who wants to learn more about five potential new markets for her family's retail chain of shoe stores.

Table 3-1 is a population chart for the five communities Alison is considering, all located in the same county. The table is an example of how secondary data acquired from a chamber of commerce can be assembled. It shows the 1980 population of each community, the 1990 population, and the projected population for the year 2000.

Additional research enables entrepreneurs to compile the types of information provided in Table 3-2.

In addition to collecting data about specific communities, entrepreneurs should collect data about geographic areas larger than the intended market so they understand the "big picture." In this case, Alison collected data about Spring County and other counties in the state. She then compiled the data (see Tables 3-3 and 3-4) so she could compare them easily.

Alison also collected data about the cities in the state with the highest rate of income growth. The results are shown in Table 3-5.

Analyze Data. After compiling secondary and primary data, entrepreneurs must analyze the information in a systematic manner. The analysis should include a written summary that includes results and an

Table 3-1   Community Population Estimates

Community	1980	1990	2000 (projected)
Spruce City	52,000	75,000	99,000
Wallington	25,000	28,000	31,000
Henry	17,600	17,800	17,500
Riceville	24,300	26,300	28,500
Newton	33,600	39,500	47,400
TOTALS	152,500	186,600	223,400

Table 3-2   Age and Ethnic Structure

Community	Median Age	White, non-Hispanic (%)	African American (%)	Asian (%)	Hispanic (%)	Native American (%)
Spruce City	32.1	87.5	6.9	1.6	2.3	1.7
Wallington	34.5	91.6	4.4	0.0	1.8	2.2
Henry	37.0	83.2	10.5	3.3	0.7	2.3
Riceville	42.5	76.4	14.6	4.8	0.0	4.2
Newton	38.4	92.0	3.2	1.2	2.6	1.0

Table 3-3   Average Head-of-Household Income, By County

County	Average Income
A—Jackson	$20,427
B—Spring	19,978
C—Concord	19,865
D—Wilson	18,696
E—Newton	18,480
F—Walton	18,205
G—Cory	17,680
H—Denton	17,435

Table 3-4   Per Capita Income—Top Five Counties in State

County	1980	1990	2000 (projected)
Atlas	$12,940	$15,540	$19,500
Spring	12,861	15,120	19,380
Desmond	12,140	14,800	18,700
Concord	11,985	13,980	17,310
Pacific	11,620	13,870	16,940

Table 3-5   Five Year Income Growth—Top Eight Cities in State

City	Income Growth (%)
Springfield	38.8
Smithville	37.8
Winston	37.0
Spruce City	35.4
Canton	34.7
Jonesborough	31.8
Green City	31.5
Howard	29.6

interpretation of what they mean. Care should be taken to ensure that all useful data collected are included in the analysis. The analysis and interpretation can provide answers to many kinds of questions.

The information in Table 3-1 provides not only basic population figures, but also an idea of growth patterns. We can see which areas of the county are growing fastest and which are likely to continue growing. If a business is to grow, it is important for the entrepreneur to consider what may happen in five years, ten years, and even after that.

The information in Tables 3-1 and 3-2 tells us that Spruce City's population is young, densely situated, centrally located, and growing faster than the population of any other community in the county. The information in Tables 3-3 and 3-4 tells us that the county's head-of-household income and per capita income are higher than average, and are expected to continue to grow. These facts are positive indicators for the possibility of opening a new business in Spruce City in Spring County.

A county map might be helpful in determining the best location for a new business. Circle or pinpoint the communities' population centers and the traveling distance between each. This allows the entrepreneur to estimate the traveling time between population centers to determine the accessibility of the business to its potential consumers.

Another item of value to the entrepreneur is a breakdown of sales in the county by industry classification (see Table 3-6).

Table 3-6   County Annual Sales, By Industry Classification

Store Type	Total Sales	Per Capita Sales
Restaurants	$7,340,000	$389.71
Apparel	3,419,000	182.61
Furniture	1,760,000	89.89
Shoes	792,000	40.18
Records, Music	388,000	20.16
Gifts/Novelties	313,000	16.85

By comparing the information in Table 3-6 with the same information from other counties, an entrepreneur can tell how the sales of a particular category of products compare, on a per capita basis, with those of surrounding counties. Major producers of the intended product can provide information about the average per capita sales of the product or service in the national or regional market. This information will let the entrepreneur know if sales of the product in the intended market area are higher or lower than average. Product manufacturers may also be able to help entrepreneurs determine how many people it will take to support a new business.

After all information has been gathered, a rough scenario of the market can be drawn. Let's use the Nichols family's shoe store as an example. Alison has learned that it takes an average of 8,000 people to support a shoe store. There are presently 16 stores that sell shoes in Spring County. Dividing the population of approximately 200,000 by 16 stores means that there is only one shoe store for every 12,500 people in this county. The average per capita shoe sales in the local market total $40 (see Table 3-6). The neighboring county has average per capita sales of $44, and the national average is $42. The intended market is evidently not purchasing its expected share of shoes. The following are indicators of a community need for more family shoe stores:

- The research showed that the per capita income is higher than normal and the unemployment level is lower, indicating a healthy economy.
- Since the neighboring county sells more shoes, it might be that consumers are shopping for shoes in the neighboring county.
- Based on the total population, this county does not have as many shoe stores as it should.

If Alison's family opens an upscale shoe store and the average per capita shoe sales increase to $42 per year, the same as the national average, the **market potential** is $8,400,000.

market potential, total potential sales dollars for a particular market

$42 (average spent per capita) × 200,000 (population) = $8,400,000

The average sales per store would be $494,117.

$8,400,000 (total sales) ÷ 17 (number of stores [16 existing plus 1 new]) = $494,117

Using primary data about the other stores and the psychographics of the consumers, the entrepreneur may be able to determine what percent of the market a new store will attract. This will depend on the location, how well the new store is managed, and how much money is available for inventory, fixtures, and equipment. A big store located in Spruce City (the largest and most central) will do more business than a smaller store located in Riceville. However, the store in Spruce City will be more expensive to open and operate.

Implement Data.   The next step in the market research process is to use the research data for decision making. A plan of action based on the information revealed in the research of the market is developed.

The shoe store is an example of how data can be used. The market research will help Alison and her family decide whether it would be better to open a big store and reach for a large, general market share, or to open a small store and sell to a smaller, more specialized share of the market.

Evaluate Action.   The last step in the market research process is evaluation. Entrepreneurs should not be satisfied with just developing a plan of action—the actions taken as a result of the analysis should be evaluated regularly after implementation.

To be sure the market research will accomplish its purpose, the entrepreneur must consider the following: (1) Demographic information is only valuable if compared to the same information for other markets. (2) The process of market research should be ongoing because the marketplace is constantly changing. It is important to stay informed about current events and changes in the marketplace and continually try to project what may happen next. (3) To keep up with and take advantage of the changes requires knowledge. Knowledge is the result of research. (4) Determination and creativity are necessary for success.

Determining Community Need

Suppose an entrepreneur wants to know how much need there is for a particular product or service within a community. Determining community need identifies the product's potential profitability. For example, anyone can open an ice cream shop and sell some ice cream, since many people enjoy ice cream. But can enough ice cream be sold to make the business profitable? If the shop owner pays $2,000 rent per month in addition to paying employees, utilities, taxes, and other operating expenses, he or she might have to sell $250,000 of ice cream per year to make a profit—$250,000 is a lot of scoops of ice cream. The owner must be sure that the community need for ice cream is that great. Deciding to sell a good product is not enough; market research must be used to determine the size of the market or the business will probably fail.

Illus. 3-2   An enterprise as simple as an ice cream shop might have to sell $250,000 worth of ice cream per year to cover rent, pay other operating expenses, and realize a profit.

Charles Gupton/The Stock Market

Gathering and using information is something that can be done by entrepreneurs engaged in any type of business activity. For manufacturing or wholesale businesses, entrepreneurs would collect information about the size of the industry to which they plan to sell their product or service, how many potential customers there are, how much competition there is, and whether there are indications that the intended market is being inadequately served.

Entrepreneurs who wish to sell to industry rather than consumers can find information about the components, or members, of an industry in reference books such as the *Thomas Register of American Manufacturers* at the local library. The *Thomas Register of American Manufacturers* includes volumes that classify products and list the companies that make them. Other volumes in the set include company listings that provide addresses and phone numbers, and others contain reprinted product catalogs. Other good sources of industry information are industry directories and membership lists from trade association publications. Beginning with this type of basic secondary data, entrepreneurs can continue the research by talking with those already established in the industry.

Many corporate entrepreneurs are product-development managers. They develop new ideas for company products or services and then complete consumer research for the company. If research shows there is a need for the new product or service, the company executives may decide to produce and sell it.

If you were to undertake a small business venture at your school, your market research might take this form. Imagine that you want to sell T-shirts imprinted with your school's name. You would collect information about the students who go to your school to identify potential customers. You would need to ask these questions:

1. How many students are there in each class year?
2. How do students spend their extra money?
3. Is anyone else selling school T-shirts?
4. What colors are most popular with students?
5. What would be the best location for sales?

You could get this information by collecting secondary data from the school office. Then reinforce this by collecting primary data—ask students questions and record the information—then compile tables and charts and study the information. If you find there is a need for T-shirts, you could go to a local T-shirt imprinter and purchase the shirts, then sell them at a higher price. How many shirts you sell will determine how much money you make. Of course, if you don't sell enough shirts to cover your investment, you will lose money. That is the entrepreneurial risk.

Illus. 3-3   Collecting primary data—by asking questions and recording the information—can help determine the need for a new enterprise.

Jay Bachemin for SWP

JEFF BURNETT—ENTREPRENEUR

Jeff has completed the first step of his market research—defining the question. He knows that if his business is to be successful, he must determine what his potential customers want and need and use this information when selecting his products.

For the second step, determining needed data, he identified the need to collect data about the buying habits of his potential customers. For the third step, Jeff collected secondary data about local radio stations, including a list of the stations, the primary type of music each station plays, and each station's ranking in the market. Finally he collected data about the amount of money spent during the previous year on musical recordings, including the amount spent for different types of music. He also collected primary data by interviewing people in three local malls.

Based on the data he collected Jeff created a pie chart (see Figure 3-2). He then decided to implement the data by carrying the styles of music included in the chart in the proportions identified—i.e., 27 percent rock, 24 percent oldies, etc.

Jeff has determined what his customers' needs are, and is ready for the next step—determining if there is a community need for a music store. He collected the following demographic information about his community, Logansville.

Figure 3-2   Product Mix for His Store

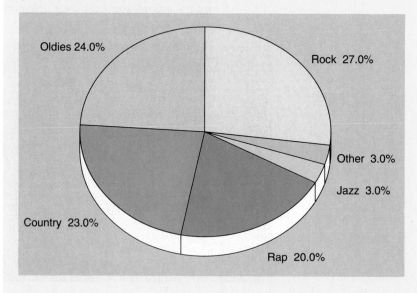

Population: 1980, 68,000; 1990, 75,000; 2000, 87,000 (projected)

Per capita income: $15,500 (12% higher than the state average)

Average age: 27.1 (3 years younger than the national average)

Average per capita spent on musical recordings: $20 ($1 less than the national average)

Average number of inhabitants per music store: 15,000 (75,000 population ÷ 5 existing stores) = 15,000 (2,500 more than the national average)

Using this information, Jeff made the following calculation:

75,000 (population) × $20 (average spent on recordings, Logansville) ÷ 5 stores = $300,000 average store revenue potential

It appeared that there might be a community need for another music store in Logansville.

SUMMARY

It is imperative that entrepreneurs do thorough studies on the size of potential markets and the makeup of potential customers before opening a business. The purpose is to determine if there are customers for the product or service and if there is a community need for the product or service.

The starting place for such a study is market research. To conduct market research, a six-step research process may be used: (1) define the question, (2) determine needed data, (3) collect data, (4) analyze data, (5) implement data, and (6) evaluate action.

Entrepreneurs must learn how to collect adequate information and put it to use effectively. Using the proper resources will significantly decrease the risk factor of the business venture. Data collected should include demographic information. The demographic study will provide information about the size of the market and the characteristics of its members. It should also indicate whether unsatisfied needs exist. Successful entrepreneurs know what needs the product or service to be offered will satisfy. By making comparisons with other markets for similar products and services, entrepreneurs will be able to project the potential for sales.

VOCABULARY BUILDER

On a separate sheet of paper, write a brief description of each word or phrase based on your reading of the chapter.

1. Customer
2. Market
3. Market research
4. Demographic study
5. Per capita income
6. Ethnic ratio
7. Gender ratio
8. Economic stability
9. Psychographics
10. Secondary data
11. Primary data
12. Market potential

REVIEW QUESTIONS

1. What is the starting point for approaching a market?
2. Why is it necessary to know the need levels of potential customers?
3. What are the six steps of the research process used to learn about markets?
4. Which of the six steps in market research involves gathering secondary and primary data?
5. What does *implement data* mean?
6. Why is it important to learn the psychographics of a market?
7. What information can an entreprenuer retrieve from a complete demographic study?
8. What is the difference between primary data and secondary data?
9. What is meant by the phrase *per capita income*?

DISCUSSION QUESTIONS

1. What factors in an individual's background would affect need levels?
2. What resources are available in your community that would help you do a demographic study?
3. What methods can be used to do a psychographic study?
4. Can the six steps of the research process apply when you are doing a school assignment?

CRITICAL THINKING

The town of Springfield has 100,000 residents. It has a healthy economy, with an above-average per capita income. It has three fine jewelry stores. The average per capita purchase of fine jewelry in Springfield is $49 annually. The national average is $52, and the per capita average for the neighboring community of Johnson City is $50. On average, a fine jewelry store serves 25,000 inhabitants. Do you think that there are enough customers in Springfield to support another jewelry store? Would you open one? Why or why not? If so, what is the potential for sales per store?

SHORT CASE: NOT ENOUGH INFORMATION

"Why not?" thought Carol. "A fine china department would add a great new look to the store and we could get out of our summer doldrums by selling to newlyweds." There were no china shops in this town of 40,000 people. The only china retailers in the area were a local jeweler, a local florist, and a department store 30 miles away. Carol was sure that a complete china department in her 4,500-square-foot gift shop would outsell the competition. She set out to research the market.

First, she talked to Victor Blanco, a sales representative for the Cardinal China Company. Victor was very encouraging and showed Carol impressive sales figures from china shops in small towns. He suggested incorporating a 600-square-foot department into her store that would sell Cardinal fine and everyday china, silverplate and sterling eating utensils, and accessories that would appeal to the newlywed market. Installing a plush white carpet, elegant wallpaper, and chandeliers would make it a very exciting department.

Carol then visited a friend who worked in the china department of a department store 200 miles away. She discussed her idea with the friend and the store manager. They both thought her idea was a good one.

Working with Victor she drew up a sales projection based on the sales history of her store. It looked great on paper, and she made plans to move ahead.

The department opened and drew many compliments from customers. "How beautiful." "Just what our town needs." "I'll be back." These were typical statements.

The china department was a failure. Sales were only 25 percent of projections. There were not very many weddings in the community. The department store, 30 miles away, still got a lot of the china business, as did the jeweler and the florist. A year later Carol liquidated the department.

Carol wondered what she had done wrong. Maybe she should have researched the idea with a demographic study similar to the one she did when she opened her store four years earlier.[1]

---

[1]Case study entitled "Not Enough Information" reprinted, with permission, from book #3511 *Why Entrepreneurs Fail: Avoid the 20 Pitfalls of Running Your Own Business* by James W. Halloran. Copyright 1991 by Liberty Hall Press/TAB Books, a division of McGraw-Hill, Blue Ridge Summit, PA 17294 (1-800-233-1128 or 1-717-794-2191).

1. What information that would relate to a china shop would a demographic study have provided?
2. Is it necessary to do a demographic study for business expansions?
3. Why was research of a department store 200 miles away not useful?

PROJECT CHALLENGE

In your business plan notebook, do a demographic study for your hypothetical business. First, determine the size of the total market. Then compare the demographic statistics to those of a nearby community. Using the information you collect, estimate the total market potential and decide what share of the market you wish to gain.

4

Getting to Know Your Competition

After mastering the information contained in this chapter, you should be able to:

4-1 Describe competitive impact.

4-2 Understand competition and its relationship to private enterprise.

4-3 Describe direct competition.

4-4 Describe indirect competition.

4-5 Explain the concept of geographic distribution of customers.

4-6 Explain the importance of analyzing competitive strengths and weaknesses.

competitor, an individual or business that sells the same products or services as another business and appeals to the same types of customers

Once aspiring entrepreneurs get to know their potential customers, they need to get to know the businesses that will compete for those customers. The reason for this is simple: new businesses need new customers. Getting the store open is only a small part of future success. Real success will occur only if there are customers—many, many customers.

Where are these customers currently shopping? Entrepreneurs must answer that question, as well as many others. After all, they start out with no customers at all. Everyone who wants to buy products similar to theirs is buying from future **competitors**. The only way to get customers is to convince them to stop purchasing from other business. To do that, entrepreneurs must have as much information about their competition as possible.

Illus. 4-1   Customers are the key to success.

THE IMPACT OF COMPETITION

competition, a rivalry between companies that sell similar products or services

competitive impact, competing effectively with other businesses

Competition, when used in a business sense, means a rivalry between companies that sell similar products or services. If you are to survive in the business world, you will have to get to know your competition. You must have **competitive impact,** which means effectively competing with other businesses.

Competition grows out of the fact that in a country such as ours, consumers have freedom of choice. They can spend their money anywhere they please. Consumers make the decision to spend their money in your store or down the street at another store that is in competition with yours.

Because there is freedom of choice in spending, you as a business person must be as competitive as possible. Your store must be of the highest quality and your merchandise of the type demanded. These positive attributes must then be combined with prices that are less than or at least equal to those of your competitor's. Every day that the doors of your business are open to the public, you must strive to develop better products and better ways to serve your customers. If you do not, your competition will. At the same time, you have to keep an eye on your competition and what they are doing. They cannot be allowed to get a competitive edge on you. Once they do, then *your* customers will become *their* customers.

COMPETITION AND PRIVATE ENTERPRISE

Competition is a very necessary part of private enterprise. If a private enterprise system is to serve the people efficiently, there must be competition among those who produce the products and among those who sell them. That competition is created by the following factors.

Similar Products and Services

Competitors offer similar products or services for sale. In the case of a sporting goods store, all businesses that sell sporting goods of any type are potential competition for the store. The management must consider all sporting goods stores as competition for customers.

Multiple Buyers and Sellers

If there is to be competition within an economic system, there must be many buyers and many sellers. When these conditions exist in a market, no individual or business can exert undue pressure. For example, if there were only one sporting goods store in town, that store's owner could charge whatever price he or she wanted for the products. Local customers would have no choice but to pay the price or travel out of town to shop. Likewise, if there were only one buyer, the buyer could exert undue pressure on the sellers to give price concessions. Multiple buyers and multiple sellers ensure competition by offering choices. Choices, in turn, help keep prices at fair levels.

Freedom To Enter or Exit Business

Competition in private enterprise means that a new business can start at any time. It also means that a company or an individual can stop doing business whenever he or she wants. This freedom is what gives private enterprise its strength. Because new people are entering the marketplace on a regular basis and others leaving, competition is assured.

The Guarantee of Fair Competition

Federal Trade Commission, a regulatory agency that enforces and monitors fair competition and other business practices

Sherman Antitrust Act, makes any business deal illegal that unreasonably restricts trade or commerce among states, and outlaws price fixing

Clayton Act, a follow-up to the Sherman Antitrust Act that further prohibits monopolies from forming and makes tying agreements illegal

Robinson-Patman Act, adds to the Clayton Act by outlawing price discrimination

monopoly, a business agreement whereby a single company controls a specific supply of products or services

price fixing, the agreement between competitors to establish and maintain prices of their goods and services

Competition is a critical component of private enterprise, but private enterprise can be effective only if fair competition is guaranteed. The United States government, along with many state governments, has taken steps to ensure fairness in competition. Through the enactment of certain laws and the creation of the **Federal Trade Commission** (FTC), the U.S. Congress has attempted to create an environment in which entrepreneurs can receive fair treatment from competitors, no matter how small or large their companies are.

Three laws that protect competition are the **Sherman Antitrust Act,** the **Clayton Act,** and the **Robinson-Patman Act.** Collectively, these laws help prevent monopolies. When a business has a **monopoly** on a market, it sets prices, prevents other businesses from entering the market, and controls the available supply of the product or service. Because these practices are anti-competitive, the government does not approve of them. The only monopolies the government allows to exist are those in industries in which the product or service offered necessitates one supplier. For example, we only have one supplier of local telephone service in the United States. The following three paragraphs describe the specific laws that help protect fair competition in the United States.

Sherman Antitrust Act.   This act, passed in 1890, makes any business deal illegal that unreasonably restricts trade or commerce among states. It outlaws **price fixing**, an illegal practice that leaves customers with few price choices. The act also makes owners or directors of violating businesses guilty of a crime.

Clayton Act. This 1914 legislation is a follow-up to the Sherman Antitrust Act that provides needed strength for dealing with companies involved in illegal deals. Specifically, it prohibits businesses from acquiring companies that would create a monopoly environment and reduce competition. It also makes illegal **tying agreements**.

tying agreements, the practice of a seller requiring a customer to buy one type of product in order to be permitted to buy another type

Robinson-Patman Act. This act extended the Clayton Act in 1936 by outlawing **price discrimination.** It also outlaws mergers in which large companies acquire all the stock of competing companies.

price discrimination, charging different prices to different customers for the same goods

Federal Trade Commission. The FTC is a regulatory agency that was established to enforce and monitor these laws. It ensures fair competition among businesses, encourages free trade, carefully reviews business mergers and acquisitions to prevent monopolies from forming, and regulates advertising so that it is not deceptive.

TYPES OF COMPETITION

As stated earlier, every business that sells sporting goods of any kind is a potential competitor for a new retail sporting goods store. Not all the businesses are the same, though. Some compete more directly than others. As entrepreneurs analyze their competition, they must first consider into which classification the competing firms fall—direct competition or indirect competition.

Direct Competition

direct competition, competition by businesses that derive the majority of their profits from the sale of products or services that are the same or similar to those sold by another business

Direct competition refers to businesses that derive the majority of their profits from the sale of products or services that are the same or similar to those sold by another business. A good way to start the analysis is by looking in the yellow pages of the telephone book for other stores that deal in the same product.

Another method of identifying direct competition is to contact the local chamber of commerce. A quick review of the list from the chamber should identify organizations that will be direct competition. Next, the entrepreneur should try the city courthouse. Many communities have planning departments that compile annual data books. In these books, cities are divided into shopping zones, and the number and types of retailers in each zone are listed.

*Illus. 4-2   The yellow pages are an excellent resource for identify-
ing direct competition.*

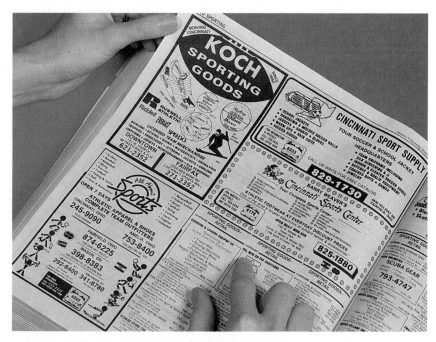

The last thing to do is a physical check of the geographic market. To do this, entrepreneurs should drive through all retail centers within the competitive area and attempt to identify competitors not already known. The check should include a walk-through of any enclosed malls.

The number of direct competitors identified and their behavior in the marketplace will ultimately have a profound effect on the new business. It is important to evaluate these findings and try to determine the reputation of the competitors. For example, these questions should be addressed: "What are they doing that appeals to customers? What could I do better? What have I seen that I want to avoid?"

Indirect Competition

indirect competition, by businesses that derive only a small percentage of their profits from the sale of products or services that are the same or similar to those sold by another business

Indirect competition is competition by businesses that derive only a small percentage of their profits from the sale of products or services that are the same or similar to those sold by another business. If a business sells sweatshirts, for example, its competitors might be Wal-Mart, K-Mart, Target, and other large general merchandise retailers.

If the entrepreneur has lived in the area for quite a while, identifying indirect competition should not be much of a problem. Entrepreneurs should take time, however, to make sure all stores that fall into this category are included.

Indirect competition can often prove to be the most dangerous kind of competition. For a business like the sweatshirt store owner's, indirect competition will almost always come from a large national chain like one of those named previously. It usually has more capital than a small business and is capable of purchasing in much greater quantities. Because the large chain does not have to rely only on the one product line, it can choose to deal in those items that produce the most profit. It can carry as little or as much of an item as is desired.

Small business owners do not have that option. Not only can they not be as selective, they cannot buy in as large a quantity, either. To attract and keep customers, the sweatshirt store owner must try to satisfy all customer needs for athletic apparel and merchandise. In addition to high profit items, the entrepreneur must also carry items in demand even though they produce much lower profits.

Just as the number of direct competitors and their behavior in the marketplace will ultimately have a profound effect on the new business, so will that of the indirect competitors. Entrepreneurs should evaluate their findings about indirect competitors and try to determine the reputations and roles of those competitors in the marketplace.

GEOGRAPHIC DISTRIBUTION OF CUSTOMERS

As entrepreneurs begin the process of formally getting to know the competition for the planned business, they need to be concerned with geography. Not geography in the sense of the *world* but instead in the sense of *customers*.

Getting to know customers is a critical ingredient in the success formula for a new company. Part of that knowledge concerns where the potential customers live. Entrepreneurs need to ask, "How far will customers travel to do business with me?"

To determine customer geographic distribution, acquire a map of the area in which the business will be located. On the map, mark in some fashion the probable location of the business. The exact location probably has not been chosen yet (see Chapter 5), but the entrepreneur should have an idea of the general business district where it will be.

Next, mark the areas on the map in all directions that represent the farthest distance customers would be willing to travel to do business. After this has been marked, a circle should be drawn on the map that includes all potential customers.

If the business is a small retail store, the circle drawn on the map may be relatively small and cover only a portion of the city. If, on the other hand, the intended business is a production facility with widely based appeal, the circle might include one or more states. It could even cover entire regions of the country.

The circle on the map represents the geographic distribution of potential customers. It also, to some extent, represents the geographic distribution of future competition. Have you ever noticed that fast-food restaurants tend to come in clusters? That's because they have all determined where their potential customers live and work and how far they are likely to drive for a hamburger and a soft drink. This is just one illustration of the fact that once you have located the customers, you have probably located the competition as well.

Illus. 4-3   The circle on the map represents the geographic distribution of potential customers as well as main access roadways.

Jay Bachemin for SWP

ANALYZING COMPETITIVE STRENGTHS AND WEAKNESSES

Now that aspiring entrepreneurs have identified their competitors, it is time to do a more detailed analysis. Identification was just the first step. Now the real work begins.

competitive analysis, identifying and examining the characteristics of a competing firm

Competitive analysis is important because understanding the competition is critical to a new business's success. From the analysis comes the information necessary to identify strengths and weaknesses. Strengths and weaknesses, both yours and the competition's, are necessary ingredients for marketing success.

Analyzing Competitors That Have Failed

Not only should all the identified direct and indirect competitors be analyzed; so should any that can be identified who have recently gone out of business. Most of these would probably have fallen into the category of direct competitors. It is important to analyze these so that you can benefit from their mistakes. To take advantage of this, though, the reasons for the mistakes must be determined. Analysis provides that information.

Table 4-1 is a form designed for analyzing competitors who have failed. To use the form, entrepreneurs should list as many competitors that have failed as possible. To identify these, they may use chamber of commerce records, community data books, personal knowledge, yellow pages from previous years, and any other source of local business data. After identifying failed competitors, the entrepreneurs should try to determine why they failed. Some of the reasons for failure are listed in the columns. They include poor management, under-capitalization, lack of knowledge about the business, and competition's influence. Also, any trends in the failures should be identified in the space given.

Analyzing Direct and Indirect Competition

The next step is to look at both direct and indirect competition from an analytical perspective. Table 4-2 is an expedient way of recording data from that analysis. As competition is examined, five factors must be analyzed: price, location, facility, competition type, and rank.

Price.   In this sense, price refers to the price range into which each competitor's prices fall for products or services that are the same or very

Table 4-1   Competitors That Have Failed

REASONS FOR FAILURE

Names	Poor Management	Under-capitalization	Lack of Knowledge	Competition	Other
1. _____	_____	_____	_____	_____	_____
2. _____	_____	_____	_____	_____	_____
3. _____	_____	_____	_____	_____	_____
4. _____	_____	_____	_____	_____	_____
5. _____	_____	_____	_____	_____	_____
6. _____	_____	_____	_____	_____	_____
7. _____	_____	_____	_____	_____	_____

Trends

1. _____
2. _____
3. _____
4. _____

similar to what the new business will offer. Based on the competitive analysis, the entrepreneur should indicate if the competition is in the high (H), middle (M), or low (L) range.

Location.   The location of competitive businesses must be examined in comparison to the new business's anticipated location. Is the competition located in a better (B), worse (W), or in about the same (S) quality location?

Facility.   Facility refers to the actual buildings occupied by competitors. In comparison to the new business's anticipated facility, is the competitor's facility better (B), worse (W), or about the same (S)?

Type of Competition.   Based on the previous information presented, determine if other businesses are direct (D) or indirect (I) competition.

Table 4-2   Direct and Indirect Competition

Names of Competitors	Price (H/M/L)	Location (B/W/S)	Facility (B/W/S)	Direct/Indirect (D/I)	Rank (1–10)
1. _____	_____	_____	_____	_____	_____
2. _____	_____	_____	_____	_____	_____
3. _____	_____	_____	_____	_____	_____
4. _____	_____	_____	_____	_____	_____
5. _____	_____	_____	_____	_____	_____
6. _____	_____	_____	_____	_____	_____
7. _____	_____	_____	_____	_____	_____
8. _____	_____	_____	_____	_____	_____
9. _____	_____	_____	_____	_____	_____
10. _____	_____	_____	_____	_____	_____

Table 4-3   New Business Strengths and Weaknesses

Strengths

1. _____

2. _____

Weaknesses

1. _____

How I will overcome this: _____

_____

_____

2. _____

How I will overcome this: _____

_____

_____

Rank. The competitors should be ranked from 1 to 10 in terms of the degree of competitiveness. Number 1 should be the strongest competitor; number 10 the weakest.

Table 4-3 on page 68 is a form that takes the competitive analysis one step further. By completing the form, entrepreneurs can use the information recorded in Table 4-2 to identify their own strengths and weaknesses. To begin, identify two strengths of the intended business. After that has been done, two weaknesses should be listed. As each weakness is identified, the entrepreneur should try to determine how it might be overcome.

By this point, an aspiring entrepreneur should have the knowledge necessary for getting to know the competition. If entrepreneurs do a good job, competitors should not be able to surprise them in the future.

JEFF BURNETT—ENTREPRENEUR

As Jeff started the process that would allow him to get to know his competition, he became very interested in the various names that were used. His interest grew out of the fact that he had not yet named his own business. Jeff knew that the name for his business was very important. He wanted a name that would identify his business for what it was—a retail music store. The name also had to be easy to remember, and it needed to bring music immediately to mind.

After much thought, and after looking at all his competitors' names, Jeff decided on a name for his new business. He then talked to several of his friends about it. They all thought it was great. Jeff's new business would be called "Rock 'n' Soul Music."

By playing off the phrase *rock and roll*, Jeff knew that his store's name would be very easy to remember. It was simply a matter of association. When people remembered the name of his store, they would associate it with rock and roll. Rock 'n' Soul would stick in their minds. With a name chosen, Jeff moved forward with the process of analyzing his competition. The first thing he examined was geographic distribution.

Jeff lives in a town of about 75,000 people. Because of its relatively small size, he figured that every retail music store selling records, tapes, and CD's in town would offer competition. These would include both direct and indirect competitors. Having defined the geographic distribution of competition, Jeff decided to complete Table 4-1 concerning competitors that had failed. Let's see how it looks.

Table 4-1 Competitors That Have Failed

REASONS FOR FAILURE

Names	Poor Management	Under-capitalization	Lack of Knowledge	Competition	Other
1. *Tunes R Us*			X	X	
2. *Joe's Music*					X
3. *Rap Store*	X	X			
4.					
5.					
6.					
7.					

Trends

1. *No real trends are evident.*

2.

3.

4.

From the data Jeff could gather, he identified three businesses that had failed. There were no real trends that he could discover. Besides, those were other people. He didn't think they had anything in common with him. Do you think Jeff made the correct decision in not trying harder to discover trends among the failed businesses?

Jeff decided to proceed with an analysis of current direct and, indirect competition. It took him some time, but he eventually completed Table 4-2. Let's see if we can figure out what he discovered.

After following all the instructions found in this chapter, Jeff was able to determine that Rock 'n' Soul Music will have seven competitors. Five of his competitors will be direct; two will be indirect. As we leave Jeff Burnett, he is still studying Table 4-2 trying to determine what other information it contains. He is also trying to see how he can identify the strengths and weaknesses of his own business.

Table 4-2   Direct and Indirect Competition

Names of Competitors	Price (H/M/L)	Location (B/W/S)	Facility (B/W/S)	Direct/Indirect (D/I)	Rank (1–10)
1. *Music Scene*	M	S	B	D	1
2. *Modern Sounds*	H	W	W	D	6
3. *Radical Tunes*	H	W	W	D	7
4. *K-Mart*	L	W	W	I	2
5. *Town Sounds*	M	W	S	D	4
6. *Wal-Mart*	L	W	W	I	3
7. *Totally Music*	H	W	S	D	5
8.					
9.					
10.					

SUMMARY

A knowledge of competition is vital to all entrepreneurs if they are to survive in the business world. Competition and private enterprise are dependent upon each other. Competition in the United States is created by the following factors: similar products and services, multiple buyers and sellers, freedom to enter or exit business, and the guarantee of fair competition. Fair competition is ensured by three acts of Congress: The Sherman Antitrust Act, The Clayton Act, and The Robinson-Patman Act. In addition, the Federal Trade Commission regulates business activities to prevent unfair competition.

There are two types of competition, direct and indirect. All competitors, whether direct or indirect, must be identified and analyzed. The geographic distribution of competition is one of the first factors for an aspiring entrepreneur to consider. Businesses that have failed in the recent past must also be identified. Those establishments that have failed should be analyzed to determine why each failed and to see if there are any trends evident among the failures.

Current competitors must be analyzed in five areas: price, location, facility, type of competition, rank. After competitors are analyzed, the information should be used to identify strengths and weaknesses of the new business.

VOCABULARY BUILDER

On a separate sheet of paper, write a brief description of each word or phrase based on your reading of the chapter.

1. Competitors
2. Competition
3. Competitive impact
4. Federal Trade Commission
5. Sherman Antitrust Act
6. Clayton Act
7. Robinson-Patman Act
8. Monopoly
9. Price fixing
10. Tying agreements
11. Price discrimination
12. Direct competition
13. Indirect competition
14. Competitive analysis

REVIEW QUESTIONS

1. What is competitive impact?
2. How does competition relate to private enterprise?
3. What is the difference between direct and indirect competition?
4. What is meant by geographic distribution of customers?
5. Why is it important to analyze competitive strengths and weaknesses?

DISCUSSION QUESTIONS

1. What are the four factors that create competition in our country? Briefly explain each factor.
2. How does a monopoly eliminate competition?
3. What role do customers play in determining the geographic distribution of competition?
4. Why is it important to analyze competitors that have failed?
5. What are the five factors to consider when analyzing current competitors?

CRITICAL THINKING

Jan Cohen lives in a small town in Mississippi called Clarksdale. Jan has wanted to own and manage a model train store ever since she was a young child. After looking around town, she decided to lease a small shop located in a strip shopping center on the northwest side of town. However, before she signs the lease, she knows she should check out the competition.

1. If you were advising Jan, what is the first thing you would tell her to do?

2. Look in the yellow pages of the telephone book and prepare a list on a separate piece of paper of all businesses that sell model trains. If your city is large, concentrate only on your section of town. (For the purposes of this activity, limit your list to about ten businesses.)
3. After you have prepared the list, indicate whether each competitor is direct or indirect competition.
4. Based on your knowledge of the businesses listed as competitors for Jan's model train store, rank them in order. Number 1 should be the strongest competitor and the last number should be the weakest.

SHORT CASE: "A GOOD JOB" FOR THE COMPETITION

Benjamin Dinges opened his new business two weeks ago. His store is called "Sporting Life." It offers a full range of athletic equipment designed for weekend athletes.

Business has been very slow for Ben and he is getting discouraged with his new business venture. It has not lived up to his expectations at all. In the beginning, he thought that once he got enough money together to open the store, customers would automatically start coming in. He managed to get the money after putting up the equity in his home as security. He did the necessary work to get the rented facility ready. He was sure that he had chosen the right kind of merchandise. He even had a few customers come in.

The problem was that most of the customers left without buying. He had been so frustrated that he even asked several of them why they didn't buy. They told him that they could get the same merchandise at a lower price from the competition. When he pressed them for names, they mentioned several. The problem was that he had only heard of one of the competing stores.

When he had been thinking about opening his new store, he knew there would be competition, but he didn't worry about it. "Just do a good job," he had told himself. "That's all it takes. Let the competition worry about me. I'm going to be the problem, not them."

1. If you were a friend of Ben's and he asked you for advice, what would you say to him at this point?
2. Do you think there is any chance of salvaging Ben's business? What is the biggest mistake he has made so far in his new business venture?
3. Do you think Ben gave himself good advice when he said, "Just do a good job?" Why?

PROJECT CHALLENGE

As you continue the planning process for your new business, it is now time to take the information presented in this chapter and use it to get to know your competition. To assist you in the process, complete the following steps in your business plan notebook.

1. Choose a name for your new business.
2. Take a map of your area and put a star in the general area of the site of your new business. Now take a marker and draw a circle around your anticipated geographic market area.
3. Using the yellow pages and other available resources, make a list of businesses that are potential competitors.
4. Try to discover if other businesses such as yours have failed in the past year. List those businesses on a separate sheet of paper.
5. Now make your own copies of Tables 4-1, 4-2, and 4-3. Complete the tables as fully as you are able.

5
Location and Facilities

After mastering the information contained in this chapter, you should be able to:

5-1 Explain the importance of choosing a proper location for a business.

5-2 Describe the different types of goods.

5-3 Describe the different types of locations available for selling consumer goods or services.

5-4 Describe the location considerations of those who produce and sell industrial and technological goods.

5-5 Explain the importance of properly evaluating potential facilities and the surrounding environments.

You might have heard that the three most important ingredients in starting a successful business are location, location, and location. Although this is something of an exaggeration, for some businesses it is close to the truth. Choosing the proper location is one of the most important decisions entrepreneurs will make.

THE IMPORTANCE OF CONVENIENCE

Our society demands convenience. Driving along a busy commercial strip with all of its fast-food restaurants, or visiting a super-sized shopping center gives us an idea of the extremes that businesses go to in order to be accessible to their customers. The question is no longer whether to eat pizza, rather it is from what pizza restaurant to order and whether to go out to eat, pick it up, or have the restaurant deliver. The aspiring entrepreneur who knows that being in the right place at the right time is important is the one who is most likely to succeed.

Entrepreneurs must understand the relationship, or correlation, between time and place. Whether the prospective purchases be consumer goods or services or industrial products, customers' decisions are affected by what they perceive to be convenient. Making a business convenient to patronize intensifies the consumer's wants. In other words, if it is convenient to buy pizza, you buy more. If you have to drive 10 miles to buy a pizza instead of 5 miles, you will buy fewer pizzas. Therefore, it is important that businesses create situations that their customers perceive as convenient.

Convenience saves time. Time is finite. By finite we mean that time cannot be created or extended. There are only 24 hours in a day. In Americans' increasingly busy lives, saving time has become very important.

By offering convenience, the entrepreneur saves time for the consumer, thus persuading the consumer to buy more.

Illus. 5-1   Choosing a convenient location is one of the most important decisions an entrepreneur will make.

The fact is, we Americans have grown accustomed to obtaining the goods we need with little effort. If we are pressed for time and cannot find what we want easily, we buy substitute goods or services. Many businesses profit from consumers' time limitations. Fast-food restaurants are examples of businesses that have grown because of people's time limitations. By being convenient to their markets, they take advantage of time limitations and sell more food as a consequence. Time and convenience are also responsible for growth in many industries, such as mail order sales and machine vending, and for the successes of small manufacturers, which are often able to deliver goods faster than large companies. It is very important to have the right assortment of goods and the right image, but if the goods are not easy to acquire, the entrepreneur will not be successful.

CLASSIFYING CONSUMER GOODS

To determine the best location for selling consumer goods and services, entrepreneurs must first classify their products as one of three types of goods.

convenience goods, products that people purchase regularly

Convenience goods are products people expect to find in many places. There is very little decision making involved in making these purchases. Soft drinks, tissues, toothpaste, and newspapers are examples of convenience goods. These products are readily available in a variety of stores, including convenience stores, drug stores, and grocery stores. It is imperative for businesses that sell convenience goods to be accessible to large markets.

shopping goods, products that people purchase occasionally

Shopping goods are products that are easily found, although they are not as widely distributed as convenience goods. They are normally available in sufficient quantity in all communities to meet expected average consumer needs. Tires, jewelry, popular fashions, and compact discs are examples of shopping goods. Purchase of these products often requires going to a particular type of store and usually requires more planning and decision making than does the purchase of convenience goods. Consumers often comparison shop for these products, looking for the best values. To sell shopping goods successfully, businesses must be convenient to intended markets.

specialty goods, products that people purchase less frequently

Specialty goods are products that people are willing to go out of their way to buy. The purchases are usually planned in advance. Wedding dresses, cars, and computers are examples of specialty goods. Since these are usually major purchases, the consumer does not mind taking extra time to get the best product. Success in specialty goods sales requires that the business be accessible, that its location be known to potential customers, and that it be located in an area that is compatible with the image of the product or service.

CHOOSING A LOCATION

The first decision to make is which community will be the best one for the business. As discussed in Chapter 3, completing a demographic study can determine this.

If demographics for his or her own community support the business idea, the entrepreneur would be wise to locate there for several reasons:

1. The business owner will be working in a familiar area.
2. There will already be a small nucleus of customers, through friends and acquaintances.
3. The entrepreneur may know bankers, attorneys, or accountants who would be part of an important support system for the new business.

The grass might look greener in another community, but the hometown is usually the best bet.

Once the community is chosen, location possibilities can be considered.

Shopping Areas

Downtown Shopping Districts.   In the past, the downtown area of a town or city was where the commercial activity was centered—almost everyone worked and shopped downtown. After World War II, a move toward the suburban areas began. More and more people chose to reside outside of cities, so retail establishments started to move to these areas.

Suburban shopping areas began as small shopping centers and have grown to major shopping facilities. As a result, the downtown stores branched out to the suburbs, which caused downtown areas in many communities to become almost deserted. In recent years, many cities have recognized deterioration in their downtown areas and have made efforts to change this. It is often difficult to rebuild these areas because of parking problems and limited shopping hours, but many towns do have attractive downtown shopping districts. These shopping districts offer advantages to business owners.

The chief advantage to locating in a downtown area is a lower cost of doing business. Since the buildings are often older, the rental costs can be considerably less. Also, the hours of operation are shorter, which

Illus. 5-2   The chief advantage of locating in a downtown area is the lower cost of doing business.

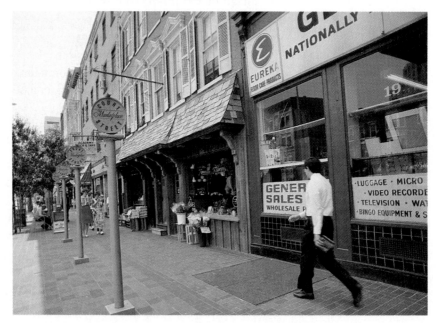

reduces operating expenses. However, if considering a downtown location, entrepreneurs must identify any disadvantages, such as parking limitations, and any repairs the facility might need. Although many of today's shoppers prefer evening shopping, if the downtown area is active during the day and the surrounding businesses are well maintained, it is certainly a location worth considering.

Shopping Centers.   Shopping centers have come a long way since they began to appear some 50 years ago. There are four classifications of shopping centers; they are indicative of the markets the centers serve.

neighborhood shopping center, small shopping centers, usually with fewer than 20 stores, that serve their immediate neighborhoods

Neighborhood shopping centers often have a supermarket and small service and convenience goods stores. The customers are nearby residents; they shop in these centers for convenience. The populations of the nearby residential areas determine the amount of activity. Rental expense is usually reasonable—businesses that sell mainly convenience goods or services can be profitable in these centers.

community shopping center, shopping center large enough to provide convenience goods and shopping goods to several neighborhoods

Community shopping centers are designed to service residents of many neighborhoods. Although rent costs are usually higher than in neighborhood shopping centers, locating in community shopping centers

Illus. 5-3   Businesses that sell primarily convenience goods or services can be profitable in neighborhood shopping centers.

Illus. 5-4 Community shopping centers are designed to service residents of many neighborhoods.

anchor store, a store large and strong enough to attract customers by itself

can mean more profit for businesses that sell shopping goods, convenience goods, or both. Normally these centers have at least one, and sometimes two, major tenants called **anchor stores,** and 20 small stores or more. Anchor stores, which are often department stores, discount stores, large supermarkets, or large drug stores, advertise actively and attract customers from an entire community. The smaller stores can then attempt to attract the customers into their stores.

regional shopping center, shopping center that usually has 3 or 4 anchor stores and more than 40 other stores

mall, an enclosed shopping center with a controlled climate

profit margin (markup), the difference between what the seller and the consumer pay for a product

Regional shopping centers are designed to attract customers from a region, or more than one community. These large shopping areas usually have three or four anchor stores and more than 40 other stores. Many times they are **malls,** which are the trend in contemporary shopping. A regional shopping center or mall usually offers convenience, shopping, and specialty goods, but due to the expense of renting space in such a center, the products sold often have a higher **profit margin** or **markup** than most convenience goods can support.

The entrepreneur who sells shopping goods or specialty goods and needs a large amount of pedestrian traffic to be successful might want to do business in a regional shopping center, but the high cost of operation might make this risky.

super regional shopping center, a colossal shopping mall made up of many anchor stores and sometimes hundreds of smaller stores

Super regional shopping centers are found in major metropolitan areas and have hundreds of stores, including the most contemporary ones. For example, the West Edmonton Mall in Edmonton, Canada, and the Mall of America in Bloomington, Minnesota, each have approximately 800 stores. These giant shopping complexes often have entertainment facilities, such as skating rinks and miniature golf courses; hotels; or amusement parks attached. They are the wave of the future. Stores in these centers are very expensive to operate and are not usually recommended for new business owners. Most tenants are part of chain operations that can make large investments in their operations.

If the new business is to be located in a shopping center, the entrepreneur must research the advantages and disadvantages of each type of center. For example, the high cost of the large center is offset by its appeal to customers and, theoretically, more people shopping means more chances to sell. However, malls charge rent based on traffic flow. A location in a high-traffic mall will cost more than one in a lower traffic mall. Entrepreneurs need to determine if the extra traffic will generate enough additional sales to offset the expense of the higher rent. Stores that depend on a large number of fairly low-cost transactions must locate where there is a large amount of pedestrian traffic. Also, larger shopping centers usually have larger advertising budgets.

The super regional, regional, and some of the community shopping centers have **merchant associations.** The dues collected by these associations are used to advertise and to pay for entertainment events that

merchant association, an organization of merchants who work together to promote shopping at their shopping area

Illus. 5-5   Within 4.2 million feet of enclosed space, the Mall of America has hundreds of specialty shops along with a seven-acre amusement park.

Courtesy of the Bloomington MN Convention and Visitors Bureau

are designed to attract customers. Special attractions at shopping centers, whether they be Christmas decorations, antique automobiles, or circus clowns, have usually been arranged by the merchant association.

Stand-alone stores. **Stand-alone stores** often depend on drive-by traffic. They must have ample parking, good signing, and effective lighting if they are to be successful. Stand-alone stores are often located away from shopping areas. They can also be located adjacent to large malls, or on streets leading to malls, to take advantage of the traffic flow. The buildings are often owned by the business owner. Even if the owner is leasing, however, rental costs are usually lower than those for shopping center spaces. Restaurants—both eat-in and carryout—and auto dealers are examples of businesses that often are successful in stand-alone locations.

stand-alone store, a store that is not located in a shopping area

Locations for Industrial Businesses

Manufacturers and wholesalers must also recognize the importance of location, but for different reasons. It is important that these businesses efficiently address transportation and communication needs. A sizable part of the operating expense of an industrial company is shipping cost, both for materials received and for products shipped. These businesses must deliver their products in a timely manner; therefore, the manufacturer

Illus. 5-6   Restaurants and auto dealers are examples of businesses that often are successful in stand-alone locations.

or wholesaler will want to locate near transportation facilities and, if possible, close to customers. Also, locating close to customers allows the business to make personal sales calls with a minimum of expense.

Industrial Parks. **Industrial parks** usually provide space at a reasonable cost and often provide good access to transportation. The cost is often partially subsidized by the community to attract industrial businesses, creating jobs and thus increasing the community's tax base. The industrial entrepreneur should investigate this option if a large amount of space is needed.

industrial park, a section of land allocated for use by industrial businesses

Incubators. In recent years a need for small businesses, particularly new ones, to locate together and share some common operating expenses has been recognized. **Incubators** allow a small number of businesses to share certain operating expenses such as rent, utilities, property taxes, office equipment, and support employee salaries. They are often found within industrial parks and are usually funded by state or local agencies using federal funds, rather than being managed by a leasing company. The entrepreneur who needs only a small amount of space, for technological development or small manufacturing, for example, should find out if there is an incubator with available space within the community.

incubator, a facility that houses a number of small businesses, usually fewer than 10, which share certain operating expenses

Home-Based Businesses

There has been a tremendous growth in **home-based businesses** during the past 10 years, and for some very good reasons.

home-based business, a business conducted from the owner's residence

- Doing business from the home is an excellent way to run a business on a limited budget. Rent charges, utility costs, and maintenance fees are avoided, so there is more money to purchase income producing inventory and for advertising expenditures.
- Home-based business owners are not subject to the restrictions and obligations imposed by lease agreements.
- The owner can be at the business site around the clock.

A home-based business is excellent for the part-time entrepreneur. Many businesses are operated from the owner's home, on a part-time basis, until a demand is established. Then the entrepreneur can better afford to move to a larger site.

You might recall the story of Mary Lawrence in Chapter 1. Mary successfully turned a part-time jewelry business into a full-time career. She started a home-based business selling hand-made jewelry to retailers. She worked in her basement to fill the orders, then took the finished products to a nearby shipping office. When a steady demand for her merchandise was established, she hired four people and moved to an industrial park to have more working space and better access to shippers.

Anyone can operate a home-based business. Many services, such as babysitting, house or office cleaning, or lawn maintenance, can be coordinated from a home. All that is needed is a telephone to contact customers and a typewriter or word processor. It is also possible to sell goods, via mail order, from a home. The goods can be offered through advertisements or catalogs or by direct mail. Orders would be sent to your home or a local post office box, then filled and shipped from a local post office or shipping company.

Professional Office Space

Many entrepreneurs need a professional office to effectively sell to their clients. Doctors, lawyers, real estate agents, accountants, business consultants, and architects are examples of entrepreneurs who need office space for their businesses. It is important that the offices present a professional image and be conveniently located. Many types of offices are available, from small suites in stand-alone buildings to penthouse suites at the tops of skyscrapers. The spaces are leased, and expenses vary depending on location, size, and what services the landlord offers to the tenant. Some office complexes offer shared office expenses in an arrangement similar to that of an incubator.

LEASING

commercial lease, a signed legal agreement that specifies the terms (length of time, cost, conditions to be met) for use of a business property by someone other than its owner

lessee, the person who promises to pay a specified sum of money for the use of space

lessor, the person who allows someone to use his or her property under certain terms

Unless they work from home-based businesses, business owners must make lease arrangements or buy a business property. Lease agreements for **commercial leases** are usually long and complex contracts that the **lessee** and possibly an attorney should review carefully. The lease should have complete details of all conditions and costs, including basic rent costs and other costs, such as maintenance fees, utility costs, insurance costs, and, in the case of larger shopping centers, merchant association dues. Since the **lessor** often requires at least three years of tenancy, the entrepreneur must feel confident that all conditions are satisfactory. Too often business owners must fulfill lease obligations for businesses that have failed and no longer exist.

EVALUATING A FACILITY

Choosing the facility for a new business is an important decision for business owners. Once the best location has been found, the owner must determine if the facility is suitable for the intended business operation. It must be large enough, and it must be structurally sound. Some leases assign responsibility for all maintenance of property to the lessee; if there is a leak in the roof or if the plumbing or air conditioning fails, the tenant will have to pay all repair costs. Therefore, it is imperative that the prospective tenant carefully examine the property for structural soundness before signing the lease.

It is very important that the chosen site fit the image of the intended business. Selling expensive, fine jewelry requires a different image than selling tires. People shopping for a $5,000 diamond ring will not shop in a rundown area of town. However, for most people, the price of a tire is more important than where it is purchased. If you are selling to a specific market, the facility and its surroundings must appeal to that market.

Different businesses have different environmental requirements. For example, the aspiring restaurateur should consider the following:

1. Restaurants should not be in areas that are noisy, have unpleasant odors, or are frequented by vagrants.

Illus. 5-7(a and b) The site must fit the image of the intended business.

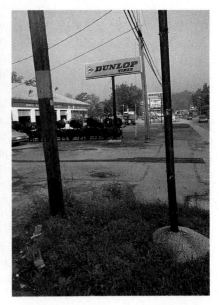

Courtesy of the Los Angeles Visitors and Convention Bureau

2. The type of neighborhood will influence whether customers come in family groups, couples, or singles.
3. Restaurants located in industrial areas will depend on surrounding businesses and their employees' lunch arrangements.
4. Restaurants in residential areas will be most dependent on evening trade.
5. Restaurants should not be located near funeral homes or cemeteries.
6. Schools or churches are not particularly desirable as neighbors to a restaurant; they may cause congestion, and they can affect the restaurant's right to sell alcoholic beverages.
7. There must be good lighting and ample parking to provide convenient access for customers.

The prospective business owner will need to research the location and facility requirements for his or her intended product or service.

JEFF BURNETT—ENTREPRENEUR

After completing his demographic research and studying his competition, Jeff began his search for the perfect location for his business. Having classified his products as shopping goods, Jeff knew he needed a location with heavy pedestrian traffic. He ruled out Logansville's deserted downtown area and concentrated on the shopping centers in the community. There were seven centers that had more than ten stores each: three were neighborhood shopping centers, two were community discount plazas, and two were community malls. There were two competitive stores that were located in shopping centers—one in a neighborhood shopping center and one in a discount plaza. Neither community mall had a retail music store.

Jeff visited the managers of the two community malls. They were both interested in adding a retail music store, so Jeff began his research to decide which would be the best location. After collecting and reviewing his information, he was confused.

Shopping mall A (see Figure 5-1), with 45 stores, had 2 anchor stores—a nationally known department store and a large supermarket. The anchor stores were located at opposite ends of the mall. Mixed in with the smaller stores were a well-known drug store, a large variety store, and a movie theater. The base rent for a 2,000 square-foot space, the size recommended by the record companies, was $1,500 per month.

Shopping mall B (see Figure 5-2) was located two miles north of shopping mall A on the same main road through town. It was

Figure 5-1   Shopping Mall A

Figure 5-2   Shopping Mall B

about the same size as shopping mall A with the same tenant mix: 2 anchors, 40 small stores, a drug store, a variety store, and a movie theater. The biggest difference was that the anchor stores were both department stores. The rent for 2,000 square feet of space in this center was $2,000 per month.

The manager of shopping mall A pointed out that the department store in his center was well recognized throughout the country and that the supermarket was the largest in the community. The manager of shopping mall B pointed out that the two competing department stores stimulated a great flow of pedestrian traffic from one end of the mall to the other. He also pointed out that a supermarket anchor is of questionable value to a music retailer; most people do not combine grocery shopping with shopping trips for other goods.

Jeff decided to do a traffic count at each mall. He stood in front of the proposed location in each mall and counted the number of shoppers who passed during specific periods of time.

When he compared the results, Jeff found that shopping mall B's traffic was almost 50 percent higher. He wondered if the extra traffic was worth the extra $500 per month in rent. If the 50 percent increase in traffic generated a 50 percent increase in sales, it could mean an additional $100,000, bringing his total projected annual sales to $300,000. After discussing his thoughts with Susan, and with Mrs. Contel at the bank, Jeff decided that an additional $6,000 of rent for a potential $100,000 increase in sales was a reasonable risk.

SUMMARY

Successful entrepreneurs know the importance of choosing the right location. Being in the right place at the right time is an important ingredient of success. Our society has become accustomed to accessibility and convenience, and we have come to expect it.

Entrepreneurs must classify the products to be sold in terms of the degree of convenience the consumer demands of the product. They can then determine what type of location should be chosen to successfully sell the products. This choice will depend on the product, the community, and the amount of money available to operate the business.

Entrepreneurs who sell or manufacture industrial goods might locate in an industrial park. Some small industrial and technological businesses locate in incubators.

Some entrepreneurs operate small businesses from their homes. Many successful businesses have been started in homes and then moved after a demand has been established. A home-based business is an excellent starting place for the part-time entrepreneur.

Unless entrepreneurs plan to buy a facility or work at home, they will need to make leasing arrangements. Commercial leases are legal contracts that should be signed only after a complete review of the document and a complete examination of the facility. The examination of the facility must include its surroundings. The location must be conducive to selling the intended product or service.

VOCABULARY BUILDER

On a separate sheet of paper, write a brief definition of each word or phrase based on your reading of the chapter.

1. Convenience goods
2. Shopping goods
3. Specialty goods
4. Neighborhood shopping center
5. Community shopping center
6. Anchor store
7. Regional shopping center
8. Mall
9. Profit margin
10. Markup
11. Super regional shopping center
12. Merchant association
13. Stand-alone store
14. Industrial park
15. Incubator
16. Home-based business
17. Commercial lease
18. Lessee
19. Lessor

REVIEW QUESTIONS

1. Why is choosing the proper business location important?
2. What are the differences between convenience goods, shopping goods, and specialty goods?
3. Why should entrepreneurs classify the products to be sold before choosing a location?
4. What are the differences between neighborhood shopping centers, community shopping centers, regional shopping centers, and super regional shopping centers?
5. What is a merchant association?
6. What is an industrial park?
7. What is the purpose of an incubator?
8. What is the primary reason for starting a business in the home?
9. What is a commercial lease?
10. Why is the environment surrounding a business important to its success?

DISCUSSION QUESTIONS

1. Why have accessibility and convenience become so important to consumers?
2. What would happen if a convenience grocery store were located in a rather deserted downtown area? Why?
3. Where do people shop most often, and why?
4. What can happen to business owners who do not take the time to study and learn leasing considerations?
5. Why would opening an expensive jewelry store in a discount shopping center be dangerous?

CRITICAL THINKING

Make a list of businesses that you could operate from your home. What are the risks of each? What is the potential for each?

SHORT CASE: THE WRONG SIDE OF THE STREET

Sally Watkins had wanted to open a gift shop on posh St. George's Avenue since moving to the area seven years ago. The tree-lined shopping area comprised four blocks of unusual boutiques. There were gift shops, fashion boutiques, jewelry shops, craft stores, European-style restaurants—a dazzling collection to please the most discriminating shoppers. The area was so successful that openings for new stores were rare. When a vacancy did occur, the leasing agent would contact the next person on the long tenant waiting list.

When Sally learned that the old movie theater across the street was to be converted into a three-story shopping complex of small stores, she contacted the developer. The developer's plan provided for 18 store spaces of approximately 800 square feet each. The developer was hoping for a balanced tenant mix of specialty retail stores and food services. The idea was to have a restaurant, a gift shop, an apparel store, and three other stores on each level. This would ensure a good traffic flow throughout the complex. Sally leased the ground floor gift shop location, just inside the entrance—a sure winner. She had carefully scrutinized the gift shops across the street; they all seemed to be very successful.

During the nine months of remodeling, Sally planned an exciting presentation. She went to the leading merchandise marts to buy her inventory and consulted with top professionals on store layout. The finished store was truly a fine one. It had the latest in fixture design, elegant color-coordinated decor, and a sophisticated cash register.

The Theatre Shopping Galleria opened with great fanfare. Of the 18 spaces, 15 opened on time, and the initial reaction was quite enthusiastic. Sally was very pleased with the first 10 days' receipts, and the compliments seemed endless. After 30 days, however, she became concerned—the initial curious shopping crowd thinned, and it was not replaced by consistent, everyday traffic. Sales were inconsistent; somedays were so hectic she could hardly keep up, and others were so slow it seemed a barricade had been placed in front of the entrance. She was puzzled when she learned that business was still at a brisk, consistent level for the gift merchants across the street.

A year later Sally contemplated closing. Six of the original merchants had already moved out. Four had been replaced, but the new tenants did not have the quality or stature of the original stores. Meanwhile, businesses on the other side of St. George's Avenue continued to prosper.[1]

1. Examine Figure 5-3. Can you see some of the reasons the Theatre Shopping Galleria had difficulty attracting shoppers?
2. Based on your knowledge of the importance of convenience, what could be done to help the stores in the Galleria?
3. Do you think Sally should close her store?

Figure 5-3   St. George's Avenue

PROJECT CHALLENGE

Choose a potential location for your business, applying what you have learned in this chapter.

If your business involves the sale of a consumer product or service you should consider the following:

1. Classify your product or service as a convenience, shopping, or specialty good.

---

[1]Case study entitled "The Wrong Side of the Street" reprinted, with permission, from book #3511 *Why Entrepreneurs Fail: Avoid the 20 Pitfalls of Running Your Own Business* by James W. Halloran. Copyright 1991 by Liberty Hall Press/TAB Books, a division of McGraw-Hill, Blue Ridge Summit, PA 17294 (1-800-233-1128 or 1-717-794-2191).

2. Visit shopping areas in your community where you would expect to find similar products. Make notes about how successful these areas seem to be, based on the number of shoppers, and how well the businesses appear to be doing.
3. Call leasing agents and inquire about costs and other leasing considerations.

If you are starting an industrial, wholesale, technological, or professional business, ask leasing agents for information about industrial parks, incubators, or professional office space, including terms and considerations.

If you want to start a home-based business, decide how you would use your home as a place of business.

Now make your location decision. Remember to consider the surrounding environment and the facility itself in making your decision. Explain why you chose the location.

6
Developing the Marketing Plan

marketing concept, the belief that consumer wants and needs are the driving force behind any product development or marketing effort

market segmentation, process of dividing the market into groups of similar consumers

target marketing, marketing to a selected group of consumers

THE MARKETING CONCEPT

Small business owners who want to become successful need to develop effective marketing plans. To develop effective marketing plans, entrepreneurs must utilize the **marketing concept.** The first step in utilizing the marketing concept is identifying the customer.

MARKET SEGMENTATION AND TARGET MARKETING

Identifying the customer begins with **market segmentation**. Since a small business cannot possibly serve an entire market, entrepreneurs must determine which portion of the market is most likely to buy the product or service offered. An example of market segmentation would be to separate country music fans from those who like to listen to rock, then classifying them as different market segments. After completing the market segmentation process, entrepreneurs identify their customers through **target marketing.** For example, a radio station concentrating its efforts on rock listeners from the ages of fourteen to twenty-two would be target marketing. It is imperative that the small business target its marketing to a small, manageable segment of the market that can be effectively reached and influenced. Entrepreneurs need to make sure, however, that the targeted market is stable, permanent, and large enough to support the business. Focusing on a manageable segment will enable the business owner to design a marketing program that aims directly at the best market for the product or service. Target marketing begins with market research, as explained in Chapter 3.

Remember Tim Holton and his baseball plaques from Chapter 1? Tim did his market research before deciding to sell his baseball plaques. He wanted to find out if there was a large enough market for his product before spending money to produce it. By researching publications, he found that there were more than 20 million collectors of baseball cards. He then continued his research to find out what publications baseball card collectors subscribe to. When he felt confident that he had found publications with good circulation to his market, he ran test advertisements in the publications to determine consumer interest. He analyzed the results by comparing the number of orders received with the circulation of each publication. With this information, he was able to determine where to place his advertisements to get enough orders to make a profit. He could then decide how many plaques to produce and how much to spend on advertisements. Tim followed the steps for market segmentation and target marketing.

As discussed in Chapter 3, to effectively sell a product or service, the entrepreneur must know as many market characteristics as possible, such as where the people who comprise the prime market live and how much money they have to spend. Identifying the ideal customer keeps the entrepreneur from spending money unwisely by trying to attract customers who are not interested in the product or service offered.

TARGET MARKETING QUESTIONS

Target marketing is achieved by answering the following questions:

1. Where do my customers live and work?
2. What level of income is needed to purchase my product or service?
3. What is the life-style of the people who are most likely to need my product or service?
4. Which of my potential customers will receive the greatest benefit from my product or service?
5. Which group of consumers will buy the most of my product or service?

customer profile, a recorded and complete description of the ideal customer for a business

The answers to these questions can help entrepreneurs achieve their target market goal which is to create **customer profiles.** An example is shown in Figure 6-1.

Place a customer profile in the center of a target as the bull's eye. The outer rings of the target will have descriptions of customers who have some of the characteristics of the ideal customer and *might* buy your product. However, the bull's-eye is where the entrepreneur's marketing arrow should be aimed. Figure 6-2 on page 96 shows the target market for a retail store that sells expensive women's clothing.

Figure 6-1   Customer Profile

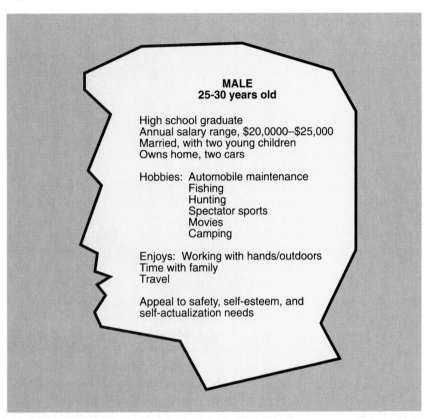

**MALE
25-30 years old**

High school graduate
Annual salary range, $20,0000–$25,000
Married, with two young children
Owns home, two cars

Hobbies: Automobile maintenance
            Fishing
            Hunting
            Spectator sports
            Movies
            Camping

Enjoys: Working with hands/outdoors
Time with family
Travel

Appeal to safety, self-esteem, and
self-actualization needs

Source: Reprinted, with permission, from book #3511 *Why Entrepreneurs Fail: Avoid the 20 Pitfalls of Running Your Own Business* by James W. Halloran. Copyright 1991 by Liberty Hall Press/TAB Books, a division of McGraw-Hill, Blue Ridge Summit, PA 17294 (1-800-233-1128 or 1-717-794-2191).

MARKETING RESEARCH

marketing research, the systematic gathering, recording, and analyzing of data relating to the marketing of goods or services

How do entrepreneurs determine what their potential customers want? A useful tool in this process is **marketing research.** As defined by the American Marketing Association, marketing research refers to the systematic gathering, recording, and analyzing of data about problems relating to the marketing of goods or services.[1]

---

[1]From American Marketing Association, "Report of the Definitions Committee of the American Marketing Association," Chicago, 1961.

Figure 6-2   Target Market Illustration

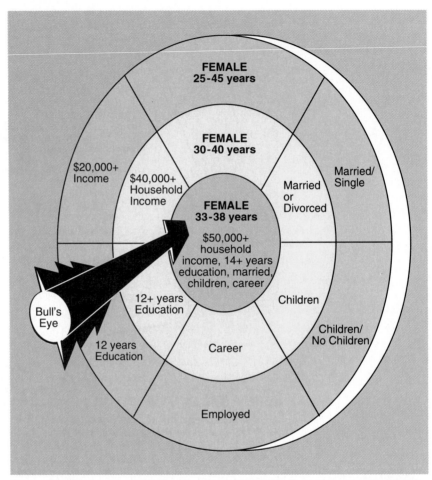

Source: Reprinted, with permission, from book #3511 *Why Entrepreneurs Fail: Avoid the 20 Pitfalls of Running Your Own Business* by James W. Halloran. Copyright 1991 by Liberty Hall Press/TAB Books, a division of McGraw-Hill, Blue Ridge Summit, PA 17294 (1-800-233-1128 or 1-717-794-2191).

There are many times when the data obtained through marketing research can prove very useful. One of those times is during the start-up phase of the business. Another is when the business has unexplained difficulties, such as low sales, reduced store traffic, or frequent merchandise returns. Expansion of the business also requires research. Any time a business owner needs to make a decision, marketing research should be considered.

Marketing Research at Work

Entrepreneurs can use the six research steps discussed in Chapter 3 (see Market Research) to make effective management decisions concerning marketing. Following these steps can solve many kinds of problems for entrepreneurs, once they learn the process.

Define the Question. Mei-ling Chan wants to open a bookstore, but she needs to decide what types of books and related merchandise to carry. She defines the problem by asking herself, "Exactly what types of merchandise and specific product lines should I offer for sale?"

Determine Needed Data. If Mei-ling makes a decision without adequate information, she is just guessing. Guessing about the solution to a problem is not a good way to run a business.

For Mei-ling, the problem is what to sell. She needs to know what kind of books and related merchandise customers want to purchase. Therefore, she has to collect data concerning the buying habits of her targeted customers.

Illus. 6-1 Entrepreneurs, like Mei-ling Chan, can use local libraries to begin their market research.

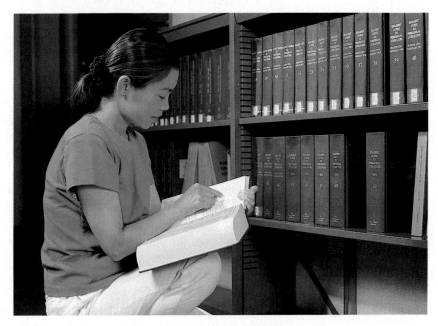

Collect Data. Now that Mei-ling has identified the data she needs to collect, she has to figure out how to collect it. Since she is basically a lone operator on a tight budget, that may be a difficult task.

Mei-ling worked in the consumer book publishing business several years ago, so she has access to some secondary data, including several lists of bestselling books. These lists were compiled and published by national newspapers, consumer book clubs, and the local newspaper. She also has access to new book reviews through the periodical index in her local library, which allows her to locate magazine reviews. These data will tell her which books will be in high demand. She also has information concerning how much money was spent the previous year on hardcover and paperback books. Finally, she has a breakdown according to type of book purchased, for example, the number of mysteries, romances, science fiction novels, and biographies that were sold in hardcover and paperback. If she adds this to her demographic research (see Collect Data in Chapter 3), her volume of data should be significant.

Secondary data can provide much useful information. The smart entrepreneur will seek out all available sources of secondary data before proceeding to more direct collection of data. If Mei-ling does not have enough secondary information to make her decision, she must collect primary data. In Mei-ling's case, the primary data will be consumer data. As an entrepreneur operating on a small budget, Meiling's task may be accomplished in one of two ways. She may either observe consumers or survey consumers using a questionnaire. Whichever approach is used, Mei-ling should observe or question as many consumers as possible.

Analyze Data. After Mei-ling has analyzed her data, she will know what her customers are most likely to buy. If an entrepreneur has a problem with frequent merchandise returns, the analysis may indicate that customers find that products made by a certain manufacturer don't operate as they should or that the workmanship is of poor quality.

Implement Data. Mei-ling Chan can now use her analysis to make good buying decisions. She decides to carry a full range of fiction and nonfiction in her bookstore, with an emphasis on self-help books. In addition, a large selection of periodicals will be prominently displayed to entice customers in to browse. Finally, a selection of specialty stationery items will round out her new store's offerings.

Evaluate Action. After Mei-ling has made her buying decisions, she will closely monitor sales to determine if changes in product selection are needed. If she does need to alter her stock, Mei-Ling can use these same six research steps to help her decide what changes to make and when to make them.

MARKETING MIX

marketing mix, four variables—product, place, price, and promotion—that must be manipulated to ensure success in marketing

After the marketing research is completed, entrepreneurs can make informed decisions about the **marketing mix.** Often referred to as the four *P*'s of marketing, the marketing mix variables form the heart of the marketing plan (see Figure 6-3).

Figure 6-3 The Marketing Mix

Product

Most entrepreneurs think that the product or service part of the marketing mix is the easiest with which to deal. After all, they chose that product or service when they decided on their business venture.

It is not always that easy. Mei-ling, for example, knew she wanted to open a book store. But what kind of books would sell best? She still has to make a product decision. What will happen if she makes the wrong product choice? Choosing the right product may be difficult. Entrepreneurs often have a little doubt about whether or not the product offered will sell.

Place

The place, or distribution, decision means the entrepreneur has to make sure that the right product is in the right place at the right time. The product must be on the shelves ready to be sold when the consumer walks in. If it isn't, then all the marketing planning in the world will not make the business a success.

Price

The price decision is critical to marketing success. The price charged for the product must be low enough that consumers will want to buy. At the same time, it must be high enough for the entrepreneur to make a reasonable profit.

Another consideration is whether or not the price is competitive with those of other businesses offering the same product or service. If it is not, there must be a reason for the difference. The reason must be readily apparent to the customers. Pricing is such a critical P in the marketing mix that Chapter 7 is devoted to pricing strategies.

Promotion

Promotion, like the other P's, is very important to marketing success. It is through promotion that the entrepreneur informs the potential customer about the product or service. Promotion includes advertising, sales promotion, personal selling, and visual merchandising.

advertising, paid nonpersonal public notice

Advertising.   Although **advertising** can be an expensive aspect of starting a business, it is a factor that cannot be ignored by entrepreneurs offering products or services directly to consumers.

Advertising is important to entrepreneurs starting new businesses and to owners of established businesses. There are several reasons for this importance. Advertising accomplishes the following:

- Lets customers know that the new business exists
- Informs customers about the products or services that the business offers
- Provides communication with customers
- Keeps the business's name in front of the buying public

As an entrepreneur, you must select the form of advertising that best suits your business. Newspaper advertisements are probably the most common form of advertisement for entrepreneurs. The other common types of advertising are radio and television (TV). Radio and TV can reach many, many people, but TV advertising, in particular, is quite expensive. Other types of advertising that might be considered are telephone directory ads, direct mail, billboards, and specialty advertising. Examples of

Illus. 6-2 Direct mail is just one of many effective methods of advertising.

specialty advertising are calendars or keyrings with the business's name imprinted on them.

sales promotion, things other than advertising and personal selling that will have a positive impact on the purchasing decision.

Sales Promotion.   To ensure effective **sales promotion,** entrepreneurs must understand the communication channel (see Figure 6-4). The communication channel consists of the five steps in sending a message—message sender, encoding, message vehicle, decoding, and message receiver. The message sender decides what message is to be relayed, creates the message (encoding), and determines the best method for relaying the message. That method may be advertising or sales promotion. Once sent, the message is interpreted (decoded) and absorbed by the message receiver. The sender waits for feedback, or a response, from the receiver. The feedback might be a returned message or an action taken as a result of the message.

In sales promotion, the entrepreneur is a message sender hoping for a positive response from the message receiver such as confirmation of a sale. To maintain an effective communication channel, the entrepreneur must recognize that distortions and interruptions will disrupt the messages. The distortions, called "noise" factors, will impose severe limitations on

Figure 6-4   The Communication Channel

Source: Reprinted, with permission, from book #30049 *The Entrepreneur's Guide to Start-ing a Successful Business* by James W. Halloran. Copyright 1987 by Liberty Hall Press/TAB Books, a division of McGraw-Hill, Blue Ridge Summit, PA 17294 (1-800-233-1128 or 1-717-794-2191).

how intended messages are received and interpreted. A simple example is the game of sending a message around a group—each person whispers the message to the next person, passing the message to each person in the group. The message received by the last person often has little resemblance to the original message. Try this in your class or with a group of friends and see what happens.

In sales promotion and advertising, the best way to get a message across is through repetition. The more times a message is sent, the better the chances that it will be received in its intended form. This is why advertisements are repeated many times. The advertiser believes that with continual exposure, the intended message will eventually be received, resulting in more sales.

One of the most common tools for sales promotion currently used by businesses is coupons. Businesses provide coupons to their targeted customers through newspapers, magazines, and direct mail materials. Other examples are free samples and free gifts. The smart entrepreneur chooses sales promotion tools carefully. Because they can be very expensive, sales promotions should be well planned and implemented for specific reasons.

personal selling, face-to-face communication between the buyer and the seller

Personal Selling.   The importance of **personal selling** to the success of a business cannot be overstated. Customers are more likely to purchase a product or service if they like the person selling it. Entrepreneurs may hire salespeople or have family members help out, but they often do the majority of the personal selling themselves. This is because of the small number of employees in most new businesses and because the entrepreneur knows the product or service being sold better than anyone else in the business. Because of their confidence, determination, and need to achieve, entrepreneurs are often natural salespeople. Nevertheless, since personal selling is critical to the success of the business, the entrepreneur should take the time to satisfy the needs and wants of customers by making use of personal selling skills. Personal selling skills—involving a sales approach, presentation, and a close—can be developed by study and observation. Time spent in this fashion will almost certainly pay off in increased sales and customer satisfaction.

Visual Merchandising. Window displays are a very common form of **visual merchandising.** Visual merchandising also includes any interior use of merchandise to attract customers' attention. Examples are the use of shadow boxes, display cases, and mannequins.

visual merchandising, creative display of merchandise for attracting customers' attention and creating a desire to purchase

Illus. 6-3   Visual merchandising includes any interior display of merchandise to attract customers' attention.

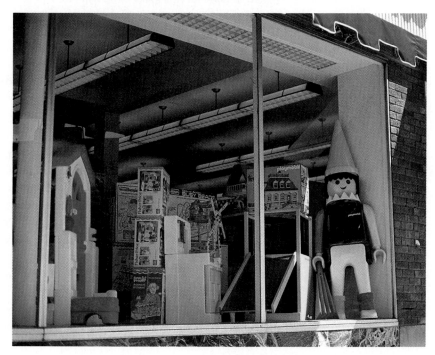

MARKETING STRATEGIES

marketing strategy, planned activity designed to increase sales of a business's products or services

To develop **marketing strategies,** entrepreneurs must analyze previously gathered data about customers, community, facilities, and competition. Once the analysis is complete, decisions about the marketing mix can be made.

Consider the 4 *P's*

Entrepreneurs who are planning to sell products must make final decisions about the source for the products and how they will get to the place of business. From whom will the products be purchased? When? How will they be transported? Can sources ensure timely delivery? What type of inventory system will be used? Remember, if the product is not there when the customer is ready to buy, the sale may be forever lost. Final pricing decisions also need to be made. What will the price range(s) be for the products or services?

When entrepreneurs get to the promotion phase of the marketing mix, they are at the point where most marketing strategies will be decided. The majority of the strategies will be promotional in nature.

Implement Marketing Strategies

Now is when entrepreneurs can put their months of research to work. They can use their accurate information to develop effective marketing strategies. Six steps must be carried out to arrive at a complete marketing strategy.

Establish an Advertising Budget. A certain amount of advertising has to be done to launch a new business toward success. Entrepreneurs need to decide what kind of advertising will best serve their type of business. To get assistance, the entrepreneur should contact the newspaper, radio station, or whatever medium is to be used. Professionals will be available to discuss schedules, costs, and other necessary information. A little extra time should be devoted to comparing the costs for different types of advertising as well as the costs between competitive advertising media, such as two radio stations or two newspapers. The information gathered from this investigation should be used in developing an advertising budget. Although the entrepreneur may feel the expense is excessive, it is necessary.

If the entrepreneur feels that no money is available for advertising, there may not be enough money to start the business. Perhaps a delay in the business start-up should be considered.

Whatever the type of business, some form of advertising is usually necessary to say, "Hey, we're open for business!" The advertising budget may be devoted to direct mail or other means of informing potential customers about the opening. Direct mail might be in the form of a sales letter or a catalog, or it might be a circular informing potential customers of the opening of the business and of special sale items.

Plan and Schedule Advertising. Once the advertising budget has been determined, a plan should be developed. Working with the media specialists discussed above, the entrepreneur should plan and schedule actual advertising.

Make Decisions about Sales Promotion. Entrepreneurs should make decisions about sales promotion well in advance of the planned opening of the business. For example, entrepreneurs who plan to use coupons as promotional tools must design the coupons (or have them designed), contact printers to obtain quotes for the work, select a printer, order the coupons, and distribute them in time for the opening. This process could take weeks or months.

Decide How Personal Selling Will Be Handled. Many decisions have to be made concerning personal selling, such as whether to hire salespeople, how many to hire, when to hire them, how to compensate them, and how to train them. These decisions and others will have to be made and acted upon long before the business is open and ready for customers.

Make Decisions about Visual Merchandising. If the new business is retail, visual merchandising is an important concern. The entrepreneur cannot wait until the merchandise arrives. Decisions have to be made much earlier so that visual merchandising supplies and props can be ordered and/or constructed.

Develop a Strategies Calendar. After strategies have been developed, they should be scheduled. Using a scheduling device (see Figure 6-5) allows the entrepreneur to plan strategy implementation. It also provides a method for keeping track of the implementation.

If a calendar is used, start by listing the strategies, then set a date to begin planning, write down the date planning must be completed, and set the date to implement (start) the strategy. When the strategy is completed, put a check mark in the last column.

Figure 6-5   Strategies Calendar

Strategy	Begin Planning	Complete Planning	Implement Plan	Strategy Complete
1.				
2.				
3.				
4.				
5.				
6.				
7.				
8.				
9.				
10.				

JEFF BURNETT—ENTREPRENEUR

Let's see how Jeff is doing. He has decided what types of music to carry and has information concerning his competition (see Chapters 3 and 4). Jeff now needs to find out who his best customers will be. He segmented the market as follows:

1. People who buy musical recordings generally shop at stores located close to where they live. Most people will not travel great distances to obtain musical recordings. Recordings are often bought on impulse.
2. Consumers purchase records, tapes, or CD's with extra income. They are not necessity items, so they must be paid for with money not needed for basic living expenses. The price range of $6-$15 requires an income level above minimum wage.
3. People who buy many musical recordings have sufficient leisure time to listen to them. They are people in whose lives music is

an integral part. They also have the necessary equipment to play the recordings.

4. Many individuals listen to musical recordings while commuting or exercising. This segment consists of people who are well versed in popular music.

5. Industry sources confirm that most records, tapes, and CD's are purchased by teenagers. They are well informed about the most popular records and buy them for social needs. They normally have extra income from allowances or part-time work. Many buy on a regular basis.

Having made these determinations, Jeff wrote a customer profile and drew a target of his market (see Figures 6-6 and 6-7).

Based on what he learned through his research, Jeff has decided on his marketing mix. He feels the most important part of the mix is product selection.

Jeff is now ready to start developing his marketing plan. The first thing he must do is establish an advertising budget. Based on

Figure 6-6   Customer Profile of Musical Recording Buyer

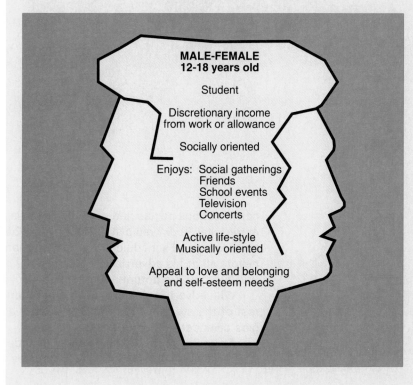

MALE-FEMALE
12-18 years old

Student

Discretionary income
from work or allowance

Socially oriented

Enjoys: Social gatherings
Friends
School events
Television
Concerts

Active life-style
Musically oriented

Appeal to love and belonging
and self-esteem needs

Figure 6-7   Target for Musical Recording Customer

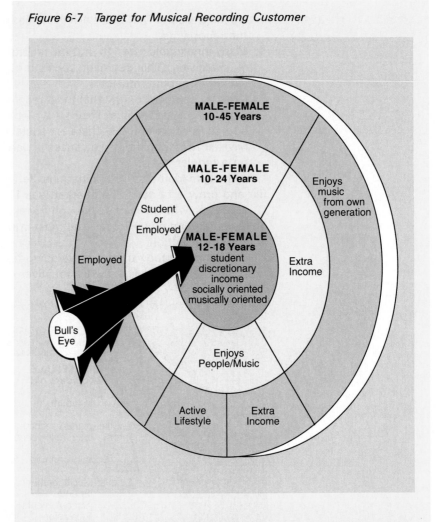

conversations he has had with the advertising sales representative at the local "rock" radio station, Jeff set $2,000 as his budget. Next, he created and scheduled his advertisements. Jeff has decided to devote all of his advertising dollars to the rock station. He figures that most of his potential customers are listening to that station.

With advertising taken care of, Jeff worked his way through the rest of the steps. The last thing he did was to develop his strategies calendar (see Figure 6-8).

As you examine Jeff's calendar, decide if you agree with all of his decisions. Look at both the strategies and the dates.

Figure 6-8 Strategies Calendar: Rock 'n' Soul Music—Opening 9/1

		(Current Date: 6/1)		
STRATEGY	BEGIN PLANNING	COMPLETE PLANNING	IMPLEMENT PLANNING	STRATEGY COMPLETE
1. Visual merchandising	ASAP	6/30	8/24	
2. Order products	ASAP	7/31	8/15	
3. Advertising— radio	7/1	7/31	8/15	
4. Hire/train salesperson	7/15	7/31	8/24	
5. Promotions— coupon free gift/ grand opening	ASAP	7/31 7/31	9/1 9/1	
6. Specialty advertising— keyrings matchbooks	ASAP	8/15 8/15	9/1 9/1	

SUMMARY

As entrepreneurs begin the marketing planning process, they must understand the marketing concept. They must then use the data collected in their market research to segment the market, breaking it down into manageable groups of potential consumers with similar characteristics. Additional information allows entrepreneurs to target the market to a very specialized group of customers with similar characteristics and needs. The final step is creating a customer profile that describes the ideal customer for the planned business.

To effectively plan, decisions need to be made regarding the marketing mix, the 4 *P*'s: product, place, price, and promotion. The promotion part of the mix includes advertising, sales promotion, personal selling, and visual merchandising.

Once the marketing plan is developed, the entrepreneur will have a list of marketing strategies to implement.

- Establish an advertising budget.
- Plan and schedule advertising.
- Make decisions about sales promotion.
- Decide how personal selling will be handled.
- Make decisions about visual merchandising.
- Develop a strategies calendar.

The ultimate goal of the business is to offer the product or service to potential customers at a convenient location at an affordable price, so the business will make a profit. If this happens, both the consumer and the business owner will be satisfied.

As each strategy is completed, the dream of being a successful business owner will be one step closer to becoming a reality.

VOCABULARY BUILDER

On a separate sheet of paper, write a brief description of each word or phrase based on your reading of the chapter.

1. Marketing concept
2. Market segmentation
3. Target marketing
4. Customer profile
5. Marketing research
6. Marketing mix
7. Advertising
8. Sales promotion
9. Personal selling
10. Visual merchandising
11. Marketing strategy

REVIEW QUESTIONS

1. Why is it important that entrepreneurs study and learn the segment of the market to be served?
2. Why must entrepreneurs concentrate on a target market?
3. What is the value of drawing a customer profile?
4. What are the six steps of marketing research?
5. List the four variables of the marketing mix. 4 P's
6. What are the five steps of the communication channel? Briefly describe each step.
7. What are marketing strategies?
8. What are the steps involved in the development of marketing strategies?

DISCUSSION QUESTIONS

1. What is the marketing concept?
2. What would be included if you were writing a customer profile about one of your classmates?
3. What is marketing research and why is it important?
4. From what sources might you obtain secondary and primary data for your own use?
5. What is advertising and why is it important?
6. What are some examples of "noise" factors that distort messages?
7. How can various forms of sales promotion help a business?
8. What is personal selling?
9. Why is a strategies calendar necessary?

CRITICAL THINKING

Gene Chin is planning to open a men's clothing store in the local mall. The majority of his products will be for professional men 30 years of age and older. At this point in his marketing planning he is working on advertising.

1. If Gene lived in your town, what would his advertising options be?
2. To give Gene some ideas, collect ads from three similar businesses. Try to get examples from at least two media. Explain how each of the ads succeeds or fails in letting customers know the business exists, informing customers about the business's products or services, communicating with customers, and keeping the business's name in front of the buying public.
3. Based on Gene's target market and your knowledge of local radio stations, recommend the local station that you think he should use. Give reasons for your recommendation.

SHORT CASE: SELECTING A PERSONAL SHOPPER

Kathy O'Neill plans to open a business in three months. Her business will offer what she considers a needed service in her community. Kathy plans to offer customized shopping for senior citizens who wish to avoid the hassle of going to the grocery store or are simply unable to go themselves.

By researching her community, Kathy has collected the following data:

- Twenty percent of her city's population are senior citizens. Current city population is 115,000.

- The average annual income for each senior citizen household is $25,000.
- Most senior citizens (80 percent) live in the same section of town, the south side, because of a concentration of retirement housing.

Although Kathy knows that she wants to sell her services as a personal shopper, she hasn't decided exactly what specific services senior citizens would be willing to buy.

1. Do you think Kathy has an idea that will work? Why?
2. What would you suggest Kathy do to determine the specific services to offer?
3. What other information (if any) do you think Kathy needs to complete her marketing plan?

PROJECT CHALLENGE

At this point in your overall business planning, it is time to concentrate on the marketing plan. In your business plan notebook, complete the following as they relate to your hypothetical business:

1. Decide if you believe in the marketing concept.
2. Determine what information you will need when developing your marketing mix.
3. Design a marketing research process for gathering the information you need. Gather the data.
4. Develop your marketing mix.

7

Pricing and Sales Planning

After mastering the information contained in this chapter, you should be able to:

7-1 Understand the importance of price.
7-2 Define and calculate a markup.
7-3 Describe different pricing strategies and understand why each is used.
7-4 Describe the steps of the selling process.

To be successful, entrepreneurs must offer products that fulfill unsatisfied needs and that are conveniently available to the intended market at an acceptable cost. They must also educate the market about the products' features, advantages, and benefits. This is how the 4 *P*'s discussed in Chapter 6—product, place, price, and promotion—are interrelated. We have discussed having the right product at the right place; now we will discuss the importance of offering the product at the right price with the right sales plan.

A product or service that is not properly priced cannot be sold successfully. Determining proper price begins with understanding supply and demand.

UNDERSTANDING SUPPLY AND DEMAND

economics, the study of how the resources of a society are allocated

If you take a course in **economics,** you will learn the relationship between supply and demand. Proper allocation of goods and services to the market at an affordable cost helps maintain a healthy economy. We can only buy what we can afford—the higher the price of the product or service, the smaller the market will be. If the price of a product is perceived as too high by the market, the demand for the product will be low. This will cause a surplus of the product in the marketplace and production will have to be slowed or stopped. Conversely, if a product is priced below the perceived value, the demand for the product will be great. This will cause a shortage in the marketplace and production will need to be increased to bring supply in line with demand.

The entrepreneur's goal is to find the price point that allows a balance of demand and supply. When a price is set high enough to ensure a profit for the seller, certain portions of the market will switch their demand to other products. This guarantees that the supply of the higher priced product will be adequate for demand. On a supply and demand graph (see Figure 7-1), the balance, or equilibrium, point is reached when the demand line intersects with the supply line. To read the graph, use the vertical (price) scale in conjunction with the supply line. Use the horizontal (quantity) scale in conjunction with the demand line. For example, if an item costs $2, read across the graph until you reach the point where the demand line intersects the horizontal "2" line. The demand for a $2 item would be eight units.

The prices that entrepreneurs set need to be low enough to encourage a high demand for the products or services, but they must also be high enough to ensure a profit. Low prices will certainly increase demand, but may mean little or no profit. High prices could mean more profit, but only if demand does not drop. Therefore, it is important to find a price point that is acceptable to the buyer and yields a satisfactory profit to the seller. In our relatively free marketplace, the determination of the acceptable price point ultimately comes from the buyers; they will not buy what they cannot afford. The entrepreneur attempts to determine what that price is, using various strategies employed in a marketing plan.

The consumer's decision about how to spend money is based on **utility satisfaction.** For example, the consumer has $15. That $15 can be

utility satisfaction, using one's money (utility) for the product or service that will bring the greatest need satisfaction

Figure 7-1 Supply and Demand Graph

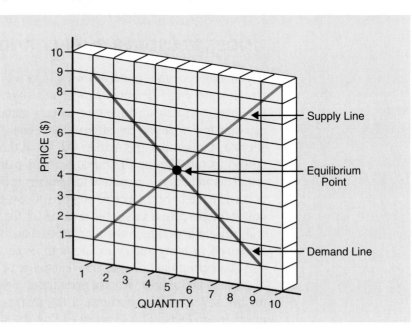

used to buy a new CD or take a friend to a movie. The decision will probably be based on what is perceived to give the greatest need satisfaction. The consumer must weigh considerations such as who the recording artist is and how popular the CD is. On the other hand, the consumer must consider the popularity of the movie and the desire to spend time with a friend. In this instance, the CD industry is competing against the movie industry. A change in price, such as a sale—two CD's for $15—or a discount for matinees might affect the decision. Ultimately, the consumer determines where the money is spent, but businesses *can* influence those decisions.

DETERMINING PRICE

Proper pricing of a product or service addresses two objectives. The first objective is for the price to serve as a customer relations tool. A fair price tells the customer that the business offers good value, encouraging a demand for the product or service. The second objective is for the price to ensure profit to the seller, thereby allowing the business to continue serving the market.

Illus. 7-1   Fixed and variable costs must be determined before pricing each unit.

break-even point, the price at which the costs of producing and/or selling a product or service are covered

fixed cost, a cost that does not vary even though there are changes in production and/or sales volume

variable cost, a cost that fluctuates with changes in production and/or sales volume

Price setting begins with determining a **break-even point.** The entrepreneur determines the break-even point by properly analyzing **fixed costs,** such as rent, utilities, and insurance, and **variable costs,** such as cost of goods or materials, salaries, and advertising, to determine the cost of each unit sold.

Once the break-even point is reached, additional sales will mean profit for the entrepreneur. The more units sold, the more profit will be made. Total profit can be projected by multiplying the amount of money that will be made per unit by the number of units that will be sold, then subtracting the total cost (fixed plus variable) of selling. Figure 7-2 is a graphic illustration of the break-even point for a small manufacturer of a product— let's call it a Gizmo. The price, $10, will cover all fixed and variable costs of making the Gizmos when 1,000 units have been sold. If fewer than 1,000 units are sold at this price there will be a loss; each sale in excess of 1,000 will mean profit.

Figure 7-2   Break-Even Point Graph

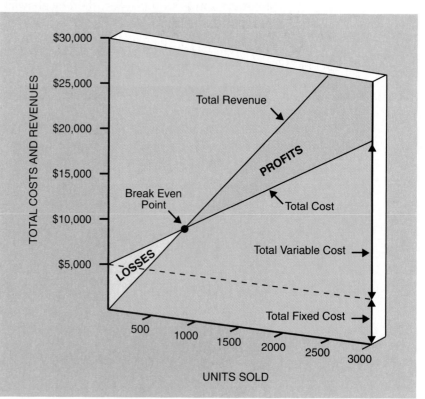

The price of a product or service must accomplish the following:

1. The total cost of the item to be sold must be covered, including the direct expenses of manufacturing or buying the product and the operating and overhead expenses incurred in operating the business.
2. A contribution to the long-term stability of the business must be made—enough profit must be made to generate retained earnings.
3. The entrepreneur must be rewarded for the effort expended and risk assumed in owning and running the business.
4. Customers must perceive the price as fair value.

By satisfying these requirements, the entrepreneur is operating under the **total pricing concept.**

Once they know the break-even point, entrepreneurs can take the next step. With the total pricing concept in mind, as well as profit goals and the condition of the market, entrepreneurs must determine the selling prices of their products.

total pricing concept, prices are set to compete successfully, build good customer relations, and ensure the long-term success of a business

Markups[1]

markup, amount added to the cost of an item to arrive at a selling price

Markups can be stated in dollars or by percentage. They vary widely depending on the industry and market conditions. If an item costs $5 and sells for $10, the markup is $5, or 50 percent, of the selling price.

To calculate a selling price at a 50 percent markup, when the cost is known, divide the cost by the reciprocal of the markup percent. To get the reciprocal, subtract the markup percent from 100. The reciprocal of a 40 percent markup is 60 percent: the reciprocal of a 45 percent markup is 55 percent. A cost of $5 divided by 50 percent, or 0.5, equals a $10 selling price. For a cost of $6 and a desired markup of 40 percent, divide $6 by the reciprocal of 40 percent, or 60 percent.

$$\$6 \text{ (cost)} \div 60 \text{ percent} = \$10$$

To calculate the cost when the selling price and the markup percent are known, multiply the selling price by the markup and subtract the answer from the selling price.

$$\$10 \text{ (selling price)} \times 40 \text{ percent} = \$4 \text{ markup}$$

$$\$10 \text{ (selling price)} - \$4 \text{ markup} = \$6 \text{ cost}$$

---

[1]These examples reprinted, with permission, from book #30049 *The Entrepreneur's Guide to Starting a Successful Business* by James W. Halloran. Copyright 1987 by Liberty Hall Press/TAB Books, a division of McGraw-Hill, Blue Ridge Summit, PA 17294 (1-800-233-1128 or 1-717-794-2191).

To determine the markup percent when the cost and the selling price are known, subtract the cost from the selling price and divide the difference by the selling price.

$$\$10 \text{ (selling price)} - \$6 \text{ (cost)} = \$4 \div \$10 \text{ (selling price)}$$
$$= 0.4 \text{ or } 40 \text{ percent}$$

These examples apply to markup for a retail business. Manufacturers, wholesalers, and service businesses use similar formulas. Determining a markup percent is a complex process that is affected by the many variables of the industry, the market, and the operating expenses of the business. Once determined, a markup percent must be closely monitored.

Many small businesses do not adequately protect their profit objectives—their markups are too low. For example, a retail store sells its products at a 50 percent markup—a $1 product has been purchased by the entrepreneur for $.50. The profit on each dollar of sales is calculated as follows:

Sale	$1.00
Cost of product	− .50
Gross profit	$ .50
Operating expenses	− .34
Net profit before taxes	$ .16

At a 50 percent markup, the owner receives $.16 in profit per item sold—this must cover the owner's salary, taxes, loan payments, and retained earnings. If the markup were only 40 percent, the product cost would be $.60, and if all expenses remained the same, the profit would be $.06. The owner would need to sell more products to make the same amount of money. Too often entrepreneurs discount their markups and severely decrease potential profits.

Markdowns

markdown, the difference between the original selling price and the price at which an item is actually sold

If a product cannot be sold at the selected price, a **markdown** must be taken. When a product is "on sale," the original selling price of the item has been reduced. To calculate a markdown, decide on the percent of the markdown. Multiply the original selling price by the percent markdown. Then subtract the result from the original selling price to get the sale price. There are a number of reasons for taking markdowns:

1. Damaged merchandise—A defective item usually cannot be sold at its original selling price.

2. Old merchandise—Some merchandise that remains in the store too long becomes out of style or obsolete.
3. Broken assortments—Merchandise intended to be sold in sets loses its appeal when part of the set is damaged or missing.
4. Special promotions—Low prices are offered to increase customer traffic and, therefore, demand.
5. Competitors' prices—If the competition is offering the same merchandise at a lower price, the entrepreneur must either lower the price or increase services to effectively compete.
6. Space considerations—Sales must be increased to make room for new merchandise.

Business owners must consider the possibility of markdowns when setting prices for new merchandise. The initial markup must be high enough to accommodate periodic markdowns.

Pricing Strategies

As previously mentioned, the customers ultimately determine price; they will not buy if they do not perceive the price as fair. However, in the initial stages, entrepreneurs must set prices for products or services to determine what is acceptable to customers. This is done by following the

Illus. 7-2 Business owners must consider possible markdowns when setting prices for new merchandise.

rules of the total pricing concept and then determining the marketing objective of the business to determine a pricing strategy. Following are some common strategies that business owners use.

Short-Term Profit Strategy. A short-term profit strategy is used for products that are not expected to remain on the market. These products are fads that take advantage of current, but temporary, demands in the marketplace. The products are sometimes tied into a current market happening, such as a popular movie, record, or fashion trends. These products are produced with the expectation of selling a lot quickly, then getting out of the market. Prices are set very high, anticipating that the short selling period will encourage customers to pay a high price for the "in" product. These products have a high risk; sales are dependent on whether or not the fad or craze catches on. The idea is to make as much profit as possible in a short period of time.

One example of a fad product is the Pet Rock—a novelty product that appeared in the late 1970's. It was an ordinary rock packaged in a small carton that looked like a doghouse. The marketing strategy suggested that you train your rock to do tricks—training instructions were included. It caught the public's imagination—millions were sold during a six-week period, then it quickly disappeared from the marketplace. The price for a common rock, a humorous box, and a sheet of instructions was $5.95—truly a price set with a short-term profit strategy.

Market Penetration Strategy. Sometimes entrepreneurs use a strategy opposite to the short-term strategy. Using a market penetration strategy means selling at the lowest possible price. Entrepreneurs often use this strategy when introducing a new product. The idea is to get people to try the product, then raise the price to a profitable level. This is a method of gaining **market share.** By gaining market share, the entrepreneur increases demand for the product.

market share, the portion of a particular market that uses a particular product or service

Loss Leader Pricing Strategy. Using the loss leader pricing strategy, retailers purposely price some of their products at a level that will produce little profit or incur a loss. This is done to increase customer traffic, thereby increasing the likelihood that other products will be sold at a normal or high profit. This strategy is frequently used in grocery stores, drug stores, and toy stores. By enticing customers to come in and buy certain products at bargain prices, business owners hope that those customers will also buy other products at full price to offset the loss on the bargain products.

Status Quo Pricing Strategy. Most businesses will settle into a status quo pricing strategy in which price levels are firmly established and remain

Illus. 7-3   Loss leaders are products that retailers sell at or below cost to increase customer traffic.

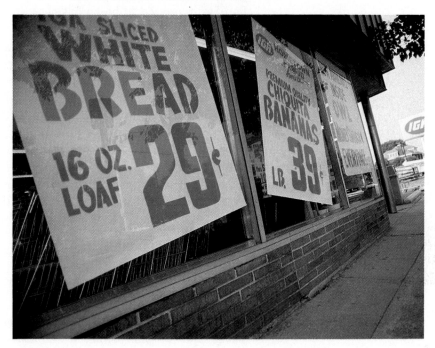

relatively fixed until something happens in the market that makes a change necessary. A price change may become necessary with new competition, changes in established competition's pricing strategies, changes in demand due to market shortages or overflows or changes in the economy.

The profit goals of the business can only be reached if entrepreneurs use the right pricing strategy. Entrepreneurs must be realistic in their expectations and knowledgeable about the supply and demand conditions of the market to be served to determine the best pricing strategy. This requires constant evaluation of pricing policies and market conditions.

THE SALES PLAN

sales plan, any planned attempt to stimulate a potential customer's attention, interest, and desire

A **sales plan** emphasizes a product, service, or business through advertising, personal selling, customer referrals, publicity, or promotional events. The major objective of a sales plan is to educate potential customers by informing them of the features, benefits, and advantages of a product or business.

The ability to sell a product or service is essential to any business. Selling keeps the activity going. Without sales there can be no production, therefore there would be no business, increasing unemployment. All businesses sell in some manner.

Entrepreneurs must design sales plans that address the needs of the markets their businesses serve. Since different products satisfy different needs, the sales strategy must be tailored to the particular needs of the target market. Selling automobiles requires a different selling strategy than selling life insurance because the two products satisfy different needs. A good sales plan is one that is designed to identify the needs of the customers and motivate the customers to satisfy those needs for themselves. Successful salespeople believe in their products and are convinced that they are helping their customers by persuading them to buy. Entrepreneurs and their employees must know their products thoroughly if they are to successfully persuade customers to purchase the products or services.

Sales Methods

There are many different ways to sell. Some methods and examples are listed below:

1. Telemarketing—customer contact by telephone
2. Retailing—the customer comes to the seller
3. Cold calling—customer contact carried out door-to-door by seller
4. Direct mail—sending promotional materials to customers
5. Vending machines—selling without direct customer contact
6. Trade shows—customers come to see products and how they can fulfill needs
7. Product demonstration—customer contact by means of in-home demonstration, initiated through door-to-door contact or customer request
8. Mail-order catalogs—customer contacts the seller

Whatever the method of selling, the entrepreneur must learn the parts of an effective sale.

sales approach, the part of the selling process that is intended to attract the potential buyer's attention and stimulate interest

Sales Approach.   In a personal selling situation, the **sales approach** might be an opening statement about the benefit of the product or service. In a retailing situation, it might be a display that draws attention to how a product looks or how it makes a buyer feel.

sales presentation, the part of the selling process that emphasizes the features, advantages, and benefits of a product or service

Sales Presentation.   The **sales presentation** should create a desire, develop a positive attitude in the buyer, and instill confidence that the product will satisfy a need. A good presentation will persuade, build trust, ask for participation, and prove the seller's statements.

sales close, the part of the selling process that requests an action, such as an order or purchase

Sales Close. The **sales close** is the final step of selling. It involves helping customers make decisions, encouraging them to purchase the product or service offered.

When making a sale, the salesperson will often encounter objections. A good sales plan provides methods for handling objections. One method is to use the objections to emphasize the benefits of the product. A common objection is price. A salesperson can easily defend the price by knowing and presenting the advantages of the product.

Entrepreneurs must also understand the importance of instilling a good feeling about the product or service in the customer, even if a sale is not made. Goodwill leads to repeat business, which is important to all businesses. A good sales plan emphasizes that the customer must feel important at all times.

Sales Strategies

A complete sales plan is supported by the tools discussed in Chapter 6. One of those tools, advertising, is used to draw attention to a product, service, or business. Advertising can be considered a sales approach. Its importance varies with the type of business or industry. Some businesses, such as automobile dealerships, invest a greater portion of revenues in advertising than others. Small manufacturers often limit their advertising expenditures to reaching a small group of potential clients within their industry. Since the purpose of advertising is attracting the attention of the business's target market, the amount of advertising needed depends on how large the potential market is. Although there is much disagreement

Illus. 7-4   A good display will draw attention to the look or feel of a product.

about the value of advertising in relation to its costs, there is no disagreement about its importance in the sales plan.

Although it is the slowest method of selling, getting the message about the business to potential customers through satisfied customers is the most effective selling strategy. Referral advertising refers to a satisfied customer telling a potential customer about the benefits of a product, service, or business. This reference is considered the most creditable of all promotion—it can be a very effective selling tool. However, if it is a bad reference, it can be very damaging. Entrepreneurs must maintain a positive image with customers to ensure that references are positive. This is done through an effective program of building sound customer relations.

publicity, advertising that does not incur cost to a seller

When a business exhibits interesting aspects that are noteworthy and newsworthy, it gets **publicity.** A positive newspaper article about a business is more valuable than a paid advertisement. Entrepreneurs should try to have news about their activities publicized through media releases. For example, if an entrepreneur is selling an unusual product or service, it is newsworthy. Publicity can also be generated from seasonal products and events. Community newspapers, television and radio stations, and industry publications are media vehicles that bring attention to a product, service, or business.

Businesses often use planned events or activities, such as contests, entertainment, or giveaways, to attract attention. Promotional events are effective elements of a sales plan; they are image-builders, designed to create goodwill and increase sales activity and profits. Creative entrepreneurs recognize the value of promotional events in relation to both customer and employee involvement—they are fun for everyone and encourage good referrals.

JEFF BURNETT—ENTREPRENEUR

Jeff was moving quickly toward his goal. Having found a location for Rock 'n' Soul Music, he set a timetable to open for business—16 weeks. He turned his attention to selecting his products and developing a pricing strategy.

After completing his research on the products he would sell, Jeff knew the following:

1. Merchandise could be purchased at a lower cost by ordering directly from recording companies than from wholesale distributors.

2. Recent recordings would be received more quickly if he ordered directly from recording companies.
3. Buying from a distributor would require less paperwork.
4. The distributor offered exchange privileges on recordings and the recording companies did not.

Jeff realized that he would have to get new recordings first if his store was to be the leading record store in Logansville. He also knew that, because he was an independent, his markup would have to be high if he was to succeed. To get a good markup and still be competitively priced, he would need to pay as little as possible for the products. He decided to order most of his products from the recording companies and use the distributor for emergency purposes.

Jeff's research of the industry and the competition indicated that various pricing strategies were being used. The markup for recorded music ranged from 30 percent at the discount stores to 40 and 50 percent at local department and independent stores. He calculated his markup as follows:

$15 CD retail price from manufacturer at a 50 percent markup

$15 ÷ 50 percent = $7.50 cost

$15 CD retail price from distributor at a 40 percent markup

$15 ÷ 60 percent = $9 cost

Jeff's goal was to maintain an average markup of 45 percent. By buying more heavily from recording companies, he could later afford to sell obsolete and slow-selling merchandise at a markdown and still achieve his goal. Selling at a 45 percent markup would give him 45 cents from each dollar of sales to cover operating expenses, his salary, and a small contribution to retained earnings.

Revenue	$1.00
Less cost of goods	.55 (45 percent markup)
Gross profit before expenses	$ .45

To achieve a net profit of $.15 for each dollar sold, or 15 percent of sales, Jeff would have to come up with an operating plan that would limit expenses to $.30 per dollar of revenue.

SUMMARY

If products or services are not properly priced, customers will not buy. The entrepreneur's goal is to set prices low enough to ensure a demand for the product and high enough to ensure enough profit to successfully operate the business. Consumers will buy what they perceive will bring them the greatest need satisfaction for their money.

Successful entrepreneurs follow the total pricing concept by pricing their products to ensure good customer relations and long-term profits. To accomplish these objectives, entrepreneurs must find the break-even point for a product, service, or business, then learn markup formulas and decide on the best pricing strategy for the business.

After determining the proper price, entrepreneurs can design sales plans that fit the target market. Since sales are essential to all business enterprises, it is important to understand the steps of making a sale—approach, presentation, and close. The total sales plan includes provision for promotional tools such as paid advertising, customer referrals, publicity, and planned promotional events.

VOCABULARY BUILDER

On a separate sheet of paper, write a brief description of each word or phrase based on your reading of the chapter.

1. Economics
2. Utility satisfaction
3. Break-even point
4. Fixed cost
5. Variable cost
6. Total pricing concept
7. Markup
8. Markdown
9. Market share
10. Sales plan
11. Sales approach
12. Sales presentation
13. Sales close
14. Publicity

REVIEW QUESTIONS

1. What is the relationship between price and demand?
2. What does the term *utility satisfaction* refer to?
3. What two objectives are to be accomplished when determining price?
4. What is the difference between markup and markdown?
5. If the cost of an item is $50 and it is sold for $100, what is the markup percent? If an item retails for $50 and has a 40 percent markup, what was its cost?

6. What are five possible reasons for taking a markdown?
7. When is a seller most likely to use a short-term profit strategy? A market penetration strategy? A loss leader pricing strategy? A status quo pricing strategy?
8. What are the three steps of making a sale?
9. What marketing tools are used to support a sales plan?

DISCUSSION QUESTIONS

1. How might you spend $100 in terms of utility satisfaction?
2. How do discount stores sell at low prices and operate profitably?
3. Bring an advertisement that appears to utilize a loss leader pricing strategy to class. What items might this business be selling at a full markup?
4. Sell a common item, such as a pencil, to the person next to you. Use a sales approach, a sales presentation, and a sales close. Be prepared to handle objections.

CRITICAL THINKING

One option for retail pricing is selling at a price that is below the suggested retail value, or discounting. To do this and be successful, the business owner must increase the number of units sold to make up for the loss of profits that results from reducing the price. If the price on a unit with a suggested retail price of $1 is reduced by 20 percent, to $.80, unit sales increase by 20 percent, and all other costs remain constant, profits will be reduced. The following example illustrates the profit difference for 100 units sold at $1 and 120 units (20 percent increase) sold at $.80.

	Before Discount	After Discount
Sales revenues	$100	$ 96 (120 @ $.80)
Cost of goods	− 50	− 60 (120 @ $.50)
Gross profit	$ 50	$ 36
Operating expense	− 34	− 34
Net profit	$ 16	$ 2

How many units would have to be sold at $.80 to make more than a $16 profit? What are the risks involved in using the discounting strategy? Discuss the aspects of this strategy that would increase operating expenses, such as the need for more inventory and, therefore, a larger investment, additional space needed to house the larger inventory, the need for more insurance coverage, and the additional personnel needed to handle the increased sales.

SHORT CASE: THE SALES "DEAL"

George was disappointed by the sales reports lying on his desk. All three of his salespeople were performing below expectations. Although the number of sales calls had increased, sales revenues were below the previous year's total for the same month. He wondered whether the new sales strategy he had introduced four months ago was doing any good.

The new sales plan was implemented after George heard a lecture at a convention. The speaker discussed "selling to the max" in a very motivating presentation, and George was impressed. The theme was to refuse to relent when selling—the more you ask for, the more you will sell. Do not give up and do not take no for an answer. Persistence pays off.

The timing of the speech was appropriate—the packaging industry was in a slump. Five years' worth of healthy sales increases had come to a halt for George and for most of the industry. It seemed everyone was searching for ways to reverse the slowdown. George had been pondering ways to get more from his sales force. They too had been disappointed, as their sales commissions had fallen. Maybe, thought George, we need to push harder.

When he presented the new sales philosophy to the sales force, George received a lukewarm response. His plan was to increase the number of calls per client, offer price discounts for immediate delivery of large orders, and remind clients of the expense of handling small orders. Judging from the reports, the new plan was not working. He asked Carla Wilson, his top salesperson, for some feedback about why she thought sales were down.

"George, I feel like a used car salesman half the time and a hatchet man the other half. I am not used to selling 'deals.' I'm used to selling pride in our product. I am also hesitant to infer that we might not be able to accept small orders. Some of our small accounts will gladly tell you how much they have ordered over the years. Add to that the extra sales calls and it is obvious that we are gaining resentment rather than sales."

George had a sinking feeling. He knew Carla was right.[2]

1. What is George forgetting about designing a sales plan that fits the needs of his clientele?
2. What support tools might George provide to his salespeople?
3. Would George be better off to review effective sales approach, presentation, and close techniques with his salespeople instead of radically changing the business's sales philosophy?

---

[2]Case study entitled "The Sales Deal" reprinted, with permission, from book #3511 *Why Entrepreneurs Fail: Avoid the 20 Pitfalls of Running Your Own Business* by James W. Halloran. Copyright 1991 by Liberty Hall Press/TAB Books, a division of McGraw-Hill, Blue Ridge Summit, PA 17294 (1-800-233-1128 or 1-717-794-2191).

PROJECT CHALLENGE

Research the price range for the product or service that you wish to sell. Make a list of competitors' prices. Determine what pricing strategies they are using, and explain why you think they are using those strategies.

What pricing strategy will you use? Answer the following questions about your pricing strategy:

1. Is it competitive with those for similar market offerings?
2. What markup percent is desirable? (Check with industry sources for opinions.)
3. Does your price meet the qualifications of the total pricing concept? (Is it a customer relations tool that will cover all costs, ensure a fair profit for you, and contribute to the long-term stability of your business?)

UNIT 3

FINANCING THE SMALL BUSINESS

8

Initial Capitalization and Financial Planning

capitalization, obtaining the necessary capital assets needed to operate a business

The obstacle that prevents many entrepreneurs from fulfilling their dreams of starting a business is initial capitalization. **Capitalization** is the activity of obtaining all capital assets necessary to operate a business. A business's capital assets include all the equipment, inventory, and operating resources (including cash) that the business owns and uses in the operation of its activities. The challenge of capitalization for the entrepreneur is determining where to obtain the money necessary to purchase and/or lease the items needed to successfully start a business.

PUTTING TOGETHER A FINANCIAL PLAN

Before a business plan is completed, entrepreneurs need to ask themselves how much money they need for the type of business they are considering. The path to the answer starts with the personal financial objective of the entrepreneur. How much income is needed for personal living expenses? What amount of profit does the entrepreneur consider necessary to make the venture a worthwhile and realistic endeavor? Entrepreneurs should write an objective statement declaring how much profit needs to be gained from the business. Whether the objective is $1,000 per year for a part-time business, or $100,000 for a heavily invested enterprise, the financial objective statement will direct the business plan.

Stating the amount of profit needed will dictate the amount of capital necessary to achieve the objective. For example, if the entrepreneur's objective is to make $25,000 per year, the financing or capitalization plan must be designed to ensure that there is enough capital purchased or leased to achieve the sales volume that will ensure a $25,000 net profit. Net profit is the income left over after all expenses, including taxes, are paid. If a business must sell $150,000 to net $25,000, the business owner must purchase or lease whatever inventory, equipment, and other capital assets are necessary to ensure he or she achieves sales revenues of $150,000. A problem many entrepreneurs encounter is that they do not develop a realistic plan of investment to earn the needed profits. When entrepreneurs are not able to obtain the resources needed to successfully complete the business's objective, the enterprise is considered **undercapitalized.** Planning the amount of capital needed starts with making the sales projection, as discussed in Chapter 3.

undercapitalized, failure of a business owner to obtain the needed resources to meet operating expenses in early stages of business

COMPUTING INITIAL CAPITAL NEEDS

As an example of computing initial capital needs, let's discuss two entrepreneurs, David and Sara, and their new store, "Novelties." David and Sara have set an objective of making a $25,000 profit selling a retail product with an average markup of 50 percent. The $25,000 objective is the minimum amount of money needed for David and Sara to maintain a desired standard of living. They hope to make more than that eventually; however, $25,000 is the amount they need to meet all of their personal obligations during the first year of operation. They need a plan to help them achieve their objectives.

In researching the industry, they learned that successful stores selling that particular product can expect to make a profit of 16 percent of gross, or total, sales. This means that their store's sales must be at least $150,000 per year, since 16 percent of $150,000 would equal a profit of $24,500. They must therefore purchase whatever inventory, fixtures, and equipment is necessary to ensure sales of $150,000.

inventory turnover, the number of times a business sells the amount of its base inventory in a year

Entrepreneurs need to estimate the number of times the inventory will turn over. If the average **inventory turnover** rate for a product is five, the owner can divide the projected sales by 5 to determine the minimum amount of inventory available at all times. To make $150,000 in sales, David and Sara's store should sell $30,000 worth of retail inventory five times each year. Since the markup is 50 percent, they must have a minimum of $15,000 ($30,000 × .50) of initial inventory to open the business.

One-Time-Only Costs

leasehold improvement, the fix-up performed on a store or business to appeal to its customers

Many starting costs are incurred only once by the business—during this start-up phase. Once the minimum amount of inventory is calculated, entrepreneurs should determine how many fixtures (shelving units, gondolas, tables, etc.) they require to house and display the initial inventory. Next they should find out how much money they need for **leasehold improvements.**

Illus. 8-1   Start-up costs are incurred only once by a business.

In addition to the inventory, fixture, and leasehold improvement costs will be the one-time costs of an appropriate sign, cash register(s), stockroom shelves, advertising for a "grand opening," utility deposits, change for the cash register, and all other miscellaneous expenditures incurred in opening the business. Building and equipment costs can be reduced considerably by leasing, rather than purchasing. Table 8-1 shows the one-time-only capital needed statement for such a retail business.

This amount of money will get the door open. However, money will also be needed to sustain operating expenses while the business gets started.

Monthly Operating Expenses

Entrepreneurs must also estimate the average monthly operating cost to keep the business running smoothly. It will take time to generate sufficient sales to cover all expenses, so the business owner must set aside money to pay the initial expenses without depending on sales revenues at all. Entrepreneurs should have three months of operating expense capital available so that they can concentrate on increasing sales without the worry of how they're going to pay the bills. To estimate operating expenses, calculate the monthly rent and employees' salaries, and determine the average cost of utility services, insurance premiums, and other charges,

Table 8-1 One-Time-Only Capital Needs

Fixtures and equipment	
Decorating and remodeling	
Installation cost	
Starting inventory	
Utility deposits	
Legal and other fees	
Grand opening promotion	
Cash on hand	
Other	
Total one-time expenses	

as shown in Table 8-2. Multiply the total projected monthly operating expenses by three (representing three months) to arrive at the amount of money that should be available in the initial capitalization plan for operating expenses.

By adding the total amount of one-time-only capital needs to the amount of initial operating expenses, entrepreneurs will know the total amount of money needed for the business idea. Once this is determined, a plan must be devised to make sure this money is available to the business owner.

PRO FORMA FINANCIAL STATEMENTS

pro forma financial statement, projected statistical report used to illustrate the expected financial status of a business at a future date

Pro forma financial statements are projected statistical reports used to illustrate the expected financial status of a business at a future date. To demonstrate the validity of a business idea, entrepreneurs must present

Table 8-2 Initial Operating Expenses

Item	Expenses (One Month)	Multiply by	Expenses (Three Months)
Owner's salary	$2,000	3	$6,000
Other salary	900	3	2,700
Rent	1,600	3	4,800
Advertising	250	3	750
Supplies	270	3	810
Utilities	300	3	900
Accounting	165	3	495
Insurance	200	3	600
Loan principal and interest	225	3	675
Taxes, licenses	125	3	375
Miscellaneous	150	3	450
Total monthly expenses	6,185		18,555

the projections of success in the form of pro forma income statements and balance sheets. These projected financial statements are an important part of the business plan.

Income Statements

income statement, financial report that shows a business's revenues collected and expenses paid out over a specified period of time

An **income statement** shows the revenues, or monies collected, and the expenses, or monies paid out, of a business over a specified period of time. It also reveals the business's profit. New business owners must make pro forma income statements for the first year of operation and also for future years. If properly done and if a realistic profit is shown, it will serve to support the reasons for starting a business. A simplified pro forma statement for the first year of operation for David and Sara's $150,000 business might look as shown in Table 8-3.

This statement makes use of the itemized expenses from the initial operating expenses statement (see Table 8-2). It shows the sales expected for a year and the accumulation of a projected year's operating expenses. In this case, it is evident that if this business is properly managed, and the location is suitable, David and Sara can expect to realize the goal of a $25,000 profit the first year.

Table 8-3   Simplified Pro Forma Income Statement

NOVELTIES

Income Statement
For Year Ending December 31, 19--

Sales	$150,000	
Cost of goods sold	78,000	
Gross profit		$72,000
Operating expenses		
Payroll	11,000	
Rent	19,000	
Maintenance and repairs	1,000	
Operating supplies	2,700	
Taxes and licenses	1,500	
Utilities	3,300	
Advertising	3,000	
Insurance	2,200	
Accounting and legal	2,000	
Miscellaneous	1,800	
Total operating expenses		$47,500
Net profit		$24,500

Future projections indicate the planned growth of the business. The growth projections can be made based on factors such as market population growth, business growth from becoming better known, and industry growth. David and Sara have determined that their business can expect growth in revenues of 15 percent in the second year ($150,000 ÷ $172,500 = 15 percent increase), and 10 percent in the third year ($172,500 ÷ $189,250 = 10 percent increase). The pro forma income statements for the second year and the third year of the business are shown in Table 8-4.

Table 8-4 Simplified Pro Forma Income Statement—Second and Third Years

NOVELTIES		
Income Statement		
	Second Year	Third Year
Sales	$172,500	$189,250
Cost of goods sold	88,000	90,200
Gross profit	84,500	99,050
Operating expenses		
Payroll	12,000	13,000
Rent	19,000	19,000
Maintenance and repairs	1,100	1,200
Operating supplies	3,300	3,400
Taxes and licenses	1,600	1,700
Utilities	3,600	3,600
Advertising	3,400	3,800
Insurance	2,500	2,600
Accounting and legal	2,100	2,200
Miscellaneous	2,000	2,200
Total operating expenses	$50,600	$52,700
Net profit	$33,900	$46,350

Balance Sheets

balance sheet, a financial
statement that shows the
worth or value of a business

A **balance sheet** is a financial statement that shows the worth, or value, of a business. A pro forma balance sheet projects the growth of a business with respect to how much capital value the business will have at a particular date in its existence. In the business plan, entrepreneurs should include a pro forma balance sheet for its opening date as well as one indicating what the business should be worth one year later. Table 8-5 shows a simplified pro forma balance sheet for David and Sara's store.

The balance sheet has two sides—assets and liabilities. The asset side shows all property and capital to which the business claims ownership. The liability side shows all the debts of the business. The net worth, or owner's equity, of a business is determined by adding all the values of what is owned (the assets) and subtracting from this the total debt of the business (the liabilities). The result is the net worth, value, or owner's equity. This table is called a balance sheet because the net worth is added to the liabilities to achieve the "balanced" totals on each side of the ledger, as shown.

Table 8-5 Simplified Pro Forma Balance Sheet

NOVELTIES

Balance Sheet
July 1, 19--

ASSETS		LIABILITIES AND OWNER'S EQUITY	
Current assets		Current liabilities	
Cash	$ 6,400	Accounts payable	$ 5,200
Inventory	$15,000	Current portion of long-term debt	3,300
Total current assets	21,400	Long-term liabilities	6,700
Fixed assets	17,900	Total liabilities	15,200
Total assets	39,300	Owner's equity	24,100
		Total liabilities and owner's equity	$39,300

current asset, property that is easily converted into cash

fixed asset, property that normally takes a longer time to convert into cash

current liability, debt that is to be paid within 12 months

long-term liability, debt that becomes due after 12 months, usually associated with the purchase of fixed assets

Assets are listed as current and fixed. **Current assets** are those that are easily converted into cash, such as cash, inventory, and accounts receivable. **Fixed assets** are those that would take a longer time to convert or liquidate into cash, such as property, equipment, or fixtures that require a special buyer.

Liabilities are listed as current and long term. **Current liabilities** are liabilities that are to be paid within 12 months of the date of the balance sheet. **Long-term liabilities** are liabilities that are often debts that will come due more than 12 months after the date of the balance sheet. Long-term liabilities are usually associated with the purchase of fixed assets such as mortgage notes on property and equipment. By understanding short- and long-term classifications, it is easy to see how much money the business could raise on short notice to use for emergency purchases or expansions. The goal of business owners is to always keep current assets greater than current liabilities, or the business will be considered "technically bankrupt."

Illus. 8-2   Fixed assets, such as this shop equipment, take longer to convert into cash.

Dan McCoy/The Stock Market

Planning Cash Flow

cash flow, how money comes in and goes out of a business operation during a specific period of time

To gain a close look at the business operation for the first year, entrepreneurs must break the year into a month-by-month projection, or a **cash flow** statement. This analysis allows business owners to gain insight into cash flow problems, which are caused by changing sales and payment patterns due to seasonal and industry fluctuations. Cash flow statements are also needed because goods are sometimes purchased and paid for by the business despite the fact that the goods are still in inventory. Cash flow statements tell entrepreneurs what their business's cash position *really* is. For example, since goods are frequently sold to customers on credit, the business may not receive payment (cash) for those credit purchases for a month or two. Although on paper it may appear that the business did receive payment at the time of sale, it was not a cash payment and the business may appear more cash-rich than it really is.

It is necessary to understand how David and Sara's $150,000 in sales will occur. Particularly in a retail business where a great portion of sales are made during the end-of-year holiday season, owners must be aware of the impact seasons have on the cash flow cycle of a business. Entrepreneurs should learn from industry sources the percent of total sales normally received each month of the year. This allows entrepreneurs to budget expenses to accommodate these fluctuations. Figure 8-1 is an example of a form that is available from the SBA for calculating and recording cash flow.

Although the final outcome of the year should support the income statement, some months have excess cash coming in, and some months have too little cash coming in to meet obligations. Entrepreneurs must be aware of these circumstances to properly plan the best allocation of money in different cycles. It is not difficult for entrepreneurs to go bankrupt if cash is flowing out of the business much faster than it is flowing in. They may be making a profit on each item sold, but if the cash flows into the business too slowly, the business may have to close.

Once entrepreneurs put together the capital needs statements, the pro forma income statements, balance sheets, and monthly cash flow projection, they will have a financial plan in place. The information gathered will indicate how much money they need to open and operate the business for the first three months; the income that the business should generate in its first, second, and third years of operation; and what the expected value of the business will be upon opening and at the end of its first year. These are essential ingredients of the business plan. Their results will determine whether the owner needs to borrow money for the idea or attract investors to share the risks and profits.

Figure 8-1   Twelve-Month Cash Flow Cycle

		Pre-Start-up Position		Month 1		Month 2		Month 3		TOTAL Columns 1—12		
NAME OF BUSINESS	**TYPE OF BUSINESS**									**DATE**		
YEAR MONTH		Estimate	Actual	Estimate	Actual	Estimate	Actual	Estimate	Actual	Estimate	Actual	
1. CASH ON HAND (Beginning of month)												1.
2. CASH RECEIPTS												2.
(a) Cash Sales												(a)
(b) Collections from Credit Accounts												(b)
(c) Loan or Other Cash injection (Specify)												(c)
3. TOTAL CASH RECEIPTS (2a + 2b + 2c = 3)												3.
4. TOTAL CASH AVAILABLE (Before cash out) (1 + 3)												4.
5. CASH PAID OUT												5.
(a) Purchases (Merchandise)												(a)
(b) Gross Wages (Excludes withdrawals)												(b)
(c) Payroll Expenses (Taxes, etc.)												(c)
(d) Outside Services												(d)
(e) Supplies (Office and operating)												(e)
(f) Repairs and Maintenance												(f)
(g) Advertising												(g)
(h) Car, Delivery, and Travel												(h)
(i) Accounting and Legal												(i)
(j) Rent												(j)
(k) Telephone												(k)
(l) Utilities												(l)
(m) Insurance												(m)
(n) Taxes (Real estate, etc.)												(n)
(o) Interest												(o)
(p) Other Expenses (Specify each)												(p)
(q) Miscellaneous (Unspecified)												(q)
(r) Subtotal												(r)
(s) Loan Principal Payment												(s)
(t) Capital Purchases (Specify)												(t)
(u) Other Start-up Costs												(u)
(v) Reserve and/or Escrow (Specify)												(v)
(w) Owner's Withdrawal												(w)
6. TOTAL CASH PAID OUT (Total 5a thru 5w)												6.
7. CASH POSITION (End of month) (4 minus 6)												7.
ESSENTIAL OPERATING DATA (Non-cash flow information) A. Sales Volume (Dollars)												A.
B. Accounts Receivable (End of month)												B.
C. Bad Debt (End of month)												C.
D. Inventory on Hand (End of month)												D.
E. Accounts Payable (End of month)												E.
F. Depreciation												F.

MAINTAINING FINANCIAL RECORDS

accountant, an individual trained in the methods and procedures used in assimilating and maintaining financial records

Most small businesses hire accountants. **Accountants** are trained in the methods and procedures used in assimilating and maintaining financial records. They are often hired by businesses to assist in making sure that all financial activity is properly documented for the purpose of reporting taxes to the government and informing banks, investors, and owners of the progress of a business.

Basic Parts of A Bookkeeping System

Too many small business owners become too dependent on accountants for assistance in keeping business records. Basic bookkeeping for a business is a relatively simple, though sometimes tedious, process that entrepreneurs should learn and maintain. By doing their own bookkeeping, business owners will be better informed of the financial condition of their businesses. The basic parts of a bookkeeping system are outlined in the following paragraphs.

Sales Journal.   This is a listing of revenues received each day from the business activity. It is also called a receipts journal. It should show the amount of cash received, any sales taxes collected, and charge account purchases. Figure 8-2 is an example of a sales journal ledger sheet.

Disbursement Journal.   This is similar to a personal checking account record. Its purpose is to show all payments made by check on a particular day, to whom the check was written, and the type of expense incurred. Figure 8-3 shows a ledger sheet from a disbursement journal.

Accounts Payable Ledger.   This is a listing, by account name, of all bills the business needs to pay. The amount owed, the due date, and the date actually paid are also recorded. Many times companies will offer a discount on a bill if it is paid promptly. If so, the amount of the discount should also be shown on the ledger. Figure 8-4 on page 147 is an example of an accounts payable ledger.

Accounts Receivable Ledger.   This record lists customers by name and the amount they owe the business for goods and services bought on credit. Figure 8-5 on page 148 shows a standard accounts receivable ledger.

Furniture, Fixture, Equipment Ledger.   All purchases of current or long-term assets should be recorded on this ledger. It will help maintain a record of business assets and the date they were purchased.

Figure 8-2 *Sales Journal Sheet*

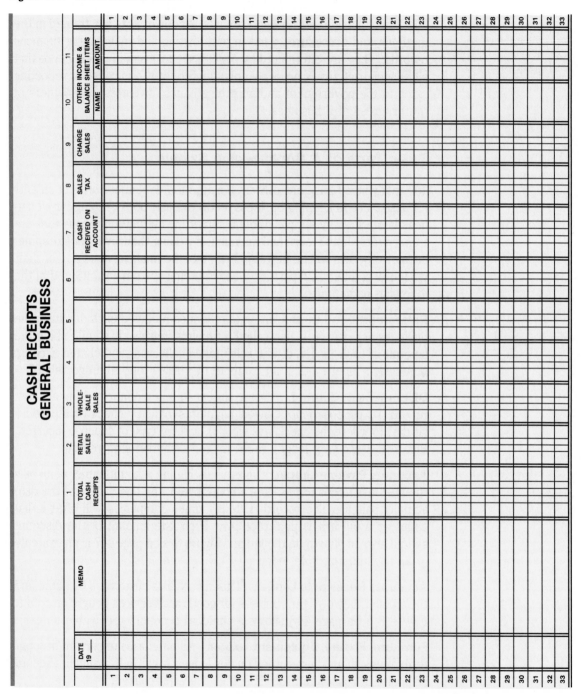

Figure 8-3   Disbursement Journal Sheet

Figure 8-3   (continued)

CASH DISBURSEMENTS

	ADVERTISING & INSURANCE	AUTO & TRUCK EXPENSES	RENT & INTEREST	SUPPLIES & POSTAGE	REPAIRS & MAINT.	UTILITIES & TELEPHONE	TAXES & LICENSES		OTHER EXPENSES — AMOUNT		BALANCE SHEET ITEMS — NAME OF ACCOUNT	AMOUNT	
1													1
2													2
3													3
4													4
5													5
6													6
7													7
8													8
9													9
10													10
11													11
12													12
13													13
14													14
15													15
16													16
17													17
18													18
19													19
20													20
21													21
22													22
23													23
24													24
25													25
26													26
27													27
28													28
29													29
30													30
31													31
32													32
33													33

Figure 8-4   Accounts Payable Ledger

Figure 8-5 Accounts Receivable Ledger

ACCOUNTS RECEIVABLE

NAME

ADDRESS

PAGE NO.

DATE 19__	NO.	MEMO	CHARGE SALES	AMOUNT RECEIVED	BALANCE
1					
2					
3					
4					
5					
6					
7					
8					
9					
10					
11					
12					
13					
14					
15					
16					
17					
18					
19					
20					
21					
22					
23					
24					
25					
26					
27					
28					
29					
30					
31					
32					
33					

NAME

ADDRESS

DATE 19__	NO.	MEMO	CHARGE SALES	AMOUNT RECEIVED	BALANCE
1					
2					
3					
4					
5					
6					
7					
8					
9					
10					
11					
12					
13					
14					
15					
16					
17					
18					
19					
20					
21					
22					
23					
24					
25					
26					
27					
28					
29					
30					
31					
32					
33					

Notes Payable Ledger.   Any money borrowed for business activity should be recorded, showing from whom it was borrowed, date the note becomes due, interest rate to be paid, and any special payment arrangements.

Using A Bookkeeping System

Entrepreneurs who keep these six basic recordkeeping devices have a basic bookkeeping system. Using this information, they will be able to produce approximate income statements and balance sheets. A monthly totaling of the sales receipts journal and the columns of the disbursement journal will allow business owners to calculate net profit. The following calculation is used:

$$\text{Sales} - \text{Purchases} - \text{Expenses} = \text{Net operating profits}$$

By keeping tabs on the accounts payable, accounts receivable, assets purchased, and notes payable, a rough balance sheet can be kept if the owner keeps track of inventory on hand and cash in the bank.

Other parts of a bookkeeping system include payroll summary sheets for each employee. These show up-to-date totals of how much each employee has been paid during a given calendar year. There should also be separate records kept for posting sales and other taxes paid, and other miscellaneous accounts that pertain to a particular business.

Successful entrepreneurs do the basic recordkeeping and bookkeeping themselves, or hire a company bookkeeper. Accountants are used to formalize, summarize, and review financial records for tax reporting purposes. Learning basic bookkeeping is essential for those who wish to open a business. Bookstores offer many sources for non-financial business people who desire easy-to-understand books on accounting and bookkeeping.

JEFF BURNETT—ENTREPRENEUR

Jeff sat down at his breakfast table with a rather large folder of information he had put together and went to work on his capitalization plan. His research had shown that $200,000 initial sales volume for a record, tape, and CD business was certainly attainable. Although he felt confident sales would be higher, since he would be located in the Lakeside Mall, he wanted to be conservative in his projection to make sure there would be no problems. His discussions with industry suppliers, combined with his own experience as a sales representative, allowed him to make a conservative estimate of four inventory turnovers annually. This meant that he would have to have a minimum opening inventory of $50,000 in merchandise, plus at least a month's worth of replacement inventory on order. Jeff would place initial orders of $50,000 for immediate delivery as well as $20,000 in merchandise to be delivered at a later date for a total inventory investment of $70,000. Using the average markup percentage of 45 percent, Jeff would need to have $38,500 ($70,000 × .55, the reciprocal of the markup percentage) available to purchase the initial inventory. Displaying and storing that much inventory in a 2,000 square foot store would require almost 100 four-foot fixtures, plus gondolas and counters, at a total cost of $35,000. In addition, Jeff decided that he needed two cash registers, stockroom shelves, carpeting, paint, a sign, and what seemed to be a million other odds and ends. Jeff figured out that his one-time-only capital needs were as follows (Table 8-6):

Table 8-6 One-Time-Only Capital Needs

Fixtures and equipment	$42,000
Decorating and remodeling	12,000
Installation cost	1,500
Starting inventory	38,500
Utility deposits	900
Legal and other fees	500
Grand opening promotion	2,500
Cash on hand	200
Other	1,200
Total one-time expenses	$99,300

Jeff also knew that he must arrange financing for initial operating expenses since it would take some time for sales to reach the expected level. He listed the following estimated monthly operating expenses (see Table 8-7).

Jeff had been advised to have three months of operating expense money available, so he multiplied $7,300 by 3 to equal $21,900. Jeff's total capitalization plan to open Rock 'n' Soul Music would be $99,300 plus $21,900 for a total of $121,200. "Wow,"

Table 8-7   Initial Operating Expenses

Item	Expenses (One Month)	Multiply by	Expenses (Three Months)
Owner's salary	$2,000	3	$ 6,000
Other salary	1,200	3	3,600
Rent	2,000	3	6,000
Advertising	500	3	1,500
Supplies	200	3	600
Utilities	550	3	1,650
Accounting	50	3	150
Insurance	100	3	300
Taxes, licenses	300	3	900
Miscellaneous	400	3	1,200
Total monthly expenses	$7,300		$21,900

Jeff said to his wife, Susan. "Where will we get that kind of money? We'll certainly have to borrow part of it, so we'll have to make sure the store's going to be profitable enough to pay back whoever loans us the money. I think I need an accountant to help me put together a pro forma income statement and balance sheet."

Jeff presented his research to Don Murphy, an accountant, who helped put together a pro forma income statement (see Table 8-8).

Using this as an operating guideline, Don cautioned Jeff that he should not enter into any loan arrangement that required a payback

Table 8-8   Rock 'n' Soul Music

**Pro Forma Income Statement
For Year Ending December 31, 19--**

Sales	$200,000	
Cost of goods sold	110,000	
Gross profit		$90,000
Operating expenses		
Payroll		
Owner's salary	24,000	
Employees' salaries	14,400	
Rent	24,000	
Operating supplies	360	
Taxes and licenses	3,600	
Utilities	7,800	
Advertising	6,000	
Insurance	1,500	
Accounting and legal	600	
Miscellaneous	2,400	
Total operating expenses		$84,660
Net profit		$ 5,340

of more than $5,000 for interest and principal the first year. Using the sales growth projections of 15 percent the second year, and 10 percent the third, and allowing a 5 percent increase in operating expenses for each year, Don roughed in the projections on Jeff's income statement (Table 8-9).

Adding the first three years of operation, profit estimates indicated this business should conservatively generate surplus cash of $40,459. This amount of money could be available for debt reduction and retained earnings for future growth.

Table 8-9   Simplified Pro Forma Income Statement — Second and Third Years

	ROCK 'N' SOUL MUSIC **Income Statement**	
	Second Year	**Third Year**
Sales	$230,000	$253,000
Cost of goods sold	126,500	139,150
Gross profit	103,500	113,850
Total operating expenses	88,893	93,338
Net profit	$14,607	$20,512

Don concluded that the business could comfortably pay back a loan of $25,000 plus interest over this period of time. The terms of the loan should allow a minimum principal reduction of 10 percent, or $2,500, the first year; 40 percent, or $10,000, the second year; and 50 percent, or $12,500, the third year.

"Jeff, assuming you can get a $25,000 loan, the pro forma balance sheet for the business on opening would look similar to this." Don placed an impressive balance sheet in front of Jeff (Table 8-10).

Much of what Don told Jeff sounded encouraging. However, it also meant that Jeff needed to get a loan for $25,000. What was even harder to swallow was that he needed $90,300 of his own money to open the business! Jeff was alarmed, to say the least. He knew he did not have that much money.

Table 8-10   Rock 'n' Soul Music

Pro Forma Balance Sheet
August 2, 19--

ASSETS		LIABILITIES AND OWNER'S EQUITY	
Current assets		Current liabilities	
Cash	$ 21,900	Accounts payable	$ 0
Inventory	38,500	Notes payable	2,500
Total current assets	60,400	Long-term liabilities	
Fixed assets		Notes payable	22,500
Fixtures and equipment	42,000	Total liabilities	25,000
Utility deposits	900	Owner's equity	90,300
Leasehold improvements	12,000		
Total assets	$115,300	Total liabilities and owner's equity	115,300

SUMMARY

In starting any business operation there must be a financial plan to arrange for the purchase of all necessary components. The plan starts with determining a realistic objective of desired profits and calculating what must be purchased to achieve that objective. Determining the amount of inventory needed, the equipment required, and how much money will be necessary to sustain initial operating expenses is done by researching industry sources and talking to suppliers.

Once a total figure is determined, pro forma income statements and balance sheets are used to validate whether or not the business is a good investment and if it is potentially profitable. These financial statements also show whether or not it is necessary to borrow money or raise money from investors to open the business.

Many business owners will use an accountant to assist in this important decision. Accountants are important to the business owner as they instruct and assist in recording and maintaining proper financial records. Successful entrepreneurs maintain basic bookkeeping systems themselves and use accountants for advisory consultation, special reports, and tax matters.

VOCABULARY BUILDER

Write a brief description of each word or phrase based on your reading of the chapter.

1. Capitalization
2. Undercapitalized
3. Inventory turnover
4. Leasehold improvements
5. Pro forma financial statements
6. Income statement
7. Balance sheet
8. Assets
9. Liabilities
10. Cash flow
11. Accountant

REVIEW QUESTIONS

1. What are the capital assets of a business?
2. What is normally the starting point in determining the financial needs of a business?
3. What causes a business to be undercapitalized?
4. What is the recommended amount of money needed for operating expenses to start a business?
5. What is the difference between an income statement and a balance sheet?
6. Why should a business conduct a cash flow analysis?
7. What is the difference between current and fixed assets? Between current and long-term liabilities?
8. Why should a business use an accountant?
9. Why should a business maintain its own bookkeeping system?
10. What are the six parts of a bookkeeping system?

DISCUSSION QUESTIONS

1. Why is the financial plan such an important part of the overall business plan?
2. How does knowing the inventory turnover of a business help determine its capital needs?

3. What problems may entrepreneurs encounter if they do not conduct a cash flow analysis for a new business?
4. If the asset value of a business increases by $2,000 and the amount of liabilities decreases by $1,000, what would be the change in the amount of owner's equity?
5. What would be the net profit of a business that has total sales of $350,000, with a 50 percent markup and operating expenses of 35 percent of total sales?

CRITICAL THINKING

Entrepreneurs often undercapitalize new businesses, believing that they will be able to make quick profits to make up the difference. Suppose an entrepreneur has calculated one-time-only capital needs at $10,000 and estimated monthly operating expense at $3,000. The entrepreneur decides to open the business with only $12,000. The first year's profits are expected to be $30,000. What would you tell this person about the problems he or she may encounter as a result of undercapitalization?

SHORT CASE: CAPITALIZATION— A CAPITAL IDEA

Paula Zelski was excited about the prospect of mass producing her own line of designer T-shirts. She had produced a limited number, 200, for distribution through three local boutiques that sold them immediately. Now, her phone was ringing requesting more stock and more designs.

Paula expanded her line from three designs to six and entered an agreement with Walt Crosby, a manufacturer's representative, to sell her shirts at a 15 percent commission. Her initial plan was to produce and sell 10,000 units, making a net profit of $1.12 per unit. If she could increase her production run to 20,000, the per-unit profit would increase to more than $3 per T-shirt.

She calculated her one-time-only capital needs at $14,500 and projected her average monthly operating expense at $3,200. She had $3,000 in the bank and borrowed $15,000 on a home equity loan. Once all the equipment was installed in her 1,000-square-foot production facility and the initial inventory was purchased, Paula had only one month's operating expense available in the bank. But outside of that everything looked great. Walt had easily sold the 10,000 units to retailers at the regional fashion show in Chicago.

Paula worked like crazy during the next three months getting the orders out. However, she ran into some difficult cash flow problems because she did a poor job of planning for accounts receivable. Although most of her shipments were made on a cash-on-delivery basis, it still took turnaround time to actually receive payment from the shipping company. She sold to several customers on terms that requested payment within 30 days of receipt of merchandise. The average collection period on these became 60 days.

She ran out of money to meet payroll and rent expenses. She also had trouble purchasing needed extra materials to produce consistently. She was forced to borrow additional monies on a short-term basis at a higher rate of interest than her home equity loan.

Eventually Paula collected all that was due and paid all her debts, including the short-term note. The additional interest charges, however, reduced her net profit. Although the profit was slim, the product's reception was excellent. Walt came back from the next show with orders for 18,000 more units.

Paula's elation quickly turned to panic as she realized she did not have enough money to pay for all the materials needed to produce that many units.[1]

Questions

1. What did Paula neglect to do in her initial capitalization plan?
2. What can Paula do now to keep the business going?

PROJECT CHALLENGE

In your business plan notebook, make a one-time-only capital needs statement for your business idea. You may need to visit someone with experience in the industry you are pursuing to receive the needed information.

Based on your sales projection, make a pro forma income statement to determine the feasibility of the idea. In addition, see if you can learn the revenue fluctuations of the business to make a monthly cash flow projection. A local Small Business Administration office or a Small Business Development Center will be glad to assist you.

---

[1]Case study entitled "A Manufacturer Obtains a Shortsighted Loan" reprinted, with permission, from book #3511 *Why Entrepreneurs Fail: Avoid the 20 Pitfalls of Running Your Own Business* by James W. Halloran. Copyright 1991 by Liberty Hall Press/TAB Books, a division of McGraw-Hill, Blue Ridge Summit, PA 17294 (1-800-233-1128 or 1-717-794-2191.)

9

Personal Finances

After mastering the information contained in this chapter, you should be able to:

9-1 Demonstrate the appropriate method of writing a personal resumé.

9-2 Explain how to select proper references.

9-3 Describe how entrepreneurs use their personal assets to start a business.

9-4 Identify what lending institutions consider good collateral.

9-5 Explain the different ways to put together initial capitalization for a new business.

When stepping out on their own, entrepreneurs realize that the personal and financial contributions they must make will come primarily from their own pockets. This stage in the start-up process requires a thorough examination of personal and financial capabilities. Some entrepreneurial pursuits will rely heavily on the individual's talents and knowledge, while others will require a sizable financial investment. All require entrepreneurs to look first at what monetary contributions they can make before looking to others for financial help.

PERSONAL RESUMÉ

A business will only be successful if the entrepreneur has the personal skills to assume the responsibility of owning and managing it. To determine if the individual has the necessary qualifications to make the business succeed, a personal resumé should be included in the business plan. Lenders and investors use personal resumés to determine whether an entrepreneur's background is suitable for the business he or she wishes to start.

If it is well written, a resumé can show that the leadership of the potential business is in good hands. A personal resumé, such as the one in Figure 9-1, includes the following information:

1. name, address, and telephone number
2. a statement declaring the individual's objective and why he or she is qualified to achieve the objective
3. a chronological list of work experiences; each position listed should include a brief description of responsibilities and accomplishments
4. a description of all formal education and training programs undertaken by the individual

Figure 9-1

PERSONAL RESUMÉ

James L. Sullivan
111 Meredith Circle
Fort Walton Beach, Florida 32548

Objective

To own and operate Precision Electronics Service Company to make use of management and vocational abilities

Employment and Business Experience

Executive Airlines
1520 Locust Drive
Atlanta, Georgia 33604
Responsibilities: Supervised ten-person maintenance crew for charter aircraft carriers. Named 1990 Employee of the Year.
1983 to present

Bureau of Land Management
907 Buena Vista Road
Boise, Idaho 68745
Responsibilities: Repaired and installed radios.
Supervised two employees.
1981 to 1983

Education

Marietta College
Marietta, Ohio
BA degree in Business Administration
GPA 3.2/4.0
1981

Vocational Technical Institute
Twin Falls, Idaho
Television Radio Repair Course
1976

Community Activities

Fulton County Chamber of Commerce, Membership Committee
South Metro YMCA Board of Directors
Kiwanis Club, Treasurer

Hobbies

Ham radio operator, golf, model train collector

References

Mr. Milton Causey, Vice President
Executive Airlines
1520 Locust Drive
Atlanta, Georgia 33604
(404) 961-3440

Ms. Phyllis Charles, Personnel Manager
Executive Airlines
1520 Locust Drive
Atlanta, Georgia 33604
(404) 961-3440

Dr. William H. Hershey, Dean
School of Business Administration
Marietta College
Marietta, Ohio 38973
(213) 774-6756

5. a list of personal activities that indicate character and ambition, including community work, significant hobbies, and awards and distinctions

6. two or three references who have witnessed the achievements of the individual

When individuals other than the owner, such as partners, active investors, or family members, will play significant roles in the start-up, entrepreneurs need to prepare a personal resumé for each person and include it in the business plan. The goal is to present a clear and complete picture of the skills and expertise the new business will have available to ensure its success. If a resumé does not show the experience and expertise needed to operate a particular business, it is necessary for the entrepreneur to gain the appropriate qualifications. This might mean taking some related courses or going to work in the industry to gain knowledge and experience.

Resumé *Do's* and *Don'ts*

A proper resumé will demonstrate the following:

1. how well a person communicates
2. how positively a person thinks of himself or herself

Illus. 9-1 A resume should reflect the qualifications necessary to make a business succeed.

Courtesy of Apple Computer, Inc.

3. ability to achieve results
4. direction and focus toward goals
5. personal character, as evidenced by community activities, personal interests, and hobbies

The following characteristics are things to avoid when preparing a personal resumé.

- excessive length (one page is sufficient in many cases)
- poor organization
- irrelevancies (a resumé should include only significant happenings that give evidence of abilities)
- poor grammar, misspellings, or typographical errors
- photos, fancy paper stock, or borders

References

A proper resumé will offer as references people who can qualify that what is represented is accurate. This can be done by listing two or three names with addresses and phone numbers or stating at the end of the resumé that references are available upon request. It is customary to ask permission from people you would like to use as references.

Illus. 9-2   Persons listed as references should be people who have witnessed the accomplishments on a resume.

It is important that the references are people who have witnessed the accomplishments listed on the resumé. A reference list should not be a list of friends or relatives. The reader expects to be able to discuss the entrepreneur's career achievements with the reference, not whether the person is pleasant to be around. The higher the authority, the more credible the reference. Previous supervisors or colleagues who have worked with the individual on career or community efforts make good references. Former teachers also make good references since they have witnessed achievements in education.

FINANCIAL CONTRIBUTION

The primary financial contribution for a new business comes from the entrepreneur's personal savings and investments. Entrepreneurs must take a careful look at what financial resources they have and how much of those resources they can contribute to the business opportunity. Although it is important to show confidence in an idea by investing personal resources, it is foolish for entrepreneurs to risk *all* of their financial assets.

Calculating Net Worth

To determine their financial capabilities, entrepreneurs should use the method of calculation shown in Table 9-1.

The format used to determine a person's financial worth is the same as that of the business balance sheet discussed in Chapter 8. It lists the entrepreneur's assets (owned property) on one side and the liabilities (debts owed) on the other. The difference between the assets and the liabilities is the net worth.

Determining Available Cash

Entrepreneurs must identify which assets can be turned into cash for financing the business and which assets can be used as collateral for borrowing purposes. Let's look at each item listed in the assets column in Table 9-1 to identify which assets can be used to start a new business.

Cash on Hand. Cash on hand refers to all money held in checking and savings accounts that is readily available upon request. Frequently, entrepreneurs seek financial assistance from family members. If a family member offers money to help the entrepreneur, a personal note should be drawn up promising repayment after the business is firmly on its feet.

Table 9–1

NET WORTH CALCULATION TABLE			
ASSETS		**LIABILITIES**	
Cash on hand and in bank	$_____	Notes payable to bank	$_____
Government securities	$_____	Notes payable to others	$_____
Stocks and/or bonds	$_____	Accounts and bills due	$_____
Accounts and notes		Real estate mortgage	
receivable	$_____	Home	$_____
Real estate owned		Other	$_____
Home	$_____	Other debts	$_____
Other	$_____		$_____
Automobile	$_____		$_____
Cash surrender value—		Total liabilities	$_____
life insurance	$_____		
Other assets	$_____		
Total assets	$_____		
Net worth calculation			
Total assets		$_____	
Total liabilities		$_____	
Net worth (total assets less liabilities)		$_____	

This should only be done after the relative or friend reviews the business plan thoroughly to make certain that the risk is fully understood. Entrepreneurs must be aware that they are required by the federal government to pay interest on such loans if they are to be considered legally enforceable.

Government Securities. **Government securities** include savings bonds and treasury notes. Individuals may invest in the U.S. government by allowing the government to use their money in exchange for repayment, including interest, at a later date. Interest is the payment made

government security, certificate that bears evidence of money on deposit with a government agency to lenders for the use of their money. Government securities can be redeemed for cash at federally insured financial institutions.

stock, certificate representing ownership in a corporation

Stocks. Stocks are certificates representing ownership in corporations. Public stocks are normally bought and sold through stockbrokers. Stockbrokers are licensed agents who are able to buy and sell stocks through stock exchanges such the New York Stock Exchange or the American Stock Exchange. If a person wishes to buy stock in a corporation, he or she could learn the price per share by asking a stockbroker or by checking the listings in the daily newspaper's business section. The stockbroker would then place a buy order through the exchange to find a seller. Buyers of stock are always available, although the selling price is never guaranteed until the transaction is actually made. To sell stock, thereby converting it to cash, individuals place a sell order with their stockbrokers. The completion of the sale normally takes only a few days and the seller of the stock will receive his or her cash at that time.

bond, certificate that verifies a debt owed to an individual by a corporation or government agency

maturity date, the predetermined time that a bond becomes payable to the bondholder

Bonds. Bonds, similar to government securities, are contracts of indebtedness issued by corporations or governmental units that promise payment of a principal amount plus interest on a specified date. The date of promised payment is called the **maturity date.** An individual holding a bond can redeem the bond at any time for cash, although it will lose some of its original value if exchanged before the maturity date.

Illus. 9-3 (a and b)   Stock certificates (left), which represent ownership in corporations, are bought and sold by stockbrokers.

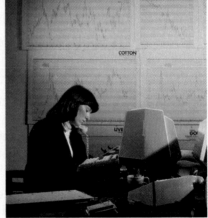

ITT Corporation

Profit Sharing and Pension Plans. Many individuals have accumulated investments in profit sharing and pension plans with current or former employers. Often these investment plans are held by the company until the time that the individual leaves the company. Entrepreneurs who have worked for such companies and plan to resign and pursue self-employment can look to these investment plans as money available to start a business. They need to be aware, however, that money withdrawn before a specified date or age may be subject to taxes and/or penalties.

Insurance Policies. Another area that is often used for available money is the cash value of a life insurance policy. **Whole life insurance** policies are insurance policies that serve as investments to their owners. Over a period of time, insurance premium payments accumulate and the policy acquires a cash value because the insurance company uses a certain portion of the premium payments to make investments. As these investments grow, the cash value of the insured's policy will grow as well. Such policies allow the owner to either redeem the cash value at any time, or to borrow against the policy at a very attractive interest rate. The policyholder must be aware, however, that any money taken out or borrowed against the policy will decrease the amount of money distributed at the time of death.

> **whole life insurance,** an investment that yields cash value from premium payments that are invested

To determine the amount of cash immediately available, entrepreneurs should add the cash on hand, easily converted investments, and any life insurance values. Automobiles are not usually considered sources of available cash since they are needed for transportation. Other assets may include personal belongings, such as furniture and jewelry, but these are also not usually counted as available assets. Entrepreneurs' homes are not considered to be readily available cash assets because they are used as residences and cannot be sold on short notice.

Borrowing against Collateral

Some assets that are not easily converted into cash can be used as collateral against which to borrow. This is true if the lender feels the assets can be converted to cash at a future date in the event that the borrower defaults on the loan.

Home Equity. The equity in one's home or other real estate is an excellent source of collateral since the real estate market is considered reasonably stable. **Home equity** refers to the amount of money owed on a home as opposed to its appraised value. For instance, the equity

> **home equity,** the difference between the appraised value of a house and the amount owed on it

Illus. 9-4 The equity in one's home or other real estate is an excellent source of collateral.

Courtesy of Philip Morris Inc. Photographer, Pierre Kopp.

of a home that has a $75,000 appraised value with an outstanding mortgage loan of $25,000 is $50,000. A lending institution might lend money against a certain portion of this equity by holding the house as collateral. In the event the borrower cannot pay, the lender would have the right to force the sale of the house to recapture the money owed. To make sure the loan is well secured, or collateralized, the lender will usually only loan up to 80 percent of the equity in a home to protect itself in the event the real estate market experiences a slump. In the previous example, the borrower could borrow up to $40,000—or 80 percent of the home equity of $50,000—if he or she is willing to place the home as collateral against a loan that would finance a new business.

Investments. Instead of selling their investments and using the cash to finance the start-up, many entrepreneurs decide to use their investments as collateral. This is particularly valid if the investments are expected to grow at a rate equal to, or higher than, the interest cost of borrowing against them. Just as in the case of home equity, the lender will loan only a certain portion of the market value of the investment to protect against a downward turn of the market.

For example, stock owned by an entrepreneur might have a collateral value of 70 percent of its current value. The borrower could place $10,000 in stock with the lender and receive a $7,000 loan. The stock stays in the name of the borrower, but remains in the possession of the lender until the loan is paid.

certificate of deposit, certificate that shows evidence of money being held by a financial institution for a specified period of time bearing a specified interest rate

Cash can be used for collateral if it is placed in a certificate of deposit with a bank. A **certificate of deposit** (commonly known as a CD) is a savings deposit that is deposited for a specified period of time (six months, one year, or longer) and cannot be withdrawn without penalty. The interest rate is higher than that of a standard savings account. And, usually, the longer the duration of the CD, the higher the interest rate. In the event that a CD is used as collateral, the bank keeps control over the certificate until the debt is paid. It is important to note that during the time stocks and/or CD's are held by a lender, interest payments from CD's and dividends from stocks continue to be paid to the borrower.

To determine their complete financial capabilities, entrepreneurs may add the total value of the readily available cash to the value of money available through collateral borrowing. Once this is calculated, entrepreneurs should carefully review the liabilities they must pay before deciding the total amount that they can contribute to the business opportunity.

It is imperative that entrepreneurs set aside enough money to provide for personal emergencies. They should also keep several months' living expenses in reserve in the event the business opportunity does not work out as planned.

Putting It All Together

In most cases, aspiring entrepreneurs use a combination of the resources discussed in this chapter as well as many financial sources that are covered in Chapter 10. Lenders do not make a habit of lending the total amount needed for initial capitalization—and often there is not enough cash available through the individual's savings and investments—so the total capitalization plan can be pieced together by gathering a little here and a little there.

Precautions

Since many new businesses go through an adjustment period, new business owners should take certain precautions. As mentioned, an ample operating reserve should be available, at least until the business is stable. There are usually unaccountable surprises in the cash flow projections—sometimes good, sometimes bad. During the developing period the owner might have to make sacrifices. One very common one is to forfeit a planned pay day. Since entrepreneurs are the last to get paid if money is short in a particular week, they may have to delay receiving their paycheck. When possible, it is wise for business owners to have alternate sources of regular income. Holding a second job on a temporary basis or, if married, having your spouse hold a steady job might be a good idea.

JEFF BURNETT—ENTREPRENEUR

As you recall from Chapter 8, Jeff was just leaving his accountant's office wondering how to achieve his capitalization plan of $115,300. Somehow, he needs to raise $90,300. His emotions ranged from being depressed and overwhelmed by the large amount of money to being exhilarated by the challenge of finding a solution. To begin, he reviewed his personal net worth (see Table 9-2).

Next, Jeff analyzed what assets he could contribute to the business. Since he knew it was wise to reserve some cash for any emergencies he or Susan might encounter, as well as three months' living expenses, he didn't want to risk all his assets.

He decided that he could contribute $18,000 in cash from his checking and savings accounts, leaving $5,000 in reserve. Next, he decided to cash in $5,000 in U.S. Savings Bonds and sell his shares of stock, worth $4,000. Then he realized that he would have to sacrifice a bit more and called his bank to find out when his CD's could be cashed in without a penalty. Luckily, the maturity date was in a month. He would cash in all $6,000.

After Jeff discussed his situation with his parents, they said they could lend him $13,000. Adding his parents' portion and his cash to the $25,000 loan that he still needed to investigate and obtain, Jeff summarized his total personal financial contribution to Rock 'n' Soul Music in his notebook (see Figure 9-2).

Still stuck with a $44,300 shortage, Jeff leaned back in his chair and said, "Whew, $46,000 down, $44,300 to go. What do I do now? Who will loan me $45,000?"

Table 9-2

NET WORTH CALCULATION TABLE JEFF AND SUSAN BURNETT			
ASSETS		**LIABILITIES**	
Cash on hand and in bank	$ 23,000	Notes payable to bank	$ 0
		Notes payable to others	0
Government securities	5,000	Accounts and bills due	
Stocks and/or bonds	4,000	Credit cards	1,000
Accounts and notes receivable	0	Real estate mortgage	
Real estate owned		Home	47,000
Home	77,000	Other	0
Other	0	Other debts	
Automobile	6,000	College loan	3,000
Cash surrender value—life insurance	2,000	Total Liabilities	51,000
Other assets			
Personal belongings	16,000		
CD's	6,000		
Total assets	$ 139,000		

Net worth calculation	
Total assets	$ 139,000
Total liabilities	51,000
Net worth (total assets less liabilities)	88,000

Figure 9-2

Goal	$ 115,300
Personal savings	-18,000
Personal investments	
Government securities	5,000
Stocks	4,000
CD's	6,000
Total personal investments	-15,000
Anticipated loan	-25,000
Family loan	-13,000
Deficit	$ (44,300)

SUMMARY

In putting together a business plan, entrepreneurs must look first at what they are able to personally contribute to the endeavor. A personal resumé gives an overview of the abilities and leadership capabilities of those who will manage and operate the business. It must be a clearly written document that demonstrates the qualifications of all persons actively involved in the proposed new business.

Entrepreneurs must also provide evidence of financial capability. A personal net worth calculation shows what financial resources can be used for the business. It indicates the amount of readily available cash entrepreneurs have and also what assets they own that can be used as loan collateral.

VOCABULARY BUILDER

On a separate sheet of paper, write a brief definition of each word or phrase based on your reading of the chapter.

1. Personal resumé
2. Reference
3. Government securities
4. Stocks
5. Bonds
6. Maturity date
7. Whole life insurance
8. Collateral
9. Home equity
10. Certificate of deposit

REVIEW QUESTIONS

1. Why is a personal resumé important to a business plan?
2. What information should a personal resumé include?
3. Why are references included in a resumé?
4. What types of people make good references?
5. How is a person's net worth determined?
6. What personal assets are considered good collateral against which to borrow?
7. What is the difference between stocks and bonds?
8. Before going to the bank for a loan, where do many new entrepreneurs find money to borrow?
9. What is a good precautionary step to take before opening a business?

DISCUSSION QUESTIONS

1. What should you avoid when preparing a resumé?
2. Approximately how much money would a bank be willing to loan as a home equity loan on a $100,000 house that has a $40,000 first mortgage?
3. Why would an individual use stocks as collateral to borrow against, rather than selling them?
4. What is the net worth of an individual with the following assets and liabilities?

ASSETS		LIABILITIES	
Cash, savings	$ 3,500	Accounts payable	$ 2,400
Stocks, bonds	8,400	Automobile loan	4,200
Automobile	9,500	Home mortgage	32,000
House	65,000		
Other, personal	17,000		

How much money do you believe this person could raise for business purposes?

CRITICAL THINKING

Many businesses encounter problems shortly after opening due to lack of capital. They turn to the bank for help and often are rejected due to lack of adequate collateral to secure a loan. What do you believe is the cause of this problem? How can it be prevented? Should banks be more helpful to these new businesses?

SHORT CASE: TOO SOON TO EXPAND

Mimi Shannon was so delighted with the results of her store after one year that she looked for a location for another. It was not hard to find — there was a need in the neighboring community.

She thought it would be much easier to open and operate the second store than the first. She had learned a great deal, and had established good credit with all of her suppliers. She did not see any reason to go through all the financial planning she did for the first store. She could order all the inventory on credit and did not have to pay for it for 30 to 60 days. By then she would have sold enough to pay for the first orders. She also knew the fixture and equipment manufacturers would give her a note for the total amount purchased since she had been paying on time for the first store's fixture and equipment note. Therefore, she opened without a cash reserve for operating expenses.

It didn't work. Business started at a very slow rate. After the first month, she had barely sold enough to cover the operating expenses, let alone the initial inventory and monthly fixture note. At the end of 60 days, she was in serious trouble. She was forced to stock the new store with inventory from her other store because she could not order from her suppliers until she paid for the initial inventory shipments. This, of course, hurt business at the original store. She had overrated the success she expected. She wondered what she should do.

Questions

1. What did Mimi fail to do?
2. What can she do now?
3. What will happen if Mimi fails to correct the situation immediately?

PROJECT CHALLENGE

Develop a personal resumé that you believe would prove satisfactory for the type of business you wish to open. (Remember that it is hypothetical, so design a background that supports your idea.)

In your business plan notebook, calculate a net worth statement that shows that you have the cash and investments to cover one half of the money you need to start your business.

10

Analyzing Financial Sources

After mastering the information contained in this chapter, you should be able to:

10-1 List potential sources of funds for a business.

10-2 List and explain types of financing.

10-3 Describe how to match financial sources to business needs.

10-4 Explain how the lending/investing decision is made.

FINANCING A NEW BUSINESS

Having access to enough capital, or money, is critical to the success of a business, especially in the start-up phase. What happens if you do not have enough capital to start your business? Should you give up your dream? Absolutely not! There are many sources of funds for entrepreneurs.

When trying to obtain additional funds, entrepreneurs must have well-developed, written business plans. Potential lenders and investors will want to see a well-prepared and reasonably accurate accounting of the business's projected development. By preparing this information carefully, entrepreneurs will be better able to determine how much money they need, when they will need it, and how decisions about sources of funds will affect cash flow and profits. Figure 10-1 shows the many sources from which entrepreneurs may obtain financing.

DEBT CAPITAL

debt capital, money loaned to a business with the stipulation that the original amount borrowed, plus interest, will be paid to the lender within a certain time period

Debt capital, also called creditor capital, is borrowed money. Sources for debt capital (see Figure 10-1) might include friends and relatives, supply vendors, equipment vendors, state and/or local business development funds, and, under certain circumstances, the Small Business Administration. In most cases, collateral is required to obtain debt capital.

Friends and Relatives

Establishing trust is usually a requirement for borrowing money. Who trusts the entrepreneur more than friends and relatives? In many cases, it was encouragement from these people that prompted the idea to start the business in the first place.

Figure 10-1 Financial Sources

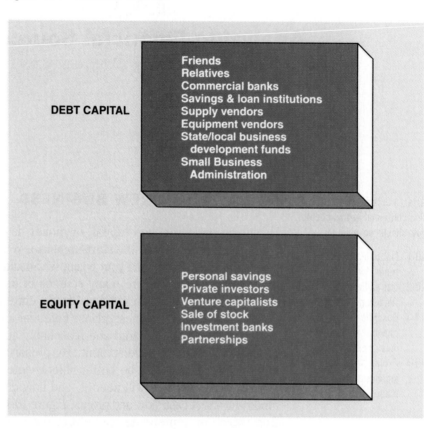

Most people use family money, if it is available, during start-up. Friends and relatives may be willing to lend more money, and they will probably allow more time for repayment. In addition, they probably will not scrutinize the business plan as another lender would, and they are usually more understanding than other lenders during times of hardship. However, borrowing money from friends and relatives may also encourage interference. They may feel that since you used their money, you should also take their advice.

Commercial Banks

Most entrepreneurs think of commercial banks when it comes to borrowing funds. Most of us have a bank we deal with on a regular basis, and we are inclined to begin our quest for funds there. However, you

Illus. 10-1 An entrepreneur's personal bank is a good starting point in the quest for funding.

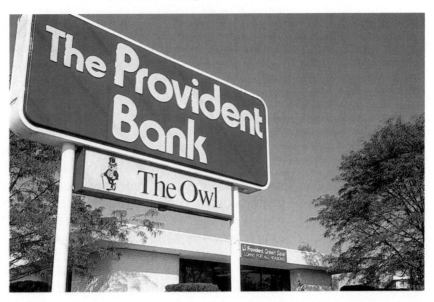

may find that your bank is not able or willing to meet your business needs. If this happens, check with other sources. The results may not be the same.

Before approaching a bank for funds, entrepreneurs should understand the various types of financing available. Seven different types are briefly described in the following paragraphs.

Traditional Loans. Often referred to as commercial loans, traditional loans are short-term loans. This type of loan is often unsecured, which means that no collateral is required. Traditional loans may not be available to new business owners.

Line of Credit. There are two types of line of credit financing—the regular line of credit and the revolving line of credit. The regular line of credit allows business owners access to a preapproved, prearranged amount of money for a specific period of time—usually one year. The revolving line of credit also allows business owners access to a certain amount of money, but it provides an option for renewal at the end of the original term.

prime rate of interest, the publicly stated rate that major commercial banks charge their most creditworthy business customers for short-term loans

The interest rate for a line of credit is usually 1.5 to 3 percent above the **prime rate of interest.** In most cases, interest is charged only on the amount drawn, but the bank usually charges a fee (1.5 to 2 percent of the total credit line) for reserving the funds.

A business owner who needs extra cash several times during the year may be able to save time and money by obtaining a line of credit. Once a line of credit is approved, loans of this amount are automatic. No additional paperwork or approval is required up to the pre-approved amount. A line of credit helps business owners through the highs and lows that can occur during the course of a year. If a retail business has a dip in sales in October, it may not have the money to stock up on inventory for the busier Christmas season. A line of credit can provide the funds to increase inventory when sales are slow.

Installment Loans.   Entrepreneurs often use installment loans to finance equipment. The term of the loan is based on the expected life of the asset purchased. If an entrepreneur purchases an expensive piece of equipment, such as a computer system, it is likely that the business will not generate enough profit to pay for it in one year. If the loan is spread out over several years, the computer will add enough value to the business to justify its expense.

The interest rate on installment loans is based on the bank's cost of funds and is usually 2 to 4 percent higher than the prime rate of interest. Installment loans for business equipment are handled in the same manner as installment loans for personal assets. They are often obtained through the private lending division of the bank rather than the commercial lending division.

Mortgage Loans.   Mortgage loans are given to businesses that have property to use as collateral for the loan. Two types of mortgage loans are usually available to entrepreneurs. The first is a loan on new property, such as a building to house the business. For this type of loan, the building becomes the collateral. The maximum amount of the loan is determined by the value of the property. Many commercial banks will approve a loan of up to 90 percent of the appraised value of a building.

The second type of mortgage uses previously owned property, such as the owner's residence, as collateral. This is known as an equity loan. The maximum amount for this type of loan is determined by the amount of equity the owner has in the secured property. Equity is the appraised value of the property, less the existing debt. Many banks will approve a loan of up to 80 percent of the equity amount.

Acquiring a mortgage loan may require payment of closing costs, including loan origination, appraisal, and other fees. Interest rates for these loans vary. Some are based on the prime lending rate, and some are based on the treasury bond interest rate.

Accounts Receivable Financing.   This type of loan is available to businesses that have accounts receivable. Accounts receivable businesses permit their customers to charge merchandise or services. If an entrepreneur has accounts receivable worth $10,000—in other words, the customers owe $10,000—then the bank will offer a loan based on that amount. Banks will loan a business up to 85 percent of the face value of the total accounts receivable. As the receivables come in, payments are forwarded to the bank. The interest rate for this type of financing is often higher than that for other types of loans, but interest is charged only on the unpaid portion of the loan.

Inventory Financing.   If entrepreneurs choose this type of financing, the inventory that is held by their businesses is used as collateral for the loan. Banks will probably require that the value of the inventory be at least double the amount of the loan. This type of loan is available only if entrepreneurs have paid for the inventory.

Sales Contracts.   Some entrepreneurs own businesses that sell products or services on a contract basis. For example, Michael Jacob owns a small furniture manufacturing plant in North Carolina. He recently obtained a contract with a large chain of retail furniture stores. He will supply them with 8,000 entertainment centers over a period of three years.

Illus. 10-2   Inventory is sometimes used as loan collateral.

Rob Nelson/Stock Boston

Michael's company has never had such a large order, and he does not have enough equipment or employees to produce the merchandise. To meet his contractual obligation, he must buy four new machines and add six employees. He does not have enough money to cover these costs. The contract is with a well-known business, so Michael can take the contract to the bank and request a loan based on the value of the contracted sales. Most banks are receptive to this type of request and will try to meet the entrepreneur's needs.

Savings and Loan Institutions

Many of the loans that are available at commercial banks are also available at savings and loan institutions, and often at a lower cost. These institutions also provide some types of financing that commercial banks generally do not, such as factoring.

Factoring is another method of using accounts receivable to obtain funds. In this case, the lender actually purchases receivables from the entrepreneur for an amount that is less than their total value. Customers are notified that their debt has been transferred, unless the entrepreneur makes other arrangements with the bank.

Supply Vendors

trade credit, a type of financing that allows delayed payment for merchandise

A company that supplies merchandise to a business can provide a source of working capital known as **trade credit** to that business. Typically, trade credit gives the business 30 to 90 days to pay for merchandise.

As discussed in Chapter 6, one of the four *P*'s of the marketing mix is place, which means having the right product at the right place at the right time. Place takes on great importance in the area of trade credit. If entrepreneurs plan carefully, their products will arrive at the time they are needed and at least part of the order will be sold before payment is due. Receipts from the sales can be used to pay vendors. By using trade credit, entrepreneurs need less working capital to maintain inventory.

Equipment Vendors

Equipment vendors often allow entrepreneurs to lease equipment or buy it on credit. The vendor will usually require a down payment of 25 to 35 percent of the cost of the equipment. The balance of the cost is paid in installments over a specified period. By allowing entrepreneurs to pay

Illus. 10-3 Equipment vendors often allow entrepreneurs to lease or buy equipment on credit.

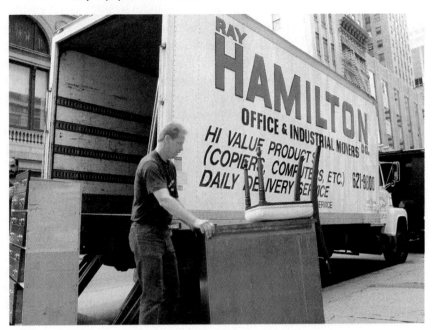

for equipment in installments, equipment vendors allow businesses to use profits from the use of the equipment to cover their costs.

A large part of the cost of starting a new business is often the purchase of equipment. When vendors allow entrepreneurs to lease or buy on credit, they provide a reduction in current expenditure and therefore, an increase in working capital.

State and Local Business Development Funds

Most states and many communities have funds available for business start-ups. An example of this type of funding at the state level is the Colorado First Customized Training Program. This program, which began with the passage of a law in 1984, provides money to new businesses for employee training.

An example of financial assistance for new business start-up at the local level is Economic Opportunity Planning Associates, Inc., in Toledo, Ohio. This fund provides loans to qualified small businesses in northern Ohio.

Small Business Administration

The SBA was established in 1953 to aid the development of small business. One of its primary purposes is to provide financial assistance to small business owners, either directly or indirectly.

The SBA's loan guarantee program is for small business owners who are unable to obtain financing through a bank or other private source. The SBA guarantees the lender that in the event the borrower is not able to repay the obligation, the SBA will use funds appropriated by Congress to pay the guaranteed portion of the loan. The maximum amount of the loan guarantee is 85 to 95 percent, depending on the amount of the loan. SBA "contact banks" include most commercial banks, some savings and loan institutions, and some finance companies.

Direct loans from the SBA are available only to a few specific groups, such as Vietnam-era veterans and certain handicapped persons. Also eligible are small firms engaged in manufacturing, selling, installing, servicing, or developing specific energy conservation methods; development companies that aid small businesses in urban and rural communities; and small companies involved with export activities. Only businesses not qualified for a guaranteed loan are eligible for a direct loan.

Illus. 10-4   Direct loans from the SBA are available only to a few specific groups.

Peter Menzel/Stock Boston

Equity Capital

equity capital, money invested in a business in return for a share in ownership and, therefore, in the profits of the business

Equity capital, also referred to as owner capital, is the money invested in a business by the owner or owners. This might include the owner's personal savings or investment by others, such as private investors, venture capitalists, stockholders, investment bankers, or partners.

Personal Savings

The best source of equity capital is personal savings. One of the advantages of using personal savings to start the business is that the entrepreneur keeps more of the business's profits.

investor, a financial source that provides capital in return for partial ownership of the business

Entrepreneurs who need additional funds and wish to finance their businesses entirely through equity capital will need to locate **investors.** Entrepreneurs who want people to invest in a business may be required to provide a substantial portion of the needed capital themselves. Many potential investors consider the amount of money the entrepreneur is willing to invest an indicator of the degree of dedication to the new venture. However, if the business is one that involves a truly innovative idea, someone may be willing to invest the entire amount needed.

Private Investors

You may be able to obtain financial assistance from people who have excess income available for investment purposes. Your banker, lawyer, or accountant may be able to provide a referral for such a source. These investors usually have a conservative investment philosophy. They may not be willing to finance businesses that involve high risk.

Venture Capitalists

venture capitalist, an investor who specializes in funding high-risk business proposals that are not acceptable by banks

Financial assistance from **venture capitalists** should usually be considered only as a last resort. Venture capitalists do not often invest in start-ups. They prefer to invest in established businesses and businesses that have potential for an extremely high return on investment.

Venture capitalists often insist on being involved in management of the business. They usually require that agreements be executed that will allow them to take full control of the business if it is not meeting their expectations. Profit becomes the highest priority, often overriding the entrepreneur's ideas about product quality or how the business should be run.

Sale of Stock

Established businesses can raise capital by selling stock, or small pieces of the business. This process will be discussed in detail in Chapter 11.

Investment Banks

Investment banks specialize in bringing together entrepreneurs who need funds with individuals or groups that have money to invest. These individuals or groups include, for example, insurance companies and pension fund administrators. Most major metropolitan areas have investment banks. Entrepreneurs in other areas may not have access to this funding source.

Partnerships

partnership, a voluntary association of two or more persons to carry on as co-owners of a business for profit

Entrepreneurs who establish **partnerships** may seek a partner or partners for two reasons. They may want to increase the business's capital or acquire expertise in areas that are unfamiliar to them. Percentages of ownership will usually be based on the portion of the capital each partner invests.

Illus. 10-5   Establishment of a partnership may increase the business's capital and/or provide greater expertise.

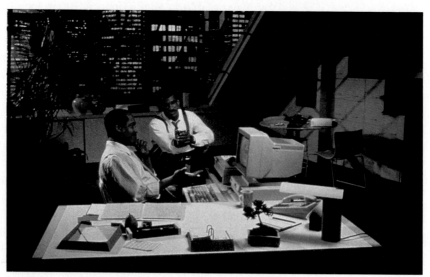

Courtesy of International Business Machines Corporation

OTHER SOURCES OF FUNDS

Some small businesses are eligible for Small Business Investment Company (SBIC) loans. An SBIC is usually one that is established by a small group of local investors. These companies can provide debt capital, equity capital, or both, to small businesses.

Debt capital is provided in the form of long-term loans to provide small businesses with funds needed for sound financing, growth, or expansion. Equity capital is usually provided as a loan and requires the business owner to issue a security to give the SBIC the right to purchase a portion of the business.

An SBIC is not permitted to control a small business on a permanent basis. The SBA may, however, allow the SBIC to assume temporary control to protect its investment in a high-risk business. All SBIC loans to small businesses have a minimum term of five years. Early repayment may be subject to penalty.

The Small Business Innovation Research (SBIR) program provides grants to small businesses for innovative research and development. These grants can only be obtained by applying to the SBA in Washington, D.C. Applications and information about the program are available at local SBA offices.

MATCHING FINANCIAL SOURCES TO BUSINESS NEEDS

When considering sources of additional funds, entrepreneurs should remember that the best source is the one that fulfills the business's particular needs at the lowest cost. Cost can refer to a monetary loss or ownership reduction, which forces entrepreneurs to give up a portion of their interest in the business.

Entrepreneurs must be knowledgeable about the sources available and how each could apply to the business. It is important that entrepreneurs take time to determine the true cost—both monetary and ownership—of capital obtained from each financial source. Alternatives should be chosen since the first choice may not be available. For example, an entrepreneur who doesn't have enough capital to purchase inventory should probably try to make use of trade credit or seek a short-term loan from a bank. If equipment is needed, entrepreneurs might consider equipment vendors or banks.

HOW THE LENDING/INVESTING DECISION IS MADE

In Chapter 9, you learned about personal financial statements, resumés and references, and types of personal collateral. Lending institutions will usually require this information, as well as information on cash flow projections and an operating statement. These documents are very important to the lender or investor.

When combined with the other elements of the business plan, this information lets the financial source know that the business venture is well planned. The thoroughness and knowledge demonstrated by the entrepreneur in putting this information together will have a direct bearing on whether or not the necessary capital is obtained.

JEFF BURNETT—ENTREPRENEUR

Rock 'n' Soul Music is well on its way to becoming a reality. Jeff has done quite a bit of research to get to know his customers and competition and to establish his pricing strategy and sales plan. He has also given his location and facilities and the marketing plan a lot of attention.

In Chapter 9, Jeff analyzed his personal financial position. With that information, he knows that Rock 'n' Soul Music may never get past the dream stage unless he obtains some kind of financial assistance.

Jeff has compiled a list of potential sources of financial assistance for Rock 'n' Soul (see Figure 10-2).

Jeff has determined how much funding is available for his music store from his own savings and investments, a home equity loan, and a loan from a relative. He knows that he still has a $44,300 shortage. It is time to investigate other sources of funding.

Jeff wants to have complete control of his business, so he eliminates the idea of acquiring a partner. He also knows that the business is not a large enough—or profitable enough—operation to attract venture capitalists. Finally, Jeff knows the SBA offers loans, but prefers to make larger loans than he needs.

For these reasons, he decides to turn to his own industry for assistance. He discovered that he could purchase fixtures and equipment on an installment note from the manufacturers. They asked for 50 percent down and financed the remainder over a five-year

Figure 10-2 Financial Sources for Rock 'n' Soul Music

Friends
Relatives
Commercial banks
Savings and loan institutions
Supply vendors
Equipment vendors
State/local business development funds
Small Business Administration
Personal savings
Private investors
Venture capitalists
Sale of stock
Investment bankers
Partners

period, with the fixtures and equipment serving as collateral in the event something goes wrong. This means that 50 percent of the cost, or $21,000, can be paid at $440 per month including interest.

Jeff was also pleased to learn that after paying for the initial inventory shipment of $27,500 in advance, he would be granted trade credit for the en route merchandise, worth $11,000. Although this credit was only granted for 30 days after delivery, it would give Jeff some time to sell some merchandise before paying for it. He deducted one half of the amount of this trade credit, $5,500, from his capital needs. His financial needs now look like this:

Deficit before industry sources	$(44,300)
Fixture and equipment note	− 21,000
Trade credit	− 5,500
	$(17,800)

"Well," Jeff thought to himself, "I'm getting closer, but I'm not quite there yet." He had enough to open the store, but not enough to give him a three-month operating reserve. He and Susan decided to visit Mrs. Contel at the bank and present all of their information to her for recommendations.

After reviewing all of Jeff's pro forma statements, his financial plan, and his resumé, Mrs. Contel responded. "Jeff, you're doing a good job on your plan. It appears to be a very worthwhile endeavor, and one that you're putting a great deal of energy into. Although we can't advance you the entire $17,800, if you can come up with an additional $7,800, I will recommend to the loan committee that the bank grant you a line of credit not to exceed $10,000. You can use this for emergencies and for short-term needs to help with expenses during months that you might be a little short of cash. You can draw on this money when you have a need. If you don't need it, don't use it; you will have to pay interest on what you use. Since your plan indicates that it is for operating reserve, you may not have to use it at all. In the event you do—in whole or in part—you must make sure that the balance outstanding is paid in full by the end of a year. As long as you meet this requirement, the line of credit can be renewed for an additional year at your request.

"The bank would like to have your business deposits here, and we'd like you to keep us up to date on your progress. I believe we can enjoy a mutually beneficial relationship for many years. Do you think you can contribute the missing $7,800?"

Jeff looked at Susan. She knew exactly what he was thinking and gave him an approving smile. "Susan and I still have $10,000 in our emergency savings and whole life insurance cash value that we were not going to use for the business, but since we are this close—and if you think the business plan looks strong—I believe we'd be willing to put another $7,800 into our dream."

Mrs. Contel smiled. "It looks like you two are in business. When you finish the final plan, bring it in and I'll arrange the line of credit."

Jeff squeezed Susan's hand. They had done it. The final pro forma balance sheet for Rock 'n' Soul Music would show the following assets and liabilities.

Assets		Liabilities	
Cash available	$ 21,900	Accounts payable	$ 5,500
Inventory	38,500	Notes payable	
Fixed assets		Fixtures/	
Fixtures/equipment	42,000	equipment	21,000
Utility deposit	900	Relative loan	13,000
Leasehold		Line of credit	10,000
improvements	12,000	Home equity loan	25,000
Total assets	$ 115,300	Total liabilities	74,500
		Owner's Equity	40,800
		Total Liabilities and	
		Owner's Equity	$115,300

SUMMARY

The entrepreneur has many financial sources to choose from, including debt capital (friends and relatives, commercial banks, savings and loan institutions, supply vendors, equipment vendors, state and/or local business development funds, and the SBA); equity capital (personal savings, private investors, venture capitalists, sale of stock, investment bankers, and partners); the Small Business Investment Company program, and the Small Business Innovation Research program.

Matching financial sources to business needs is very important. The entrepreneur should remember that the best source of financing is the one that fulfills the business's needs at the lowest cost.

The lending/investing decision is based on several factors, including, but not limited to, personal financial statements, resumés and references, collateral, cash flow projections, and operating statements. The degree of skill shown by the entrepreneur in putting together the required documentation will have a direct bearing on whether or not financing is secured.

VOCABULARY BUILDER

Write a brief description of each word or phrase based on your reading of the chapter.

1. Debt capital
2. Commercial bank
3. Savings and loan institution
4. Prime rate of interest
5. Trade credit
6. Supply vendor
7. Equipment vendor
8. Equity capital
9. Personal savings
10. Private investor
11. Venture capitalist
12. Sale of stock
13. Investment banker
14. Partnership

REVIEW QUESTIONS

1. What are the sources of equity capital?
2. What are the sources of debt capital? Name some of the advantages and disadvantages of each.
3. What are seven types of financing available from commercial banks?

DISCUSSION QUESTIONS

1. Why is it important to prepare well before seeking financing?
2. Describe the advantages and disadvantages of using venture capitalists.
3. How can entrepreneurs use a line of credit effectively?
4. What two costs must entrepreneurs consider before accepting financing from a source? Why?

CRITICAL THINKING

Mary Slovic is planning to open a small engine repair shop in your community. She has asked you for advice. What would you tell her if she asked these questions?

1. Should I use friends and relatives as a source of capital?
2. What are the advantages or disadvantages of using a commercial bank instead of a savings and loan institution?
3. How can I purchase the equipment and supplies I need without working capital?

SHORT CASE: TO BUY OR NOT TO BUY

Mike Joyner is planning to open a karate studio in a large city in your state. Mike is a fifth-degree blackbelt who has won the state title in his weight class for the last four years. He has received a great deal of publicity concerning his karate skills. As a result, he is very well known in the city and has become something of a hero to the young people in town.

Mike has been doing a lot of work on his business plan during the past few months. He is now ready to start thinking about financing his new studio. Although Mike will not need very much equipment for his studio, he does feel that he needs a certain type of building in the right part of town.

Mike does not like the idea of renting. He thinks that renting a building is a poor investment of his money. He would much prefer to buy a building.

A friend of Mike's, who happens to be a realtor, recently found a building that he thinks is perfect for the new karate studio. It is in the right part of town and is definitely large enough for the business. After seeing the building, Mike agreed enthusiastically.

In addition to planning for the building, Mike has also started to sign up students for the new studio. Because of his reputation and popularity in town, he has already signed up 100 students. Each student signed a one-year contract agreeing to pay $30 per month for karate instruction.

Since Mike really liked the building his friend found for him, he has decided to buy it. His only problem now is to find a source of financing.

Mike already has a little experience in financing real estate. He feels fairly comfortable in this area because he bought a home five years ago. He has equity of $20,000 in his home.

Questions

1. Where is the first place Mike should go to get financing to buy his building?
2. What type(s) of financing do you think will be available to Mike?
3. Do you think Mike will be successful in obtaining financing? Why?
4. Should Mike consider venture capitalists as a possible source of financing? Why or why not?

PROJECT CHALLENGE

Your hypothetical business planning has now progressed to the point where you need to start thinking about acquiring capital. Begin this process by doing the following:

1. Develop a list of all possible funding sources in your community. (Not all of the sources discussed in this chapter are available in all communities.)
2. Include all information pertaining to the type and amount of funding available from each source and what the cost will be.
3. Rank the sources based on the type of business you are planning. The first source on the list should be the source you consider to be your best alternative for financing.

UNIT 4
MANAGING THE SMALL BUSINESS

11
Forms of Ownership

QUESTIONS OF OWNERSHIP

A key decision for any entrepreneur is one of ownership of the new business. Will you choose to make a go of it by yourself? Will you establish a business with one or more other people? Or will you decide that you want a business in which many people share ownership?

All of these questions have to do with forms of business ownership. The form of ownership the entrepreneur chooses will have important legal, financial, and personal implications throughout the life of the business. Each form has its own set of advantages and disadvantages. As you read through this chapter, keep in mind the type of business you would like to start some day. Try to determine which form of ownership is right for you.

The three basic forms of business ownership are sole proprietorship, partnership, and incorporation. Which of these is best for the entrepreneur thinking of starting a new business? To answer that question, let's look at the various ownership options in detail. Carefully considering each will help you make the best ownership decision for you and your business.

SOLE PROPRIETORSHIP

Do you want to make a go of it by yourself? If you are willing to be solely responsible for all aspects of a new business, a **sole proprietorship** may be the best form of ownership for you.

sole proprietorship, a business established, owned, and controlled by a single person

Sole proprietorships come in all shapes and sizes. They may be very small businesses with only one employee, the owner. Or an entrepreneur may own a sole proprietorship, but he or she may hire a manager to run the business on a daily basis. Or a sole proprietorship can be a very large business with hundreds of employees. The owner realizes all the profits

Illus. 11-1 In a sole proprietorship, the owner realizes the profits, but also assumes responsibility for the losses.

from the business and assumes responsibility for any losses. In this sense, the owner of a sole proprietorship is truly an entrepreneur.

Formation of a Sole Proprietorship

Of the three forms of ownership, the sole proprietorship is by far the easiest to form. The government exercises very little control over the establishment of new sole proprietorships. Start-up can be immediate and simple, providing you have all the necessary resources—capital, knowledge, and merchandise or a service to sell. You may need to obtain licenses or permits for your particular type of business, such as the license needed to operate a hair salon.

The sole proprietorship is the most prominent of the three forms of ownership. In fact, more than 95 percent of all businesses in the United States are sole proprietorships. Because of the ease of formation and the almost unlimited control of the business, this form far outnumbers the other two forms of ownership. The very same characteristics that prompt individuals to be entrepreneurs—the desire to control one's own destiny, to achieve freedom from direct supervision, and the potential to achieve profits greater than a salary from someone else—prompt them to choose the sole proprietorship form of ownership.

One important thing entrepreneurs do need to consider is the selection and registration of the business name. This should be done whether the entrepreneur is forming a sole proprietorship, a partnership, or a corporation. Most states require any business name that doesn't fully include the personal name of the business owner to be registered with a local government agency. For example, take Dana Simpson. Dana has decided to open a video rental store in a small town. She has narrowed the choices of names for the new business down to two possibilities: "Dana's Video" and "Dana Simpson's Videos To Go." If Dana chooses "Dana's Video," the name will have to be registered. On the other hand, if Dana chooses "Dana Simpson's Videos To Go," she can start the new store without registering its name. The difference is that most states require any business name that does not include the full name of the business owner to be registered with a local government agency.

Depending upon the state, entrepreneurs register the name with a county government office or with the Secretary of State's office. It is a very simple process to fill out the necessary form. The advantage of registering a business name is protection. Once the name is registered, it goes into state records and may not be used by anyone else in the state. This protects your future profits by ensuring that you are the sole user of the business name.

Operation of a Sole Proprietorship

Owners of sole proprietorships make all of the decisions regarding the operation of the business. Even though they have the luxury of "being the boss," sole proprietors are not exempt from financial risk. They must still obtain the necessary funds to open and run the business, and they must pay taxes.

The assets of entrepreneurs who own sole proprietorships are not considered legally separate from the assets of the business. This means that if the business does not succeed and if any debts remain, the entrepreneur's assets may be taken to pay those debts. Despite this drawback, reporting taxes is fairly simple. Owners of sole proprietorships report the business income and expenses on their personal income tax return.

Advantages of a Sole Proprietorship

To summarize, some of the advantages of sole proprietorship are as follows.

- Sole proprietorships are simple to start.
- No formal action is required to establish a sole proprietorship.

- They may be started immediately.
- The owner has total control of all aspects of the business.
- The owner receives all the profit.
- The business itself pays no income tax; the owner pays income tax as an individual.

Disadvantages of a Sole Proprietorship

Listed below are some of the disadvantages of sole proprietorship.

- The owner has unlimited responsibility for losses, debts, and other liabilities the business might develop.
- The owner must make all the decisions.
- The owner is the only person who can arrange financing or capitalization.
- The existence of the business ends upon the owner's death.

PARTNERSHIP

partners, individuals who voluntarily agree to conduct a partnership

A partnership, according to the Uniform Partnership Act, is an association of two or more persons to carry on as co-owners of a business for profit. **Partners** with complementary skills or knowledge often team up to form a partnership. For example, a person experienced in manufacturing may form a partnership with an individual with marketing expertise. Entrepreneurs who may have originally wanted to form a sole proprietorship may choose to form a partnership because of the benefits of combined talents and finances.

The Uniform Partnership Act (UPA) has been adopted by almost every state in the nation to provide a degree of uniformity among states concerning partnership laws. Entrepreneurs should check to see if the UPA has been adopted by the state in which their new business is to be located. If it has not, then entrepreneurs should approach the formation of a partnership all the more cautiously. Without the UPA, there are no guidelines to protect entrepreneurs seeking to form partnerships.

Partnership Agreement

partnership agreement, the official document forming the contract between partners

One of the first things that must be done when two or more entrepreneurs are considering a partnership arrangement is to write a **partnership agreement.** Written partnership agreements are not required by law in all partnerships; oral agreements are perfectly legal for some types of

Illus. 11-2   A partnership is an association of two or more persons working as co-owners of a business.

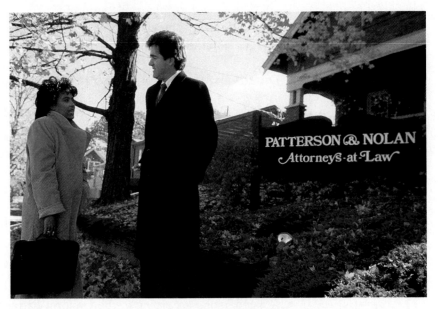

partnerships. However, a written agreement is strongly recommended. Many future conflicts can be avoided by defining in writing all important aspects of the partnership. At a minimum, partnership agreements should contain, in detail, the following points.

- name of the business or partnership
- names of the partners
- type of investment of each partner (such as cash, equipment, real estate) and its value
- managerial responsibilities of each partner
- accounting methods to be used
  rights of partners to review and/or audit accounting documents
- information about how profits will be divided and how losses will be shared
- salaries/money to be withdrawn by partners
- duration of the partnership
- information concerning dissolution of the partnership
- how assets will be distributed upon dissolution
- procedure relating to the death of a partner

Figure 11-1 is an example of a partnership agreement.

Figure 11-1   Sample Partnership Agreement

PARTNERSHIP AGREEMENT

We, L. J. Doray, Jake Meyer, and Janet Feldman, do mutually agree to conduct a business as general partners under the fictitious trade name of STYLE 'N SPEED, on the following terms and conditions:

PURPOSE,
LOCATION

I The purpose of the business shall be the operation of an automobile body customizing shop to be located in rented quarters at 5500 Auto Row, Atlanta, Georgia.

DURATION,
DISSOLUTION

II The partnership shall continue for a period of five (5) years, with the expectation that it will be renewed thereafter for additional five-year periods by unanimous mutual consent. However, any partner may withdraw without liability on ninety (90) day notice in writing, sent by registered mail to the other partners, with time to commence five (5) days from date of posting. In such event, either or both of the other partners may decide to terminate the business. In the alternative, either or both may elect to continue the business, buying the interest(s) of the withdrawing partner(s) at book value with no allowance for goodwill. Book value shall be determined as of the date of withdrawal, by the firm's certified public accountant. Payment shall then be made in equal monthly installments over a three (3) year period, unless otherwise agreed, with interest at ten (10) percent a year on the unpaid balance. The continuing partner(s) may accelerate the payments at will. In the event of death of any partner, the same terms shall apply.

CAPITAL

III The initial capital shall be the sum of thirty thousand dollars ($30,000) to be contributed in equal amounts by the partners within ten (10) days of this agreement. Additional contributions of no more than ten thousand dollars ($10,000) from each partner may be required by majority vote at any time within one year from date. Any further contributions of capital shall require unanimous agreement.

DUTIES
AUDIT, BANK

IV Doray and Meyer shall work in the shop; Feldman shall run the office, promote sales, make all necessary purchases and disbursements, and keep or supervise

fiscal year by allocating the year's total profit to all working days equally. Any sum thus deducted shall be added to the share of profits of the partner(s) who remained at work on the days(s) in question.

COMMENCEMENT,
WORK DAYS

VII Business shall commence on the day this agreement is signed. The work of this partnership shall constitute the full-time, gainful occupation of each of the partners. Unless and until otherwise agreed, the business shall be open from 8:00 a.m. until 6:00 p.m. every weekday. It shall be closed on Saturday, Sundays, and officially designated federal holidays.

IN WITNESS WHEREOF WE HAVE SET OUR HANDS THIS _____ day of September, 19—.

L. J. Doray
L. J. DORAY

Jake Meyer
JAKE MEYER

Janet Feldman
JANET FELDMAN

Source: Reprinted from Mietus, Adamson, and Fisk, *Applied Business Law,* 12th edition, p. 645. © 1984 by South-Western Publishing Co.

Types of Partnerships

Partnerships may take many forms, but the general partnership and the limited partnership are the most common. Entrepreneurs should be familiar with the characteristics of each.

General Partnership.   A general partnership is made up of two general partners. A **general partner** is a partner who actively engages in the day-to-day management of the business and is fully liable for any actions for, by, and against the business. General partners are sometimes referred to as "ordinary" or "regular" partners. Partnership agreements are not always required by law for this type of partnership. They are, however, advisable.

general partner, a partner who actively engages in the day-to-day management of the business and is fully liable for any actions for, by, and against the business

Limited Partnership.   A limited partnership is made up of one or more general partners and one or more limited partners. A **limited partner** is a partner who does not actively engage in the day-to-day management of the business and has liability limited to the extent of his or her investment in the business. They are investors in the business. For example, if Marty Junkin wants to be a limited partner in Dana Simpson's business, she is limited in two ways. First of all, Marty could not participate in the day-to-day management of the video store. Secondly, Marty's liability would be limited to the amount invested in the business. If, for example, Marty invested $3,000 in the business, then $3,000 is the maximum amount that she could lose.

limited partner, a partner who does not actively engage in the day-to-day management of the business and has liability limited to the extent of his or her investment in the business

In a limited partnership, there must be at least one general partner. This means that there is at least one partner in the business who is both fully liable for losses *and* involved in the daily management of the business.

Unlike the minimal start-up requirements for a general partnership, there must be a partnership agreement in a limited partnership. States generally require that the limited partnership agreement be filed with the state in which the limited partnership is located. Entrepreneurs considering forming a limited partnership should seek the assistance of a competent attorney when writing and filing the limited partnership agreement.

Termination of a Partnership

A partnership may be terminated for any number of reasons. Any time a partner leaves or is added to the partnership, the partnership (as well as any partnership agreement) is terminated. Such circumstances include the following situations.

- Expelling a partner—the partnership agreement may provide for the expulsion of partners under certain circumstances, such as the unauthorized use of funds.
- Adding a partner—if a partner is added, the old partnership is terminated and a new one must be initiated.
- Partners agree to terminate the partnership.

The law also dictates the termination of partnerships under certain circumstances. These include the death, bankruptcy, or insanity of a partner. In addition, a partnership may be terminated if the purpose of the business is determined to be illegal.

Advantages and Disadvantages of Partnerships

Numerous advantages exist for the partnership as a form of ownership. They include the following:

- Start-up can be simple because the law does not always require a partnership agreement.
- The partnership, as an entity, pays no income tax.
- Partners share responsibilities of decision making, management, and capitalizing the business.
- Partners share any and all liabilities.
- Liability is limited in the limited partnership.

Just as there are advantages to the partnership form of ownership, there are also disadvantages. They include the following:

- There is a high percentage of partnership break-ups.
- Partners carry unlimited financial liability (in the general partnership).
- Each partner carries liability for the errors of his or her partners.
- Partners, potentially, have less control due to shared decision making and shared management.
- Partners must share profits.
- Partnership termination may disrupt business.

CORPORATIONS

corporation, a legal entity created by law

A **corporation** is a legal entity created by law. A legal entity is like an artificial person. As an artificial person, a corporation can do all the things that a real person can do, such as pay taxes, accrue debt, enter into contracts, be held liable for negligence, and make a profit.

Illus. 11-3 (a and b)   Both large and small corporations are legal entities created by law.

Starting a Corporation

A corporation has to be created by one or more people. The individuals who start the process of incorporation—creating the corporation—are called **promoters.** The promoters file **Articles of Incorporation** with a state agency, usually the Secretary of State. Typically, Articles of Incorporation must contain the following information.

- the name of the proposed corporation
- the promoters' names and addresses
- the address of the corporate office
- an explanation of why the corporation is being formed
- the number of years desired for operation of the corporation (most states allow an indefinite number)
- the names and addresses of people who will direct the corporation

Once the Articles of Incorporation are in order, the promoters pay state taxes required for incorporation. When all requirements have been met, a state official—again, usually the Secretary of State—issues the **charter.** Entrepreneurs should have an attorney file the papers. The cost of incorporation varies from state to state.

Ownership and Management of a Corporation

Ownership of corporations is handled through the possession of stock. Stock represents a share of ownership in a corporation. The promoters

promoter, a person who starts the process to create a corporation

Articles of Incorporation, an application asking the state for permission to form a corporation

charter, document that allows a new corporation to do business in that state and/or executives of a corporation divide a specified amount of stock into a certain number of shares. People who buy these shares are called shareholders, or stockholders. All shareholders hold partial ownership in the corporation, according to the amount of stock they own.

The amount of ownership represented by one share of stock is determined by the amount of stock issued upon incorporation. If 1,000 shares of stock are initially issued, each share represents 1/1,000 ownership of the corporation. If the initial issue is 50,000 shares of stock, each share represents 1/50,000 ownership. The greater the number of shares of stock issued, the lower the value of each share.

After the charter has been issued for a new corporation, a shareholders' meeting is held. Any person owning stock in a company has the right to attend and vote on issues during this and all future meetings. During the first shareholders' meeting, a board of directors is elected. The board of directors is responsible for electing the senior officers of the corporation, setting their salaries, and deciding the corporation's rules for conducting business.

Classifications of Corporations

Corporations are usually classified in five categories. The categories are domestic, foreign, public, private, and closely held.

Domestic or Foreign. A corporation doing business within the state of incorporation is referred to as a domestic corporation. When employees of the corporation go out of the home state to do business, the corporation is considered a foreign corporation in the other states in which it does business. As an example, consider Leonard, Inc., a business that sells musical greeting cards. It is incorporated in the state of North Carolina. When it does business in North Carolina, it is a domestic corporation. When it does business in Texas, in a state outside of its chartered state, it is a foreign corporation. Foreign corporations sometimes need to obtain permission to do business in other states.

Public or Private. Corporations can be either public or private. Public corporations are owned by government entities. For example, public utility companies fall into this category.

A private corporation is one owned by one or more individuals. It is, as a rule, more free to operate than public corporations because there are fewer regulations. Most entrepreneurs who choose to incorporate form private corporations.

Closely Held. Closely held corporations are similar to private corporations. Closely held corporations are private, but the difference is that stock is sold to people other than the promoters, but only on a small scale. Even though the corporate structure is used and shares of stock are issued, there is nothing in corporate law that requires large-scale or public sale of the stock. The promoters may choose to retain all or most of the stock themselves. Some notable examples of closely held corporations are Mary Kay Cosmetics and the Amway Company.

Advantages of the Corporation

Because of the legal structure of corporations, there are numerous advantages to this form of ownership. They are discussed in the following paragraphs.

Limited Liability. This is probably the primary reason many entrepreneurs choose the corporate form of ownership. In many ways it is less risky than other forms of ownership. In the corporation, the shareholders' liability—for debts, taxes, and lawsuits—is limited to the amount of money

Illus. 11-4   Mary Kay Cosmetics is an example of a closely held corporation (photo of Mary Kay Ash).

Photoreporters, Inc.

actually invested in the purchase of stock. However, you should be aware that most lenders require a top executive, such as the chief executive officer (CEO), of an incorporated small business to sign both personally *and* as the business owner, so liability may *not* be limited for that individual in some cases.

Ability to Raise Capital. The ability of a corporation to raise additional capital through the sale of stock is a very important advantage of this form of ownership. Lenders are generally more willing to loan money to corporations than to sole proprietorships or partnerships.

Continuity of Business. Unlike the sole proprietorship and partnership, in which business is directly affected by things such as the death or bankruptcy of an owner, the corporation is not directly affected by such occurrences. The business continues to operate and exist regardless of what happens to individual shareholders.

Transferable Ownership. Since shareholders (owners) do not manage the business, ownership can change through the buying and selling of stock without disrupting the day-to-day business of the corporation.

Disadvantages of the Corporation

The legal structure of the corporation can also lead to certain disadvantages. Such drawbacks are discussed in the following paragraphs.

Double Taxation. There are several instances in which individuals are taxed more than once on income generated from a corporation. Functioning as a legal entity, the corporation pays income tax on profits earned. Furthermore, shareholders pay additional income tax on any dividends they receive from the corporation. Employees who are shareholders must, of course, pay income tax on their salaries, so they are taxed one more time. This is especially a disadvantage for a closely held corporation.

Charter Costs. The cost to incorporate a business can be high. There are fees associated with attorneys and state requirements.

Regulation. A corporation is subject to a considerable amount of regulation that would not apply to the sole proprietorship or partnership. Examples include keeping records of board meetings, holding required board meetings, and completing public disclosure reports. A corporation's business activities are also regulated; they may only pursue the business activities stated in the charter. If the owners wish to expand those activities or, in some cases, do business in other states, they must complete the necessary paperwork.

Lack of Control. Ownership in a corporation does not guarantee any control or say in the day-to-day operation of the business. Remember, ownership of stock only allows the ability to vote for the board of directors. The president or CEO actually decides how the business is run. Even if you are a major stockholder, you may not be the president or CEO and, therefore, may not have much control over the management of the company.

COMPARING FORMS OF OWNERSHIP

Table 11-1 summarizes selected advantages and disadvantages of the three forms of ownership.

Table 11-1   Forms of Ownership—Pros and Cons

Factors of Ownership	Sole Proprietorship	Partnership	Corporation
Simple to start	A	A (except for limited)	D
Liability	D	D (except for limited)	A
Regulation	A	A (except for limited)	D
Ownership control	A	A (except for limited)	D
Initial costs	A	A	D
Ability to raise capital	D	A	A
Taxes	A	A	D
A—This factor is an advantage of this particular form of ownership. D—This factor is a disadvantage of this particular form of ownership.			

JEFF BURNETT—ENTREPRENEUR

One of the main reasons Jeff left his previous job in sales was the fact that he felt somebody else was always in control of his life. As he thought about which form of ownership was best for Rock 'n' Soul Music, he kept remembering how he felt in his old job. He didn't want to ever feel again that somebody else controlled him. The form of ownership he chose would be one that left him in control.

As he examined the advantages and disadvantages of the sole proprietorship, partnership, and corporation, he paid careful attention to the factor of control. It didn't take him long to realize that if he wanted control, he should choose either sole proprietorship or partnership rather than incorporation.

First, he examined and considered the sole proprietorship. It was simple to start and involved less regulation. His taxes wouldn't be too complex. He learned that he would need to use the standard 1040 tax form for his personal income tax and Schedule C to report his business income and expenses. He would be in total control—in terms of financing, merchandise, the marketing plan, and more—and initial costs would be low. The disadvantages were in the financial liability he would have and the low ability to raise capital.

The partnership, on the other hand, spread the liability among the partners and gave him increased potential for raising capital. Taxes would be handled in much the same way as with the sole proprietorship. Even though liability was still a disadvantage, it wasn't as great as with the sole proprietorship. He would also still have control, just not as much. He would have to allow a general partner to have some control.

Jeff had to decide what was the most important advantage. He decided it was control. If he had total control, he felt he would also have total freedom. Even if he made mistakes, they would be his mistakes. Freedom meant risk, Jeff knew, but he felt it was worth it. He had tried business the other way; now he would try it *his* way. Jeff chose to form a sole proprietorship.

SUMMARY

There are three basic forms of business ownership: the sole proprietorship, partnership, and the corporation. A sole proprietorship is a business established, owned, controlled, and operated by a single person. The advantages of the sole proprietorship are that it is simple to start, may require no formal action to start, may be started immediately, owners have total control, owners receive all profits, and the business as an entity pays no income tax. Some disadvantages of the sole proprietorship are unlimited responsibility for any losses or debts, owners must make all the decisions, and owners have sole responsibility for capitalizing the business.

A partnership is an association of two or more persons to carry on as co-owners of a business for profit. The two major types of partnerships are general and limited. Some advantages of the partnership form of ownership include the following: It is simple to start; it pays no income tax as a business; partners assist in decision making, management, and capitalizing the business; shared liability; and limited liability in limited partnership. Some disadvantages of the partnership are liability for errors of partners; entrepreneurs must share decision making and management, which may result in less control; partners must share profits; and partnership termination may disrupt the business.

A corporation is a legal entity created by law. Corporations may be domestic or foreign, public or private, or closely held. Some advantages of the corporation include limited liability, little difficulty in raising capital, the continuity of business is not tied to individuals, and sale of ownership does not disrupt the business. Some disadvantages of the corporation include double taxation, charter costs, regulation, and lack of control.

VOCABULARY BUILDER

On a separate sheet of paper, write a brief description of each word or phrase based on your reading of the chapter.

1. Sole proprietorship
2. Partnership
3. Partner
4. Partnership agreement
5. General partner
6. Limited partner
7. Corporation
8. Promoters
9. Articles of incorporation
10. Charter
11. Stock
12. Shares of stock
13. Shareholder

REVIEW QUESTIONS

1. What are the three basic forms of business ownership?
2. What are the two major types of partnerships?

3. What is the difference between a general partnership and a limited partnership?
4. What are the five categories into which corporations may be classified?
5. What advantages are there to forming a corporation?

DISCUSSION QUESTIONS

1. What are the characteristics of sole proprietorship, including the advantages and disadvantages?
2. What are the characteristics of partnerships, including the advantages and disadvantages?
3. Why is having a written partnership agreement important to the individual partners?
4. What are the characteristics of the corporation, including its advantages and disadvantages?

CRITICAL THINKING

Allen Huang is planning to start a business that manufactures horse trailers. He has two friends who have expressed an interest in the business. One friend knows quite a lot about horse trailers, but the second knows very little.

1. Of the three forms of ownership, which one would you recommend to Allen? Why?
2. Is there a way the second friend could be involved in the business, but with limited liability? How?
3. If Allen decides to go into business with one or both of his friends, what is the first agreement they should negotiate? Do you think it is really necessary, since they are friends?

SHORT CASE: OWNERSHIP— SAFETY IN NUMBERS

Stan Beasley has been working for the past two months on a business plan involving a health club. For most of his life, Stan has been a very successful athlete. In high school he excelled in football and went on to earn a scholarship to a major university. After college he joined a professional team and, for ten years, he was the best defensive safety in the National Football League.

Because the only thing Stan really has any experience in is athletics, he decided that was the best area to pursue for starting a new business. With his tremendous success in the NFL, Stan is independently wealthy.

He doesn't really have to work again, but thinks he needs to stay busy at something to be happy. Opening a health club seemed to be the perfect business since he had been involved in athletic training for many years—after all, he had spent most of his adult life in training. He felt he possessed the level of technical knowledge necessary to start such a business and keep it running.

Stan is at the point in his business planning where he needs to give serious thought to the form of ownership he will use for his new business. As part of his deliberation, he has listed the following points as factors to consider before making the final decision about the form of ownership his business will assume.

1. Capitalization is no problem.
2. I possess technical expertise.
3. Health clubs have experienced great financial difficulty in recent years.
4. Lawsuits against health clubs have been increasing.
5. Several friends (ex-football players) have indicated an interest in participating in some way in the venture.

Stan has a very difficult decision to make. Give him some help by answering the following questions.

1. Should Stan give serious consideration to sole proprietorship? Explain your answer.
2. There are at least two ways that Stan could involve his friends as owners of the new business. What are they?
3. If you were Stan, what would be your primary area of concern in relation to form of ownership?
4. What form of ownership would you recommend to Stan? Why?

PROJECT CHALLENGE

Now it is time for you to decide what form of ownership will be the best for your hypothetical business. Make this decision only after careful deliberation.

1. List at least five aspects of your hypothetical business that would be considerations in your decision about form of business ownership.
2. Take the list from question #1 and rank the items in order of importance.
3. Choose two forms of ownership that are possibilities for your business. List the advantages and disadvantages of each form, being specific about your hypothetical business.
4. Choose your form of ownership and list the two most important reasons why you chose it.

12
Personnel

The successful entrepreneur knows the importance of having the right personnel. Capital, equipment, and inventory are resources that are essential to success, and so are people—they are the human resources. Without the right personnel, the business will flounder. Finding and keeping good personnel requires competent performance of three management functions—staffing, directing, and controlling.

STAFFING

Staffing begins with determining how much money is available for personnel. Entrepreneurs use sales projections as guides for purchasing initial inventory and equipment. They also use sales projections to determine how to staff the business. Entrepreneurs should first determine how much money is available to pay employees, perhaps by checking with industry sources to find the percent of sales revenues normally available for payroll expenses and multiplying their own projected revenues by that percentage. This process will establish an approximate amount to use as a guide. The next step is finding out how much other businesses are paying for similar help. This information will help determine how much employees should be paid. Then calculate the approximate payroll cost, including employer-paid taxes, for each potential employee and subtract it from the amount available.

After entrepreneurs determine how much money is available for personnel, they must determine how many employees are needed. The type of business determines what skills are needed to effectively serve customers. To decide how to staff the business, owners must carefully analyze the business's needs by means of organization charts.

Organization Chart

An **organization chart** is a picture of a business's distribution of its human resources. It identifies the positions in the organization and the general work responsibilities of each. The names of the individuals who hold the positions are added to the chart as personnel join the work force. The organization chart should show primary job responsibilities. Organization charts are both planning tools and management tools (see Figure 12-1).

Figure 12-1   Organization Chart for Small Retail Store

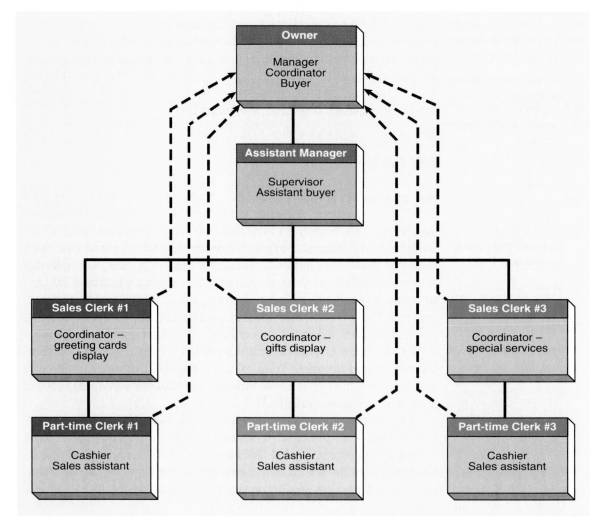

Illus. 12-1   A common staff position often found in a small business is that of bookkeeper.

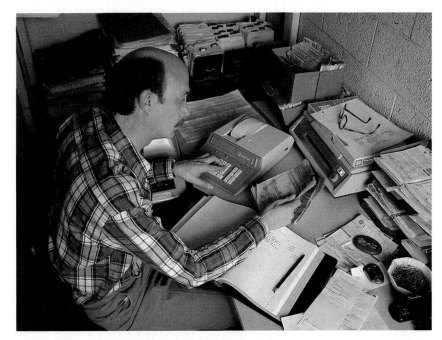

The lines on the chart indicate reporting relationships. It is important to include specific instructions about who oversees whom, or the **chain of command.** As Figure 12-1 shows, the solid lines indicate formal reporting relationships. The broken lines indicate that in small businesses all employees have direct access to the manager. Illustrating supervisory relationships in graph form eliminates confusion.

chain of command, the reporting relationship of positions depicted on the organization chart

Management uses the organization chart to identify the positions that must be filled and the skills needed for each. It is an important part of the business planning process because it gives business owners a clear picture of their personnel needs. To identify the positions to be filled, entrepreneurs need to determine what type of organization the business is.

line organization, an organization in which all members are involved in performing duties directly related to creating and/or selling products or services

Small businesses are normally characterized as **line organizations.** A line organization's mission is to create and sell the products or services. Larger organizations, characterized as **line and staff organizations,** may have, for example, a personnel manager, safety officer, or company accountant to assist those line employees who perform the work involved with creating and selling the products or services. One staff position that is sometimes found in a small business is that of bookkeeper.

line and staff organization, an organization that has staff positions to assist the line functions

The organization chart is also a very important tool for employees. All employees have the right to know what their areas of responsibility are, to whom they must report, and what other positions they may pursue within the organization. If this information is not readily available, employees may not be motivated to do their best work, and morale—and productivity—may suffer. No matter how large or small the organization, an organization chart should be established as a reference tool for management and employees.

Too many small businesses overlook this tool, believing that because their organizations are small their employees automatically know what is expected of them. It is usually not that clear, particularly in a small business where responsibilities may overlap. As is the case in most areas of small business management, personnel management must ensure a great deal of flexibility. A flexible staff is essential if all employees are to carry out their business activities efficiently.

Recruiting

Finding and recruiting the right personnel for a new business is a difficult task. Entrepreneurs usually have capital limitations that can make the task even more difficult. Because they have limited capital, small business owners—and especially *new* small business owners—cannot always offer the same wages or salaries to prospective employees as large business. The benefit packages they can offer may not be as lucrative as those offered by large businesses, which often offer incentives such as well-funded profit sharing plans, comprehensive insurance packages, and paid vacations. For these reasons, small business owners are often forced to hire less experienced individuals. This obstacle can, however, be overcome and, in some cases, works to the business owner's benefit. With efficient training, these employees can attain the desired skill levels and perform the same functions as employees who join a company with prior training.

How do small business owners find and recruit quality personnel? The first step is to decide how to "shop" for applicants.

Classified Advertisements. Placing ads in the Help Wanted sections of local newspapers is usually an effective method of attracting large numbers of applicants. Write a descriptive ad that lists job requirements, such as education or previous experience, as well as the responsibilities of the open position. Request resumes from applicants in addition to cover letters. It is sometimes helpful to ask that specific information be included in the cover letter, such as salary requirements, date of availability, or other

Illus. 12-2   College career fairs offer entrepreneurs one means of finding employees.

Courtesy, University of Cincinnati

pertinent information. If you do not wish to disclose the name of the business, many newspapers offer mail box facilities for use in conjunction with their classified ads. The business owner can then screen the resumés to determine which applicants are worth interviewing.

Employment Agencies.   Employment agencies keep records of people who are looking for work and their qualifications. Seeking applicants through an employment agency will save some of the time involved in screening applicants, but the cost is much higher than that for classified advertising. Employment agencies charge a fee from either applicants or employers, or sometimes both.

College Placement Services.   Many colleges offer a no-charge placement service. Placement departments keep records of students and alumni who are looking for work and their qualifications.

In-store Advertising.   Posting a sign in the business's window might attract pedestrians or motorists. When using this method, business owners have two options. They may either have applicants complete applications and inform them that they *may* be called for an interview, or have them complete applications and interview the applicants immediately. The first option allows the business owner to do some initial screening of the applicants. The second option requires the business owner to interview all applicants. This often means dedicating several days to interviewing alone, knowing that not much other work will get done during those days.

Referrals.   An entrepreneur's friends or employees are often good sources of referrals. If the entrepreneur considers the person who is making the recommendation reliable, a referral may require very little screening. However, many business owners are reluctant to hire people related to, or too closely affiliated with, other employees. This practice is risky— there is a possibility of alienating one at the expense of the other, creating conflicts within the organization, or losing two employees if one decides to leave or must be let go.

Regardless of the methods, it is to the business owner's advantage to attract a large number of applicants. Having more people to choose from allows more opportunity to be selective and find the *right* person.

Applications

Tailoring an employment application to a specific business is a good idea. By using a tailored application, business owners gather specific information that may not be included on a resumé, and they can use that information to decide what to ask during the interview.

Interviewing

Once job descriptions are written and candidates have been selected, the interview process can begin. As with any interview, the interviewer should plan carefully and have a written list of questions. A lot of information must be gathered in a relatively short period of time, and it is easy to get caught up in conversation and forget to ask important questions.

Interviews should be held in a quiet, relaxing environment. When conducting the interview, the business owner should focus on the applicant's personal characteristics with regard to teamwork and cooperation. Two characteristics to look for in applicants are a positive attitude and reliability. Skills are important, but, if inadequate, they can normally be taught; personal characteristics cannot. The discussion should enable the interviewer to determine if the applicant will do well in the team environment of a small business.

In many cases, more than one interview will be needed before the final decision can be made. If the interview indicates that the applicant is right for the position, the business owner should take time to fully explain the job, show the applicant the operation, and give the applicant good reasons for joining the team. Following is a list of ways that a small business owner might appeal to a prospective employee.

- Appeal to the excitement of participating in a new venture. Many people prefer to work in an environment where they are able to see the outcome of their work. Employees of small businesses know their contributions are important to the operation of the business. They have strong self-actualization needs. For these people, working for a small business is worth a possible sacrifice of financial benefits.
- Tell potential employees how much the company needs them. By being direct about this, the business owner helps them visualize the roles they will play. They will understand that they will be direct participants in the business's activities.
- Share your values with the applicant. If it is clear that the goal is to create an ethical and responsible business, the employee will feel proud to be a part of the organization.
- Create an environment of flexibility and caring, and be sure to describe that environment to potential employees. Small businesses should not need to enforce the rules that are necessary in businesses with many employees. Explain that the management understands that additional time off is sometimes required for family responsibilities. The owner should give the employee the impression that there are many benefits to working in a friendly, informal environment.
- Establish a bonus system whereby employees benefit from the success of the company. Emphasize that if the business does well, the employees will benefit financially. When extra profits are generated, employees should receive bonuses in recognition of their contributions.

New employees should be hired on a probationary basis for a certain period of time—four to six weeks is common. Both parties must clearly understand that if either party is dissatisfied at the end of this period, the relationship will be terminated. Specific reasons for termination should be reviewed by emphasizing the importance of teamwork. Tardiness, dishonesty, unreliability, and poor attitude disrupt the activities of all and cannot be accommodated in a small business.

Thorough interviewing is important, because training new employees is expensive. An employee in training is not usually able to produce at full speed, and neither is the trainer. Therefore, two employees are performing at below-normal levels for a certain period of time, which

Illus. 12-3   Thorough interviewing is important because training new employees is expensive.

McDonald's Corporation

ultimately results in added payroll expense. If the interview and selection process is inadequate, the payroll expense will be high. There will be excessive turnover of employees and, therefore, a continual need for training.

DIRECTING

Once the business is staffed, efficient management is necessary to keep valuable employees. The business owner's success in keeping an efficient team together will depend on leadership abilities and management skills. Successful small business owners understand that they lead by example. A small business does not have an "ivory tower" where the boss sits and looks down on the employees. The boss is right in the middle of things, participating with the workers. If the boss is not willing to pick up the trash, the employee won't be either.

Motivating

The owner, as teacher and organizer, decides what must be done—a planning function—and how it will be done, a directing function. Enthusiasm for the work—and efficiency in completing that work—are dependent on employers' abilities to motivate employees.

Good teachers are patient when giving instructions. They do not expect the students to do the impossible, but they do expect the students to do their best. By allowing plenty of time and creating a proper learning environment, the business owner can supply the employee with the tools needed for good performance. This requires coordination and attention to detail. The ability to give directions and assign tasks is one ingredient of success. Just as important is the owner's ability to continually motivate employees to do their best.

Management Styles

Theory X manager, a manager who directs with little consideration for human relations

Douglas MacGregor, a professor of industrial administration at Massachusetts Institute of Technology, observed two distinct management styles that he termed Theory X and Theory Y. He defines **Theory X managers** as those who direct with little consideration for human relations. They are very task oriented and are most concerned with being sure assigned jobs are completed in the most expedient manner. They operate under the assumption that workers prefer to be directed and do not wish to take on responsibility. They also believe that workers do not like work, and that getting paid is the prime motivation for their presence in the workplace.

Theory Y manager, a manager who is very concerned with human relations

Theory Y managers are very concerned about human relations. They direct under the presumption that workers like their work and enjoy responsibility. They believe that if given the opportunity, people will use their creativity and intellectual capabilities.

Effective small business managers operate under a Theory Y philosophy. They realize that, to build an effective team and accomplish all the work on hand, the workers must receive satisfaction from the job itself and not just from the pay received.

This theory is reinforced by a study of job satisfaction factors made by Frederick Herzberg in 1959. The results of his study showed that worker enthusiasm is created by the following job satisfaction factors, ranked in order.

1. Sense of achievement
2. Recognition for achievement
3. Interest in the work itself
4. Opportunity for growth
5. Opportunity for advancement
6. Responsibility
7. Peer and group relationship
8. Compensation
9. Supervisor fairness
10. Reasonable company policies and rules
11. Status
12. Job security
13. Supervisor friendliness
14. Good working conditions

Illus. 12-4 Supervisor friendliness helps create worker enthusiasm.

Courtesy of International Business Machines Corporation

This study clearly showed that employees are most concerned with job contentment. They prefer an environment that allows a sense of achievement and personal growth. They desire recognition for accomplishments and enjoy working with others who have similar goals.

Herzberg went on to separate job-related factors into two categories—**motivators** and **hygiene factors.** Motivators in the work environment include the following:

motivator, a work environment factor that provides workers with satisfaction and motivation

hygiene factor, a work environment characteristic needed to ensure job satisfaction

- The work itself
- Achievement
- Recognition
- Responsibility
- Growth and advancement

Herzberg identified the following as hygiene factors:

- Salary
- Supervision
- Company policies
- Interpersonal relationships
- Working conditions

Workers will perform their assigned duties in a satisfactory manner when the hygiene factors are present, but if management expects peak performance, the workplace must also offer the motivators.

Many small businesses can offer a combination of Theory Y management and Herzberg's motivators better than large organizations. Due to their size, large organizations must generally rely on rigid company policies and structured supervision to control operations. Small business managers can work with all employees and instill a sense of involvement, achievement, and challenge.

CONTROLLING

The controlling function is often the most difficult function of personnel management to master. To excel in this function, business owners must constantly consider employees' roles in the business.

Listening

Employees who are in line positions work directly with the customers, and often with suppliers. A good manager listens to employees because employees know what customers want and expect. Entrepreneurs will better serve their markets if they are open to suggestions from employees.

Small business owners should seek input from the people they work with and include them when setting goals. Large businesses, of necessity, tend to set objectives from the top down; upper management sets sales goals and company policies without employee input. Decisions made without collecting information from the people most affected—the employees—result in forcing new policies on the employees, which in turn hurts organization morale. The small business owner, who works so closely with employees, should always get direct input from them before making important decisions. For example, a retail store owner who is considering adding a new product line should ask sales personnel for suggestions. It only makes sense, since they work with the customers daily. The same is true for a business owner who wants to make an accurate sales forecast. Asking sales personnel what they think is happening in the market and listening to their responses enables business owners to make better predictions about future growth.

If decisions are made at the top of the organization without valuable employee input, problems arise for employees at the lower levels of the structure. For example, when ABC company, a large organization, sets its sales goals for the upcoming year, they are typically set from the top down. The president of the company reports the results of the past year to the Board of Directors and awaits a response. If the company achieved a five percent increase the previous year, the response might be to try for a six percent increase in the coming year. The president, not wanting to disappoint the board, agrees to accept the challenge. He meets with the vice president of sales and sets a goal for a seven percent increase—he wants to be sure that he will look good to the Board of Directors even if the sales team misses the mark. The vice president meets with the regional sales managers and sets their objective at achieving an eight percent increase, using the same protective strategy the president did. The regional sales managers relay a nine percent sales increase objective to the district managers who, using the same safety valve strategy, relay a ten percent sales increase objective to the sales personnel. In this case, the original goal has almost doubled by the time it reaches the unfortunate sales representatives. During the coming year, pressure to reach the objective will build, particularly for the sales representatives, who have received the most difficult assignment. This is top-down management; managers neither listen nor request information from the bottom up (see Figure 12-2).

Business owners should obtain information from the customer contact level before making decisions. Most small business owners find that they are most successful when they are willing to listen.

Performance Evaluation

Large businesses usually have an elaborate system for appraising employees' work. This system often requires rating employee performance in selected areas of responsibility such as dependability, punctuality, attitude toward job and coworkers, and, sometimes, statistical analysis of success in achieving predetermined objectives. The ratings are used to let the employees know how their supervisors perceive their performance. They also serve as useful management control tools because they provide a means of determining if the objectives for a particular job are being met. Performance evaluations are conducted at regular intervals, usually every 6 or 12 months. They are an important management tool and should be utilized in every business.

Small business owners must realize the value of listening to employees during their evaluations. Evaluations are most productive if conducted away from the business, allowing employer and employee an uninterrupted amount of time to share thoughts about the direction of the business.

Figure 12-2 Top-Down Goal Setting

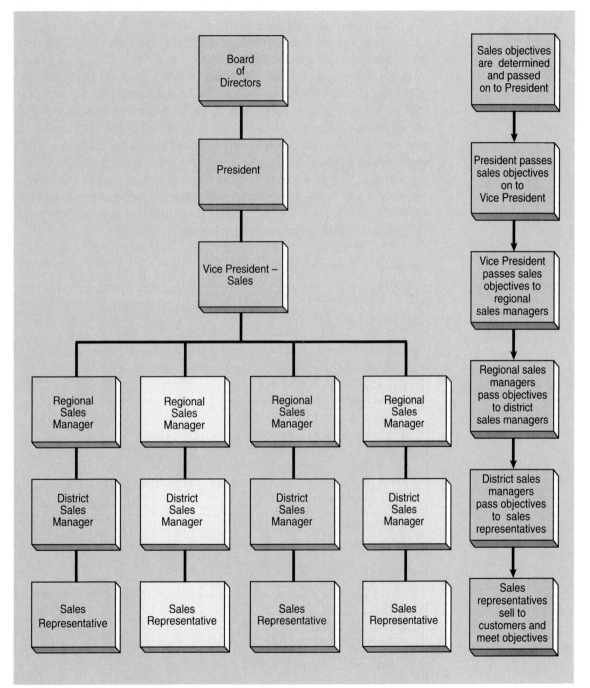

Results can be reviewed and new objectives set in a nonthreatening way that proves helpful to all. Employees need to know how their employers feel about their performance.

Employee evaluations provide an excellent opportunity for praise and, when necessary, suggestions for improvement. Small business owners must devise employee evaluation plans. These plans may differ considerably from those of a large business. The best system does not use rankings or ratings—it uses comments. A list of the areas to discuss should be prepared ahead of time, with space to record comments during the discussion. It is important that employer and employee ultimately agree about the comments and the objectives set for work performance. Clearly stating work objectives makes it easy to determine what has or has not been achieved. A good employee evaluation session focuses on positives rather than negatives. Figure 12-3 is an illustration of an effective evaluation form for a small business employee.

Figure 12-3   Employee Evaluation Form

Jan's Shoe Emporium
Employee Evaluation

Employee Name_____   **Date** _____

1. Employee's personal evaluation of his or her work accomplishments:

_____

Employer's comments: _____

_____

2. Employee's personal evaluation of the company's overall performance, including areas that could be improved upon:

_____

3. Employee's specific comments regarding   (a) employee morale, (b) customer relations, (c) policies and procedures:

_____

_____

4. Manager comments as to employee's contribution toward goals:

_____

_____

Employee's comments, including points on which he or she agrees or disagrees:

_____

_____

5. Goals agreed upon for future development of the company:

_____

LABOR LAWS

Entrepreneurs who plan to hire other people must learn the regulations that protect them and their employees from unfair labor practices. There are many laws, and new ones are constantly being added, so the business owner must keep up with legislative activities that concern employment.

Small businesses can be susceptible to personnel trouble because often the person doing the hiring is *not* a trained personnel specialist. That is why familiarity with these laws and their provisions is important. Without the necessary knowledge, small business owners may infringe upon applicants' or employees' rights without knowing it. The five laws listed below are the ones with which every business owner *must* be familiar.

- The Fair Labor Standards Act of 1938 established a minimum wage and required overtime pay for employees working in excess of 40 hours per week.
- The Civil Rights Act of 1964 prohibited discrimination based on sex, race, color, religion, or national origin.
- The Age Discrimination in Employment Act of 1967 prohibited personnel practices that discriminate against people aged 40 to 60. An amendment outlaws company policies that require employees to retire before age 70.

Illus. 12-5   Owners of small businesses must be aware of the legal rights of applicants and employees.

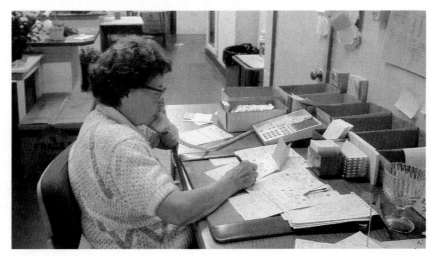

- The Occupational Safety and Health Act (OSHA) of 1970 ensures workers in the United States a healthy and safe working environment by regulating exposure to hazardous substances and setting requirements for safety equipment.
- The Immigration Reform and Control Act of 1986 requires employers to check identification for employees hired after 1986 to ensure that they are legal citizens of the United States.

These laws and others are regulated by the Equal Employment Opportunity Commission (EEOC), a government agency established by Congress in 1972.

JEFF BURNETT—ENTREPRENEUR

Jeff knew that he would need employees to help operate Rock 'n' Soul Music. He reviewed his projected budget and determined that he could allocate 10 percent of his projected sales of $200,000, or $20,000, to personnel. He learned that the average starting wage for sales personnel in his type of business was slightly above the minimum wage of $4.25 per hour. He decided that he would start his employees at the minimum wage and give them each a raise of $.25 per hour after successful completion of a probationary period of 30 days. By dividing the amount he could spend —$20,000—by the wage he planned to offer—$4.50 per hour— he determined that he could pay for 4,450 hours per year. He divided the 4,450 hours by 52 weeks to determine that he could pay for 85 hours per week. Allowing for employer-paid payroll tax expenses, he decided to hire one full-time employee (40 hours) and two part-time employees at 20 hours each—a total of 80 hours. He then drew his organization chart (see Figure 12-4).

Jeff decided to place advertisements for the positions in the Help Wanted section of the local newspaper, and he called the placement office of a local community college. He was delighted to receive more than 20 responses to his classified advertisement, and the placement office recommended five candidates. All of the candidates from the placement office seemed qualified. He screened the advertisement responses, found that he had five more candidates, and scheduled ten interviews during a two-day period. He planned to allow one hour for each interview.

Jeff decided to ask the applicants to come to the store, where he would be assembling fixtures. He would show them the store,

Figure 12-4   Rock 'n' Soul Organization Chart

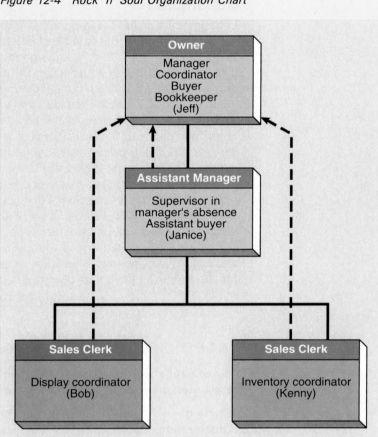

then invite them to join him for coffee or a soft drink at the restaurant across the mall. The days of interviewing arrived, and six of the applicants were very appealing. They were neat, had good attitudes, and seemed to have the necessary capabilities. Two of the six were eliminated because of schedule conflicts, and one was not satisfied with the starting pay. Jeff's new team would include Janice, who had three years of retail experience, as the full-time employee; Bob, a college student; and Kenny, a recent high school graduate. Jeff was pleased with the team. Its members represented three different backgrounds and would appeal to three different kinds of customers. Training sessions would begin three days before the grand opening.

SUMMARY

Entrepreneurs realize the importance of creating a well-coordinated team of employees that is well schooled in creating and/or selling the product or service. Creating a good team is achieved through effective leadership in a challenging and responsive environment. Entrepreneurs who are good managers participate with employees as coworkers, not exclusively as supervisors.

Developing an effective team requires creating an organization chart that clearly defines all positions, responsibilities, and reporting relationships. Small business owners must interview candidates carefully and train employees well. They must stay within budget guidelines when deciding how many people to employ.

Once the team is in place, the owner must be a skillful manager. Use of proper employee evaluation procedures and the ability to listen are essential. Employers can motivate employees by making them feel like integral parts of the business and allowing them to assume challenging responsibilities. Finally, entrepreneurs must be familiar with the laws that govern employment.

VOCABULARY BUILDER

On a separate sheet of paper, write a brief definition of each word or phrase based on your reading of the chapter.

1. Staffing
2. Organization chart
3. Chain of command
4. Line organization
5. Line and staff organization
6. Directing
7. Theory X manager
8. Theory Y manager
9. Motivator
10. Hygiene factor
11. Controlling

REVIEW QUESTIONS

1. How do entrepreneurs determine how much money to allocate to payroll expenses for new businesses?
2. What is the purpose of an organization chart?
3. What do the connecting lines on an organization chart represent?
4. What effect may capital limitations have on the recruiting process?
5. What are five methods of finding potential personnel?
6. In what ways can a small business owner interest potential employees?

7. Why are inadequate interviewing and employee selection methods expensive for small business owners?
8. What is the difference between a Theory X manager and a Theory Y manager?
9. What are the two kinds of job satisfaction factors and what effects do they have?
10. With what five labor laws should small business owners be familiar?

DISCUSSION QUESTIONS

1. What can happen in a business that does not have an organization chart?
2. What are some of the advantages of working for a small business? What are some disadvantages?
3. Have you ever worked for a Theory X manager? A Theory Y manager? Relate your experiences to the class.
4. What aspects of a job do you consider motivators? Hygiene factors? Does your list differ from Herzberg's?
5. Do you think minimum wage laws can cause increases in the cost of living? Why or why not? Could minimum wage laws affect job availability for certain groups of people (e.g., teenagers)?

CRITICAL THINKING

Report cards are a form of performance evaluation. Are you glad you receive report cards? What changes do you think could be made to improve your school's grade reporting system? Write a description of a better reporting method or form and explain the changes that you are suggesting.

SHORT CASE: INCONSISTENT MANAGEMENT

"I think you will find this store an enjoyable place to work, Susan. What we can't provide in wages we more than make up by providing a comfortable environment. I try to be as flexible as possible. Come with me, and I'll introduce you to Sharon and Jim. They'll be teaching you the ropes."

Roger felt good about his new employee. It seemed likely that she would stay for a while, not the usual two or three months. He was anxious to get her trained.

Susan was happy to have found a nice store to work in that was not far from her home. Roger seemed sincere and she thought it was going to work out well.

Sharon and Jim were cordial, but somewhat reserved. They taught her the cash register procedures and explained the inventory control system. After two weeks, she felt comfortable with her assignments, but still felt like an outsider with Sharon and Jim. She learned that although they liked the store and the customers, they were fearful of Roger's moods. Some days he was easygoing, but other days he was temperamental and very impulsive.

Susan's first encounter with one of Roger's mood swings occurred when she was at the cash register writing a ticket for a customer refund. "Who told you to write the ticket that way?" Roger demanded.

"Jim did," Susan answered.

"Well it's all wrong. Doesn't he know anything? I'll go talk to him. Meanwhile, please pick up that paper on the floor. This place looks like a pig sty." Roger abruptly took the refund ticket, went directly to Jim, and reprimanded him in front of a customer.

After this incident, Jim and Sharon accepted Susan. They often complained to each other about their boss's erratic behavior. Jim often vented his frustrations. "I will *not* be treated that way. When he is in one of those moods, I'm staying out of his way. I'll spend time in the stockroom, or say that I'm sick and leave early."

It wasn't long before Roger lost his temper and fired Jim. His replacement lasted less than two weeks; he was also fired on one of Roger's bad days. Sharon and Susan started looking for new jobs because they never knew when their turn might come. Susan didn't want to leave, but living with such inconsistency was causing anxiety—both on the job and off.[1]

Questions

1. What management style is Roger exhibiting in his bad moods?
2. What effect is Roger's inconsistency having on the production and payroll of his business?
3. What can Susan do about her situation?

PROJECT CHALLENGE

Develop a personnel plan for your hypothetical business. In your business plan notebook, write the decisions you make about the following issues.

1. Determine how many employees you will hire.
2. Create an organization chart.
3. Write a job description for each position. Include areas of responsibility. Determine if all positions are line positions.
4. Decide how much you will pay your employees.
5. Decide how you will find and recruit your employees.
6. Describe your intended management style.

---

[1]From James Halloran, *Why Entrepreneurs Fail: Avoid the 20 Pitfalls of Running Your Own Business* (Blue Ridge Summit, PA: Liberty Hall Press/TAB Books, a division of McGraw-Hill, 1991).

13

Management Control Tools

management by objectives, a management technique that clearly states the goals of the business and meshes them with the goals of the employees

In Chapter 12 we discussed how employee performance evaluations act as management tools to monitor progress toward stated objectives. There are many tools managers can use in all aspects of operating small businesses to ensure that employees meet objectives in a timely and efficient manner. Entrepreneurs must make sure that their businesses are operating as planned in terms of sales, inventory control, financial responsibilities, and operating procedures.

MANAGEMENT BY OBJECTIVES

By clearly stating the goals of the business and meshing them with the goals of the employees, entrepreneurs make use of a management technique called **management by objectives** (MBO). MBO serves as a planning tool when the objectives are being set, and as a control tool when the results are monitored and measured. Objectives should be set in all areas of business operations to ensure that resources are used efficiently. The planning function—setting objectives—should follow the steps shown in Figure 13-1.

The control function—monitoring results—can only be effective if the standards to measure against are fairly and uniformly established. Properly set measuring standards will allow an effective feedback system that will be consistent and clearly understood by all concerned. Figure 13-2 illustrates the steps involved in the controlling function of an MBO technique.

Both large and small businesses benefit from the MBO technique. Entrepreneurs must devise a system tailored to their particular business that fairly establishes and monitors the objectives of the business. It is not enough just to announce what you expect to be achieved in a particular area of the business operation. Detailed objectives must be defined,

Figure 13-1   MBO planning steps

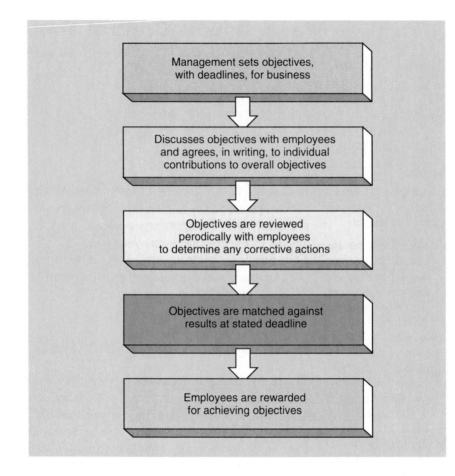

Figure 13-2   MBO control cycle

discussed, and agreed upon by any and all employees and managers concerned, and the results should be closely monitored. Small business owners use a variety of reports that serve as checklists for achieving objectives. Sales objectives are the first objectives that should be set. Nearly every aspect of the business is dependent upon sales dollars. Therefore, business owners must effectively estimate what sales totals will be for different time periods. Sales affect inventory levels, cash flow, personnel scheduling, and all other operating conditions.

CONTROLLING REVENUES

If an entrepreneur sets the business's sales objective at the beginning of the year at $200,000, the business would be in sad shape if the owner waited until November to find out that sales were running 40 percent behind objective. It would be too late at that point to take corrective action. By monitoring the sales income daily, weekly, and monthly, the entrepreneur will discover any problems early and can design and implement a plan to correct the deficiency. The sales plan that calls for sales to total $200,000 per year might require that seven percent of sales should be received in January. Therefore, the January sales objectives would be $14,000—approximately $3,500 per week or $500 per day. The comparison of actual sales results to sales objectives can be shown on a daily or weekly sales report, or a monthly report. Examples of these reports are shown in Figures 13-3 and 13-4 on pages 232 and 233.

If the results of a daily or weekly report are higher or lower than the objective, the owner might need to make changes in the weekly and monthly sales objectives. For example, if the sales income for Monday and Tuesday was $1,400, and not $1,000 as projected, the business owner might wish to reset the weekly sales objective at $3,900 instead of the $3,500 originally set. If this objective is achieved, the monthly objective might be reset for an additional $400. The same logic would apply if sales were *not* meeting the daily or weekly objectives.

CONTROLLING INVENTORY

inventory, the number of units and the value of the units a business has available for sale or manufacture

There is a direct correlation between sales and inventory. **Inventory** is the number of units, and the value of the units, that is available for sale or manufacture. Theoretically, the more units a business has on hand to sell or manufacture, the more it should sell. In this way, inventory affects

Figure 13-3

DAILY AND WEEKLY SALES REPORT

Week of _____

Daily Sales	**Objective**	**+ / (−)**
Monday _____	_____	_____
Tuesday _____	_____	_____
Wednesday _____	_____	_____
Thursday _____	_____	_____
Friday _____	_____	_____
Saturday _____	_____	_____
Sunday _____	_____	_____
Weekly total _____	_____	_____

Comments:

---

sales, and inventory levels are controlled by sales levels. If the inventory is not sufficient, there will be a drop in expected sales revenues. If a business sells more units than expected, its inventory level will fall below the desired level. If a business does not sell the number of units the owner expects, the inventory will be higher than the desired level. Monitoring sales revenues closely allows the business owner to adjust inventory levels to the demands of the market.

Figure 13-4

MONTHLY SALES TO OBJECTIVES REPORT 19				
Month	Sales	Objective	+/(−)	Comments
January	$21,200	$20,500	+700	Increase open to buy $500
February	18,400	18,550	−150	No action necessary
March	23,000	24,500	(1,500)	Decrease open to buy $1,000
April	26,700	24,300	+2,100	Increase open to buy $1,500
May	23,100	22,900	+200	No action necessary
June	19,650	19,900	−250	No action necessary

Business owners attempt to have the amount of goods available that
will give the greatest amount of sales without over-investing in inventory. It is impossible to always have the exact amount of inventory that
will yield the greatest profit. However, with proper controls in place, the
business owner can maintain a level that will produce a healthy sales income and provide a profitable return on investment. For example, if an
entrepreneur invests $10,000 in inventory and the gross profit received
from the sale of that inventory is $5,000, the entrepreneur has received
a return on investment of 50 percent. Business owners want and need
to make a profit from the purchase of inventory. If they get stuck with left-
over or unwanted inventory, they must sell it at a price that yields less
profit. Therefore, it is important to avoid having too much inventory because if it doesn't sell, it will most likely decrease the return on investment. Having too little inventory is just as dangerous. This will cause lost
sales, lost profit, and dissatisfied customers. Manufacturers who run out of
parts are forced to shut down production until the replacement parts arrive.
Retailers who run out of merchandise before a major holiday lose business

Illus. 13-1   Business owners strive to maintain an inventory of goods that will provide the greatest number of sales.

at the time when they should be making great profits. As you can see, it would be hazardous to guess at inventory levels. Inventory objectives must be planned carefully and monitored closely or the business could get into serious trouble.

Inventory Purchase Plan

The amount of inventory to purchase for a business can be derived from the sales forecast. Entrepreneurs need to ask the question, "How many units must I add to what is presently available to reach my sales objective for a particular period of time?" They also need to know the amount of inventory they want to have at the conclusion of that time period. For instance, if a business owner wishes to increase the amount of inventory on hand at the end of the period, he or she must add the amount of increase to the purchase plan. If less inventory is desired, the amount is subtracted. The formula used to plan inventory purchases is as follows:

beginning inventory + purchase − sales − markdowns = ending inventory

Suppose that a merchant has a $45,000 inventory and projected sales of $100,000 for a period of six months. He or she wishes to increase the inventory on hand to $50,000 at the end of six months and plans that $10,000 of the inventory will be marked down and sold at cost. Since markdowns represent inventory that is sold without profit, that amount should be subtracted from the plan. To find the planned purchase, the merchant inserts these figures into the formula, as shown.

$$\underset{\text{inventory)}}{\underset{\text{(beginning}}{\$45,000}} + \underset{\text{(purchase)}}{??} - \underset{\text{(sales)}}{100,000} - \underset{\text{(markdowns)}}{10,000} = \underset{\underset{\text{inventory)}}{\text{(ending}}}{\$50,000}$$

In this case, the amount of inventory to purchase would be $115,000.

Once the inventory purchase amount is determined, the entrepreneur must make sure that the inventory arrives at the proper time. If all inventory arrived at the same time, such as at the beginning of the period, it would all have to be paid for at one time. This could cause serious cash flow problems. If this were to happen, there would be no controls available to raise or lower the inventory level in the event sales were higher or lower than planned. The entrepreneur must break the plan into smaller periods of time and stagger inventory purchases. When a purchase plan is detailed, it is easier to maintain the desired inventory levels. A six-month purchase plan for the previous example could be broken into a month-by-month plan, which would resemble Figure 13-5.

Figure 13-5 Six-Month Sales and Purchase Plan

		July	August	September	October	November	December	Total
Inventory Fluctuations (in dollars)	**Beginning Inventory**	45,000	45,800	47,600	48,200	50,600	55,600	
	+ Purchases	14,000	15,000	16,000	20,000	27,000	23,000	115,000
	(−) Sales	12,000	12,000	14,000	16,000	20,000	26,000	100,000
	(−) Markdowns	1,200	1,200	1,400	1,600	2,000	2,600	10,000
	= Ending Inventory	45,800	47,600	48,200	50,600	55,600	50,000	

Note that the example in Figure 13-5 applies to a retail store. A manufacturing company would have a new materials inventory, a work-in-process inventory, and a finished goods inventory. However, we will address the purchase plan in terms of a retail operation. Also note that in Figure 13-5, the merchant plans to gradually increase the inventory level as the Christmas selling season approaches. It is imperative that the inventory level at the beginning of each month be sufficient to produce the projected sales of that particular month. The key to proper inventory levels is being flexible and changing course midstream, when necessary, due to sales that are higher or lower than projected.

In other words, if September's sales are $5,000 lower than objective, there will be a $5,000 inventory surplus (in terms of sales dollars) on hand at the beginning of October. As soon as the entrepreneur sees sales slipping, such as on September 10, he or she should alter the purchase plan swiftly to reflect this situation. Otherwise there is a risk of ending up with the $5,000 inventory surplus at the end of the month. Conversely, if sales are higher than projected, the entrepreneur may have to order additional inventory.

perpetual inventory, an approximate written record of the amount of inventory available

Small business owners should keep a running written record, called a **perpetual inventory,** at all times. By recording the amount of inventory a business receives and how much it sells on a daily, weekly, or monthly basis, entrepreneurs will have a record available that shows the approximate inventory level at all times. This record will not be exact because it does not accurately take into account defective or stolen inventory and, often, the amount of markdowns taken. It must be corrected

physical inventory, an actual count of all inventory on hand

at least once a year with a **physical inventory,** which is an actual physical count of all inventory the business owns. Physical inventories are often taken twice a year. The actual number of units of goods is counted by hand and recorded on a list detailing every good and its size, color, and/or stock number. Figure 13-6 shows a physical inventory report.

Finding Inventory Suppliers

Entrepreneurs must find the best sources from which to buy inventory. Inventory suppliers, called vendors, must be carefully chosen. Entrepreneurs should seek out vendors who are dependable, stand behind their products, ship efficiently, and care about their customers. They should avoid purchasing from vendors who are out to make a quick profit.

Entrepreneurs actually begin to purchase inventory after they establish their purchase plan objective. Equipped with the purchase plan, entrepreneurs set forth into the marketplace in search of goods. Depending

Figure 13-6   Physical Inventory Report

Description	Quantity	Sizes	Colors	Wholesale Each	Retail Each	Wholesale Total	Retail Total
Bags, duffle, equipment, nylon	9	n/a	black, navy gray	3.50	7.00	31.50	63.00
Bags, duffle, equipment, canvas	9	n/a	same	4.50	9.00	40.50	81.00
Belts, stretch, cinch, women's	45	S, M, L	yellow, white, pink, gray, lt. blue	2.50	5.00	112.50	225.00
Gloves, Triangle, leather	24	n/a	gray, white	10.00	20.00	240.00	480.00
Jump rope, heavy rope, rubber	3	3½ lbs	black	12.50	25.00	37.50	75.00
Jump rope, heavy rope, rubber	3	5 lbs	black	15.00	30.00	45.00	90.00
Jump rope, aerobic	6	n/a	white	5.00	10.00	30.00	60.00
Legwarmers, Softouch	72	n/a	yellow, white, pink, orchid, gray, black, navy, lt. blue, off-white	7.00	14.00	504.00	1008.00

on the industry, goods might come from one or more of the sources discussed in the following paragraphs.

Trade shows. Industry representatives frequently gather at central points in the marketplace and invite potential buyers to visit their exhibits. Trade shows can be as small as a few companies renting space at a local motel to show their goods, entertain customers, and make new contacts. It is an opportunity for networking. Networking is the process of making business contacts by meeting people who can assist in business development. Trade shows can be exciting ventures whether entrepreneurs are shopping for goods or selling their own. For potential buyers, trade shows are an opportunity to discover what is new in their industry that can help increase profits. They can buy unique goods, compare prices of several vendors, or purchase merchandise that the competition is not offering.

Sales calls. When not selling at trade shows, sales representatives are usually traveling through their assigned sales territories demonstrating their goods or services to customers—business owners, purchasing agents, and store managers, among others—at their places of business. Quite often, sales representatives make contacts and presentations at trade shows and then close sales deals with entrepreneurs at the business itself. Or buyers

Illus. 13-2   Trade shows allow entrepreneurs to market their goods, entertain customers, and make new contacts.

may purchase a certain amount of inventory at a trade show and a certain percentage of it from sales representatives who visit their businesses.

Catalog ordering. Just as people use mail order catalogs at home for convenient buying, business owners can also use them to purchase inventory. Vendors often spend considerable amounts of money on making catalog presentations of their products or services. By providing these catalogs to customers they offer a convenient method of ordering inventory. Using a catalog allows entrepreneurs to order whenever it is convenient.

Telemarketing. Business owners may be contacted by some vendors over the phone. Obviously, when acquiring inventory, business owners cannot rely on telemarketers. However, the telephone is an excellent means for sales follow up and sometimes for a sales closing. However, it is not normally effective as an approach or presentation, since it does not allow the customer—in this case, the business owner—to see or touch the product.

INVENTORY AND SALES FLUCTUATIONS

Let's look at what happens when objectives are either not met or exceeded. Using the sales and inventory purchase plan in Figure 13-5, let's assume that August's total sales are a disappointing $10,000, as opposed to the $12,000 projected. The immediate result is that the cash flow projection is $2,000 less than planned and the inventory level is $2,000 higher. Unless there is reason to believe that lower sales are a long-term trend, simple short-term corrections should be made.

By cutting back on the planned inventory arrivals by $2,000 in the next 30 days, the inventory level will be corrected by October 1. At the same time, the business owner could reduce planned inventory purchase expenditures by $2,000. By doing this, the cash flow projection will also be back in line in 30 days.

If sales had exceeded the projection by $2,000, the business owner should increase the planned inventory arrivals. If he or she fails to do this, the $2,000 inventory shortage will cause a decrease in anticipated sales sometime in the near future. As you can see, fluctuations in sales can easily get out of hand if they are not closely monitored. If immediate corrections are not made, a string of three or four months of sales revenues not meeting the objectives will seriously disrupt the entire operation. This is why control reports must be kept up to date.

Scheduling Inventory Arrival

Because sales projections never exactly match actual sales, the business owner must build flexibility into the purchase plan. Most businesses will make planned purchases well in advance of the planned period of sales. For example, a retail store might place orders for the Christmas selling season six to nine months beforehand to ensure receipt of the best selection of merchandise from vendors. In doing this, entrepreneurs must recognize that numerous conditions might change that could cause them to alter a sales projection made that far in advance. For this reason, the entire amount of planned purchases should not be ordered at one time.

Astute business owners place orders in advance for the sales about which they feel most confident. Cash should be set aside in a reserve fund from which additional purchases may be made depending on sales performance. Money that is allocated for inventory purchase, but not yet spent, is called the business's **open to buy.** Open to buy money is used to place orders for immediate delivery during the planned sales period. As an example, a business owner operating with the purchase plan in Figure 13-5 might place orders totaling $70,000 at a trade show at the beginning of the sales period and keep $45,000 available as an open to buy. If sales are higher than expected, more than $45,000 in inventory should be purchased. If sales are lower, some amount less than $45,000 will be used.

open to buy, money that is available for the purchase of inventory

Terms of Sale

It is very important to buy from sources that offer fair terms. Payment terms on goods sold vary from industry to industry. However, in most industries, vendors give discounts to those buyers who pay the fastest and order the largest quantities. The terms of sale are shown on the invoice, a statement the seller gives to the buyer that lists the contents of a shipment or delivery, the terms of sale, the number of units or items delivered, the unit price, and the total cost. Some examples of the more common terms of sale are as follows:

- C.O.D. (cash on delivery)—Amount of invoice is collected upon delivery of goods.
- 2/10/n30, R.O.G.—Buyer receives a two percent discount if the invoice amount is paid within ten days of receipt of delivery. The net (*n*) amount is due on the thirtieth day from the date the entrepreneur receives the goods. R.O.G. represents *receipt of goods.*

- 2/10/n30, E.O.M.—Buyer receives a two percent discount if the invoice amount is paid within ten days from the end of the month in which delivery is received. The net amount is due by the thirtieth day from end of the month. E.O.M. stands for *end of month*.
- 3/10, 1/15, n60—Buyer receives a three percent discount if invoice amount is paid within ten days of delivery, or one percent if paid within 15 days. The net amount is due in 60 days.
- E.O.M.—The amount billed is due at the end of the month; no discounts apply.

The terms of the sale will have an important impact on the cash flow projections. Business owners wish to have as much time as possible before paying for inventory purchases. Ideally, they would prefer not to pay the vendor until after there has been ample time to sell the inventory. If purchased cash in advance (C.I.A.) or C.O.D., the money for the inventory is invested immediately and taken out of cash flow. If generous terms such as n/60 are granted to the buyer, the total sales price, including the profit, might be collected before taking the money out of cash flow. This can make quite a difference to a business that sells a high percentage of its annual sales during the holiday season. Paying in January for merchandise sold in November and December, instead of paying in September when the merchandise was delivered, can be a big help. If merchandise must be paid for before having a chance to sell it, business owners often find it necessary to borrow money from the bank until the merchandise sells. This requires paying interest on the borrowed money, thereby decreasing the potential net profit. On the other hand, the benefit of discounts on invoices means additional profit for the business.

Since entrepreneurs wish to tie up money in inventory for the shortest time possible, they must devise an inventory system that allows the most efficient use of money as possible. Many businesses use an inventory system called just-in-time inventory control. By working closely with vendors and operating a very tight inventory control system, inventory is scheduled to arrive "just in time" to fill empty shelves or manufacturing parts bins. This allows business owners to avoid having money tied up in inventory that simply sits in a stockroom. The key to this is knowing the capability and dependability of suppliers and closely monitoring inventory levels.

Most businesses will assign a reorder point for inventory used on an everyday basis. When the stock level of an item falls to this level—the reorder point—the item is automatically reordered. The reorder point is influenced by delivery time of the replacement inventory. Some businesses use a computerized cashiering system to alert management to reorder a product. Others use a manual system to check stock levels of inventory daily or weekly.

EFFECTS OF INVENTORY AND SALES FLUCTUATIONS ON OTHER BUSINESS OPERATIONS

Poorly planned and controlled sales and inventory purchase objectives can have a ripple effect throughout the entire operation. In addition to cash flow problems, the business will experience disruptions in personnel scheduling, insurance expenditures, and promotional efforts.

Personnel Scheduling

The organization chart and personnel needs are designed to accommodate the projected sales objectives. In the event these projections get out of line, the business owner will have to adjust the personnel. If sales are too low, there will be employees with not enough work to do. Some may have to be laid off, or their hours may need to be decreased. Some companies will reduce the pay rate of employees. All of these measures have a negative impact on employee morale. Poor morale could, in turn, cause excessive personnel turnover, which could result in the expensive task of employee recruiting and training.

If sales are in excess of objectives, the owner may have to hire extra personnel to handle the added volume. If the business is understaffed, customers may not receive the quick, efficient assistance to which they are accustomed, and might go to the competition instead.

Personnel schedules, like inventory purchase plans, should be designed with flexibility. Successful business owners have a plan of action to handle excess or decreased sales periods. They should also cross-train employees so that they can handle additional responsibilities. Names of people who can work on a part-time, temporary basis should be on hand.

Business owners should warn employees in advance of possible courses of action the company will take to handle periods of high or low sales. For example, there might be times they are asked to work overtime, or circumstances in which their working hours may be cut back. Entrepreneurs and their families should be prepared to work extra hours

Illus. 13-3   High sales periods, such as at Christmas, require flexible personnel scheduling.

Rob Crandall/Picture Group

when needed. In the event it is necessary to lay off employees due to poor sales, owners should provide as much notice as possible to the affected personnel to give them time to search for other jobs.

Insurance

Unexpected changes in sales and inventory plans will also have an impact on the insurance requirements of the business. Entrepreneurs must carry insurance to protect them from losing their investments due to fire, accidents, or other unexpected occurrences. Owners pay insurance premiums based on the value of the business. The more property that is insured, the higher the premiums. Additional inventory increases the value of the business, which means the entrepreneur should purchase additional insurance coverage. If the value of inventory increases by $25,000, the amount of insurance coverage should increase by the same amount. Entrepreneurs must inform their insurance company of changes in the value of the business or coverage will not be sufficient. Many businesses carry a "peak season" coverage that automatically increases insurance coverage during times of the year when inventory increases are anticipated. In case of a fire or other emergency, the owner will not receive reimbursement for lost property that has not been reported to the insurance company.

Promotional events

Promotional events and advertising campaigns are planned in advance. If there is a change in sales and inventory levels prior to a promotional event, it might have an effect on the event. A business should not spend money advertising a product if it does not have sufficient stock to satisfy customer demand. If inventory levels are not sufficiently monitored and controlled, the business runs the risk of being embarrassed by advertising a product or service that it cannot provide. Customers may lose their trust in the business, and its reputation could suffer. Advertising plans, budgets, and schedules must also be flexible to accommodate circumstantial changes. If the business owner is able to buy something unusual on short notice and wishes to inform the public, there should be a method available to allow the business to do so.

Security Controls

Unfortunately, it is a fact of life that some people steal. Businesses are often victims of theft from customers and employees. If business owners do not take proper security measures, inventory theft can have a serious impact on a business's inventory control system—and its profits.

The best method of controlling inventory theft is through prevention techniques. Some techniques for preventing customer theft include the following:

- Train the staff to watch all customers closely, but not in an annoying manner. If potential thieves know they are being watched, they generally will not steal. In a retail environment, all customers should be acknowledged as they enter. It is not only polite, but also gives notice to shoplifters that the employees are aware of their presence.
- Teach employees the procedures to follow in the event that they witness a theft. Call your local police department to learn about procedures or training for business owners. If a shoplifter is apprehended and arrested, it serves as notice to others that the business does not tolerate shoplifting.
- Invest in security prevention devices. Alarm systems, hidden cameras, and security tags on merchandise are commonly used methods. The cost of some security systems might be partially offset by reduced insurance premiums. As a prevention tool, it is usually a good idea to post the security measures being used.

Illus. 13-4 *Hidden cameras, security tags on merchandise, and alarm systems are commonly used as loss prevention devices.*

Lawrence Migdale/Stock Boston

Businesses must also establish prevention measures against employee theft, which is actually far more common (in many industries) than customer theft. Common methods to utilize include the following:

- Check or search all articles taken out of the business at closing time or employee work shift changes. Articles that may be searched include purses, tote bags, briefcases, and lunch bags.
- Administer periodic lie detector tests on a random basis.
- Devise a system of checking inventory levels against sales results. If an item is not accounted for, compare sales receipts to physical inventory to determine if it may have been stolen.

The best method of ensuring employee honesty is through creating an open working relationship between employees and management. Employees who work as a team and take pride in their work are less likely to be tempted to steal from the business.

The amount of stolen inventory can be calculated at the time the physical inventory is taken. Business owners can presume that merchandise, products, or parts not accounted for by sales, use, or damage have been stolen. If there is a significant amount of theft, it will reduce inventory levels, causing problems in achieving objectives.

USING COMPUTERS AS A CONTROL

Personal computers have become great tools for small business owners. There are many choices to make concerning the type of equipment to purchase for a business's computer system. The most important consideration is choosing the software that best fits the particular business. Computer software refers to programs that instruct the computer how to operate. There are many software packages available. Some are suited for manufacturing, while others are designed with a service business or retail establishment in mind. For example, one type of software can compute long columns of numbers, while another is designed to arrange graphic symbols on a page to produce signs.

Entrepreneurs must shop carefully for the system that best fits their own business, then find the computer hardware that accommodates the chosen system. Computer hardware is the actual equipment and accessories needed to run the software. Small business owners typically begin by purchasing a central processing unit (CPU), a monitor or screen, a keyboard, and a printer. Generally speaking, entrepreneurs may expect

Illus. 13-5   Personal computers allow entrepreneurs to maintain records as efficiently as large businesses.

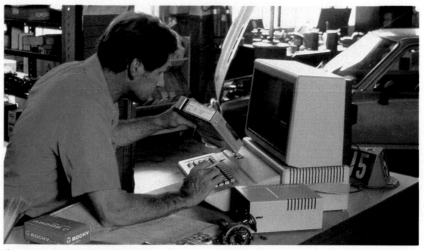

Courtesy of Apple Computer, Inc.

to spend $1,500 to $5,000 on computer hardware and software. They may upgrade and add to their initial investments as the business grows and/or changes. Courses are available through local colleges, community centers, and retail computer stores to learn computer applications. New business owners should take whatever educational courses necessary to become proficient in the use of the computer.

With proper training, entrepreneurs have the ability to keep records as efficiently as large businesses. What was once a tool for only large businesses because of the expense has now become affordable to all business operations. Businesses can use computers for the following functions:

- Financial statements—Updated income statements and balance sheets can be easily maintained and reproduced when needed.
- Inventory control—Perpetual inventory totals can be tracked by product line as well as business total. Some businesses have computer systems tied into sales terminals that automatically subtract the item sold from its product classification.
- Personnel payroll records—It is possible to maintain year-to-date records showing all tax deductions per employee. An employee payroll program also calculates all tax and other deductions automatically for each pay period. This can save considerable time for the person preparing the payroll checks.
- Accounts payable and receivable—By recording all incoming or outgoing invoices, the business is able to keep current and convenient records of all monies owed by vendors and customers.
- Correspondence—Word processing software programs make writing and keeping records of all business correspondence simple. These programs also can be very helpful when designing advertisements or brochures for promotional activities.

JEFF BURNETT—ENTREPRENEUR

Jeff needed to design a purchase plan for the first six months of operation of Rock 'n' Soul Music. Since he planned his business opening for July, he would have to include the upcoming Christmas selling season in his initial plan. He knew that his initial inventory would be $38,000, and he wanted to increase his inventory by $3,000 at the end of the period. Since he knew his sales projection was $100,000 for the first six months, he was able to plug these numbers into the purchase formula.

		(beginning inventory)	(purchase)	(sales)	(markdowns)	(ending inventory)
		$38,000 +	??	− 100,000	− 10,000	= $41,000

Calculating the formula showed a total open to buy of $113,000. He went to work devising the purchase plan for each month, keeping in mind he had to build Rock 'n' Soul's inventory to accommodate the busy Christmas season. His completed purchase plan is shown in Figure 13-7.

Satisfied with the plan, Jeff went to the regional trade show in Dallas, Texas. He spent a good amount of time at the show getting to know the representatives of the various recording companies and their distributors. When he felt convinced that they were reliable and sincere in their offers of assistance, he began to place orders for both immediate and future deliveries of merchandise. He ordered all opening inventory—$38,000—and approximately half of what he needed for the first six months after opening, or

Figure 13-7   Six-Month Purchase Plan Rock 'n' Soul Music

Inventory Fluctuations (in dollars)

	July	August	September	October	November	December	Total
Beginning Inventory	38,000	38,900	39,600	40,100	45,500	47,500	
+ Purchases	13,000	15,000	17,000	23,000	24,000	21,000	113,000
(−) Sales	11,000	13,000	15,000	16,000	20,000	25,000	100,000
(−) Markdowns	1,100	1,300	1,500	1,600	2,000	2,500	10,000
= Ending Inventory	38,900	39,600	40,100	45,500	47,500	41,000	

$60,000. This left him with an open to buy of $53,000 to order new releases and promotions during the six months. He planned to order most of these from the various sales representatives when they visited his store. This also allowed him a reserve of cash to use if sales conditions changed or if he wished to increase his orders for particularly popular recordings.

Since his was a new account for most vendors, he was not able to receive trade credit for the opening inventory orders, but did receive 2/10/n30 credit terms on most of his orders.

Upon his return to Logansville, Jeff set to work installing a new computer system. With the help of a friend who was knowledgeable in computer applications, he was able to install a program for making financial statements, inventory record keeping, accounts payable and receivable, payroll reports, and a word processing program to allow him to write and keep track of correspondence. Except for setting up the store, Jeff was almost ready to open for business.

SUMMARY

Small business owners must control all aspects of business operations if they are to reach their objectives. Management by objectives clearly states the goals of the business and meshes them with the goals of the employees to ensure everyone is involved. Objectives are stated for all operational aspects of the business.

Once sales objectives are set, sales results are monitored on a daily, weekly, and monthly basis to make sure everything is operating as planned. If sales objectives are off line it will have a ripple effect throughout the operation. Missed sales objectives force changes in inventory levels, personnel and scheduling needs, insurance requirements, and promotional plans.

Entrepreneurs should carefully design their inventory purchase plans and choose suppliers. The purchase plan must be flexible to accommodate changes in sales revenue forecasts.

Personal computers have become valuable control tools for small business owners. By using a computer and various reporting procedures, entrepreneurs can control business operations quickly and efficiently.

VOCABULARY BUILDER

On a separate sheet of paper, write a brief definition of each word or phrase based on your reading of the chapter.

1. Management by objectives
2. Inventory
3. Return on investment
4. Perpetual inventory
5. Physical inventory
6. Just-in-time inventory planning
7. Open to buy
8. Networking
9. Invoice
10. C.O.D.
11. R.O.G.
12. E.O.M.
13. Software
14. Hardware

REVIEW QUESTIONS

1. Why is the management by objectives technique both a planning and a control tool?
2. Why is it necessary to monitor sales results daily, weekly, and monthly?
3. What happens to inventory if sales exceed projections?
4. What is the starting point for designing a purchase plan?
5. What is the difference between a perpetual and a physical inventory?
6. In what four ways can small business owners acquire inventory?
7. Why should inventory arrivals be scheduled over a period of time instead of all at once?
8. What do the following notations mean: 2/10/n30; 3/10, 1/15, n60?
9. What is the advantage of a just-in-time inventory control system?
10. In what five ways can small business owners make use of computers?

DISCUSSION QUESTIONS

1. How can you use a management by objectives method in doing your homework assignments?
2. What happens to your personal budget when you receive less money than you expect? How is a business affected when sales are lower than projected?
3. What do you usually do if a store is sold out of an item that you need? Why?
4. What do you think is management's responsibility to employees when poor sales force a reduction in payroll?
5. What are the advantages of using a computer in a small business?

CRITICAL THINKING

The business that you manage has experienced sales far in excess of what was projected. After the first month of operation, sales are twice what you had expected. Do you think the sales forecast and the inventory purchase plan should be doubled for the entire first year? If so, what risks might you incur? What other plan of action could you take that would be less risky?

SHORT CASE: TOO MANY SUPPLIERS

Carlotta needed help. She sat in front of a desk stacked with invoices and folders discussing her situation with Henry Carson, a consultant with the local Small Business Development Center. "I can't keep up with all these bills. I am totally confused about which ones to pay and which ones I can hold off until later." Henry was not surprised. Carlotta's business was a mess—a gift shop with shelves stuffed with miscellaneous gifts. There really was no theme or direction. "How many suppliers do you have, Carlotta?"

"I'm not really sure, Henry—maybe 50 or 60. When I go to trade shows I buy whatever looks good. I don't pay much attention to who the seller is."

Henry handed Carlotta a blank tablet. "Carlotta, let's get this place organized. A gift shop this size does not need that many suppliers. Make a list of all your suppliers by classification. Then we will determine what percentage of your total sales comes from each classification. We need to design a plan to control your buying procedures."

Carlotta presented the following list to Henry a week later.

Classification	Number of Suppliers	Percent of Sales
Greeting cards, paper products	14	31
Novelty gifts	21	38
All-occasion gifts	15	23
Fine gifts	4	8

"Carlotta, you have 54 suppliers! You can't operate a store with an average of 2 percent of sales per vendor (100% ÷ 54). By consolidating your buying, you will receive better service from the suppliers, have a better grip on your business, and make a more focused presentation to your customers. If you cut the list to 20 suppliers—5 percent of sales from each supplier—you will save on shipping costs, receive some discounts for buying larger quantities of merchandise, and cut down your administrative duties greatly."

Working together, Henry and Carlotta made a new list.

Classification	Number of Suppliers	Percent of Sales
Greeting cards, paper products	5	31
Novelty gifts	7	38
All-occasion gifts	6	33
Fine gifts	2	8

"I recommend that you pay careful attention to your choice of vendors. Buy only from those you know you can depend on, and who will offer assistance when needed. By choosing the best vendors, your inventory selection will be better than ever. I believe you will also find that the more established the vendor, the better your payment terms will be. Design a purchase plan of needs and budget before you go to the next trade show—and stick to it."

Questions

1. What do you think caused Carlotta to have an inventory problem in the first place?
2. What control tools should she implement now for the future?
3. Have you seen stores that seem to be overcrowded and do not seem to focus their offerings to their customers? What is your impression of such places?

PROJECT CHALLENGE

In your business plan notebook, prepare a six-month purchase plan for your hypothetical business. Start by stating your beginning inventory and your potential ending inventory. By inserting your six-month sales forecast and calculating a percentage for markdowns, you will be able to determine your initial open to buy. Use a table such as the one in Figure 13-5.

Then determine from which vendors you will purchase inventory. You can accomplish this by visiting would-be competitors in your community. Find out if there are trade shows for your hypothetical industry and where and when they are held.

14

Small Business Assistance

After mastering the information contained in this chapter, you should be able to:

14-1 List federal and state government agencies that small business owners may contact for assistance.

14-2 Understand the importance of Small Business Development Centers to business owners.

14-3 Identify sources of assistance in your community.

14-4 Identify the services that various professionals might provide to small businesses.

Because entrepreneurs are often the sole creators and/or directors of small enterprises, they sometimes work in isolated environments. As we have seen, entrepreneurs must become knowledgeable in many areas to successfully operate their businesses and compete in today's sophisticated marketplace.

FEDERAL AGENCIES

Many types of support and assistance are available to entrepreneurs, primarily through numerous government agencies and private professionals. Entrepreneurs can usually obtain most information, education, and direction they need through these sources.

Small Business Administration

The United States government recognizes the importance of the role that small businesses play in our society. Congress authorized the formation of the Small Business Administration (SBA) to encourage small business development and the important inventions and innovations that these businesses provide.

The SBA was created to assist in the development of small businesses. It helps small businesses secure government contracts and acts as a special advocate with other federal agencies and state and private agencies. The SBA also helps increase revenues and profits for small businesses, thereby increasing tax revenue for the government and helping to maintain our standard of living. There are more than 100 SBA offices located throughout the United States. Assistance available through the SBA includes loans, counseling, and publications.

SBA Loan Assistance.   The SBA provides assistance in financing thousands of businesses that would not qualify for conventional financing. It offers two basic types of business loans—guaranteed and direct—which were discussed in Chapter 10.

Counseling.   One of the sources of SBA counseling services is the **Service Corps of Retired Executives** (SCORE). There is no cost for these services—SCORE is a volunteer organization. Members use their business experience to advise and guide small business owners. SCORE volunteers come from all areas of business, including commercial and industrial. They are individuals who contribute their time to help others succeed. SCORE counselors can provide business owners with information about business basics, but may not be able to answer questions specific to a particular business. SCORE also provides comprehensive workshops for prospective and new business owners (see Figure 14-1).

Another source of free counseling is the Small Business Institute (SBI). SBI counseling services are provided by student teams at many colleges. Contact the SBA office to obtain information about these services; they are available only for certain periods of a school's term.

Service Corps of Retired Executives, a counseling service—staffed by volunteers who have business experience—for new and established small business owners

Illus. 14-1   SCORE counselors are volunteers who use their business experience to advise and guide small business owners.

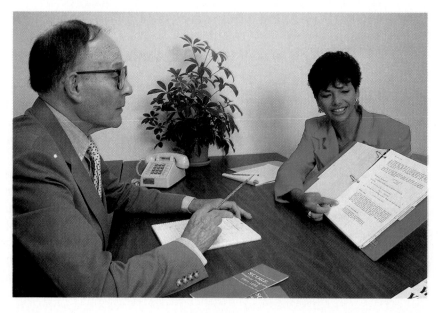

Figure 14-1   SCORE Workshop Announcement

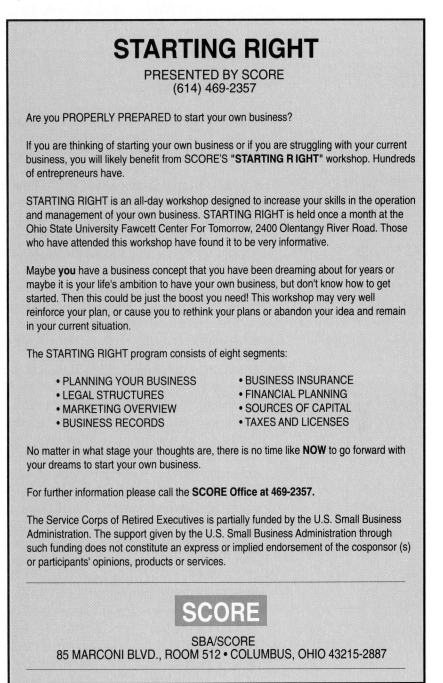

STARTING RIGHT

PRESENTED BY SCORE
(614) 469-2357

Are you PROPERLY PREPARED to start your own business?

If you are thinking of starting your own business or if you are struggling with your current business, you will likely benefit from SCORE'S **"STARTING R IGHT"** workshop. Hundreds of entrepreneurs have.

STARTING RIGHT is an all-day workshop designed to increase your skills in the operation and management of your own business. STARTING RIGHT is held once a month at the Ohio State University Fawcett Center For Tomorrow, 2400 Olentangy River Road. Those who have attended this workshop have found it to be very informative.

Maybe **you** have a business concept that you have been dreaming about for years or maybe it is your life's ambition to have your own business, but don't know how to get started. Then this could be just the boost you need! This workshop may very well reinforce your plan, or cause you to rethink your plans or abandon your idea and remain in your current situation.

The STARTING RIGHT program consists of eight segments:

- PLANNING YOUR BUSINESS
- LEGAL STRUCTURES
- MARKETING OVERVIEW
- BUSINESS RECORDS
- BUSINESS INSURANCE
- FINANCIAL PLANNING
- SOURCES OF CAPITAL
- TAXES AND LICENSES

No matter in what stage your thoughts are, there is no time like **NOW** to go forward with your dreams to start your own business.

For further information please call the **SCORE Office at 469-2357.**

The Service Corps of Retired Executives is partially funded by the U.S. Small Business Administration. The support given by the U.S. Small Business Administration through such funding does not constitute an express or implied endorsement of the cosponsor (s) or participants' opinions, products or services.

SCORE

SBA/SCORE
85 MARCONI BLVD., ROOM 512 • COLUMBUS, OHIO 43215-2887

Publications.   The SBA offers a number of publications and videotapes to provide information to small business owners. Most are available at a nominal cost and can be ordered through any SBA office (see Figure 14-2).

Other Federal Agencies

Small business owners can also obtain assistance from numerous government offices. These offices are widely distributed throughout the United States and their services cover the full range of business needs.

The United States Department of Commerce.   The Department of Commerce encourages, serves, and promotes international trade, economic growth, and technological advancement. The Department provides a wide variety of programs that offer assistance and information, including social and economic statistics for business and research and support for scientific, engineering, and technological development. It also grants patents, trademarks, and service marks; provides assistance to promote economic development; and assists in the growth of minority businesses. These functions are served through 12 different bureaus within the Department of Commerce, the most prominent of which are listed here.

- The Office of Business Liaison, which develops and promotes a cooperative working relationship between the Department of Commerce and the business community. This office keeps the business community aware of the Department of Commerce's administration, resources, policies, and programs, and keeps administration officials within the Department of Commerce aware of issues that concern businesses. It also promotes business involvement in departmental policymaking and program development, and provides technical assistance to businesses that need help in dealing with the government. The Office of Business Liaison is the focal point for all communication between the Department of Commerce and the business community.
- The Office of Small and Disadvantaged Business Utilization (OSDBU) works in conjunction with the SBA to assist some small and minority-owned businesses to secure contracts, both private and federal.
- The Bureau of the Census collects, tabulates, and publishes a wide variety of statistical data about the people and the economy of the United States. The principal means by which the Bureau

Figure 14-2   Partial Listing of SBA Publications

VIDEOTAPES

Each VHS videotape below comes complete with a workbook.

Marketing: Winning Customers With A Workable Plan

This program, developed by two of the country's leading small business marketing experts, offers a step-by-step approach on how to write the best possible marketing plan for your business. You'll also learn the best methods for determining customer needs, how to identify and develop a working profile for potential customers and much more. PLUS… the workbook that comes with each video provides easy-to-follow examples of how to use this information to meet your marketing goals.

| | VT1 | $30.00 |

The Business Plan: Your Roadmap To Success

This videotape teaches you the essentials of developing a business plan that will help lead you to capital, growth, and profitability. It tells you what to include, what to omit, and how to get free help from qualified consultants. You'll also find out what an SBA executive, a venture capitalist, and a banker will be looking for when reviewing your business plan. The workbook that comes with each video includes a checklist of information to include as well as samples of the income statement, balance sheet, and cash flow forecast.

| | VT2 | $30.00 |

Promotion: Solving The Puzzle

Advertising, public relations, direct mail, and trade shows are the parts of the promotion puzzle. Each piece is important to the whole and each piece works to reinforce the others. This videotape and workbook package shows you how to put the pieces together to present a sound promotional plan aimed at targeting new customers, increasing sales and getting the most for your promotional dollar. Learn how to choose the best advertising medium for your needs, write a press release that grabs attention, and much more.

| | VT3 | $30.00 |

PUBLICATIONS

PRODUCTS/IDEAS/INVENTIONS

Ideas Into Dollars

This publication identifies the main challenges in product development and provides a list of resources to help inventors and innovators take their ideas into the marketplace

| | PI1 | $2.00 |

Avoiding Patent, Trademark And Copywrite Problems.

Learn how to avoid infringing the rights of others and the importance of protecting your own rights.

| | PI2 | $1.00 |

Trademarks And Business Goodwill

Learn what trademarks are and are not and how to get the most protection for your commercial name.

| | PI3 | $1.00 |

FINANCIAL MANAGEMENT

ABC's Of Borrowing

This best seller tells you what lenders look for and what to expect when borrowing money for your small business.

| | FM1 | $1.00 |

Profit Costing And Pricing For Manufacturers

Uncover the latest techniques for pricing your products profitably.

| | FM2 | $1.00 |

Basic Budgets For Profit Planning

This publication takes the worry out of putting together a comprehensive budgeting system to monitor your profits and assess your financial operations.

| | FM3 | $1.00 |

Understanding Cash Flow

The owner/manager is shown how to plan for the movement of cash through the business and thus plan for future requirements.

| | FM4 | $1.00 |

A Venture Capital Primer For Small Business

Learn what venture capital resources are available and how to develop a proposal for obtaining these funds.

| | FM5 | $0.50 |

Accounting Services For Small Service Firms

Sample profit/loss statements are used to illustrate how accounting services can help expose and correct trouble spots in business financial records.

| | FM6 | $0.50 |

Analyze Your Records To Reduce Costs

Understand the nature of expenses and how they interrelate with sales, inventories, and profit. Achieve greater profits through more efficient use of the dollar.

| | FM7 | $0.50 |

Budgeting In A Small Service Firm

Learn how to set up and keep sound financial records. Study how to effectively use journals, ledgers, and charts to increase profits.

| | FM8 | $0.50 |

Sound Cash Management And Borrowing

Avoid a "crash crisis" through proper use of cash budgets, cash flow projections and planned borrowing concepts.

| | FM9 | $0.50 |

assists small businesses is its provision of printed reports, computer tapes, and special tabulations.

- The Bureau of Economic Analysis (BEA) strives to provide a clear picture of U.S. economy through analysis of national economic statistics, including personal income, business activity, and investment activity. Results of BEA analyses are published monthly in *Survey of Current Business* and *Business Conditions Digest.*
- The Economic Development Administration (EDA) was established to generate new jobs, protect existing jobs, and to stimulate commercial and industrial growth in economically distressed areas. The EDA provides assistance to state and local governments, public and private nonprofit organizations, and industrial and commercial businesses. One of the ways in which the EDA provides assistance to businesses is by providing loan guarantees. Proceeds from EDA loans can be used for working capital, to maintain or expand operations, or for purchasing assets.

The remaining seven offices of the Department of Commerce provide technical information; assistance for international trade (both import and

Illus. 14-2   The EDA helps economically distressed areas generate new jobs, protect existing jobs, and stimulate commercial and industrial growth.

John Elk III/Stock Boston

export) and minority business development; extensive research for scientific and technological businesses; environmental monitoring; telecommunications development; incentives for invention, research and development, and commercialization; and information about travel and tourism.

Government Printing Office.   The Government Printing Office (GPO) executes orders for printing and binding for all divisions of the federal government. Although government publications are not produced by this office, it does produce and distribute catalogs of all publications that are available and processes orders for these publications.

Federal Trade Commission.   The primary purpose of the Federal Trade Commission (FTC) is to ensure that business practices in the United States are fair. Meeting this responsibility requires constant monitoring of all aspects of business to ensure accurate product representation, fair competition, fair pricing, accuracy in credit reporting, fair cost for credit, and fair export trade. The FTC has the authority to make and/or enforce rules to regulate trade and protect consumers. To protect their own interests, entrepreneurs may report competitors' unfair or illegal business practices to the FTC.

Internal Revenue Service.   An office of the Department of the Treasury, the Internal Revenue Service (IRS) is a division that all of us come in contact with on a regular basis. The IRS is responsible for collecting taxes and for ensuring compliance with tax laws. The IRS also provides services to taxpayers. It issues federal taxpayer identification numbers for businesses, distributes (upon request) publications that explain tax rules, and assists with tax-related questions, both by telephone and through IRS representatives at local IRS offices.

FEDERAL/STATE COOPERATIVES

Small Business Development Center, an agency funded by both the federal government and state governments to provide counseling and training for small business owners

Some sources of assistance are funded by both the federal government (through the SBA) and state governments. One such agency is the **Small Business Development Center** (SBDC). The SBDC program is a cooperative venture between the SBA and each state's business development department, with active participation of local chambers of commerce and colleges and universities. A typical SBDC consists of these three components:

1. An administrative unit, which is generally housed with other departments of state

2. Several sub-centers, which provide small business information, in-depth counseling, referrals, and owner/manager education programs
3. Satellite offices, which offer some, but not all, of the services offered by the sub-centers

The programs and seminars offered (see Figure 14-3) cover all aspects of business operation. Entrepreneurs can obtain much valuable information by attending a "How To Start A Business" seminar. While developing a business plan, entrepreneurs can attend a wide variety of seminars that will provide information about many phases of business development. Some sample seminar titles include "Legal Aspects of Operating A Business," and "Preparing Loan Proposals." Many of the seminars will also help established business owners.

A typical SBDC sub-center's staff includes a director and several consultants who have experience in operating small businesses. They act as advisors for preparing business plans, completing loan applications, developing marketing programs, or planning any business activity.

SBDC offices are an excellent source for help in designing a business plan. Since they often involve the state's university system, they have access to information and research in almost any field. They are also backed by the SBDC Connection, a central library that provides information to all centers. Many states' SBDC's also have specialists in international trade, minority business development, and government procurement available to provide information. There are 650 SBDC's in the United States.

STATE DEPARTMENTS OF DEVELOPMENT

Department of Development, a state agency that works to advance economic growth and to encourage new and existing businesses to operate within the state

Assistance is also available to small businesses at the state level. Each of the 50 states has a **Department of Development** (DOD). This department administers federal community development programs, and is usually made up of several divisions, such as the following:

• The Division of Business Development coordinates the various business programs, including tax incentive and financial assistance programs, that are designed to enhance the state's business climate. Subdivisions of this department promote state to out-of-state industries and businesses, and encourage existing companies to maintain and/or expand their facilities. They also provide information about locations, markets, labor, taxes, and finances, and often provide customized job training programs.

Figure 14-3   SBDC Brochure Cover

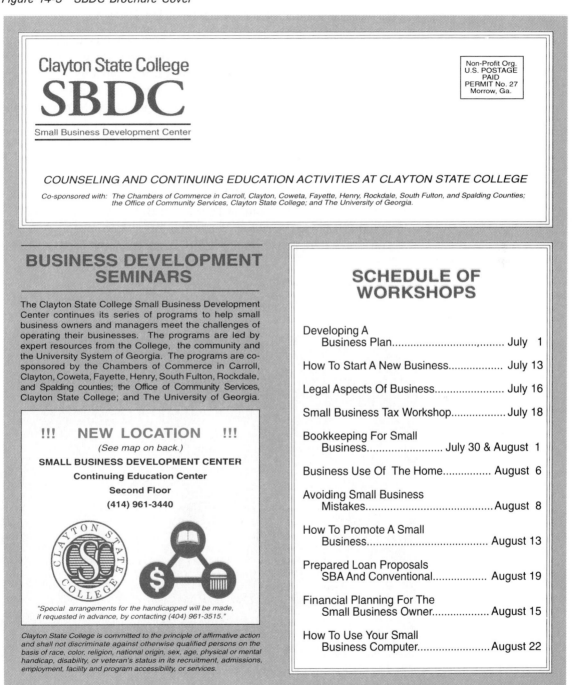

Clayton State College
SBDC
Small Business Development Center

Non-Profit Org.
U.S. POSTAGE
PAID
PERMIT No. 27
Morrow, Ga.

COUNSELING AND CONTINUING EDUCATION ACTIVITIES AT CLAYTON STATE COLLEGE

Co-sponsored with: The Chambers of Commerce in Carroll, Clayton, Coweta, Fayette, Henry, Rockdale, South Fulton, and Spalding Counties; the Office of Community Services, Clayton State College; and The University of Georgia.

BUSINESS DEVELOPMENT SEMINARS

The Clayton State College Small Business Development Center continues its series of programs to help small business owners and managers meet the challenges of operating their businesses. The programs are led by expert resources from the College, the community and the University System of Georgia. The programs are co-sponsored by the Chambers of Commerce in Carroll, Clayton, Coweta, Fayette, Henry, South Fulton, Rockdale, and Spalding counties; the Office of Community Services, Clayton State College; and The University of Georgia.

!!!   NEW LOCATION   !!!
(See map on back.)
SMALL BUSINESS DEVELOPMENT CENTER
Continuing Education Center
Second Floor
(414) 961-3440

"Special arrangements for the handicapped will be made, if requested in advance, by contacting (404) 961-3515."

Clayton State College is committed to the principle of affirmative action and shall not discriminate against otherwise qualified persons on the basis of race, color, religion, national origin, sex, age, physical or mental handicap, disability, or veteran's status in its recruitment, admissions, employment, facility and program accessibility, or services.

SCHEDULE OF WORKSHOPS

Developing A
   Business Plan.................................,........ July   1

How To Start A New Business................. July 13

Legal Aspects Of Business...................... July 16

Small Business Tax Workshop................. July 18

Bookkeeping For Small
   Business........................ July 30 & August 1

Business Use Of The Home............... August 6

Avoiding Small Business
   Mistakes...August 8

How To Promote A Small
   Business...................................... August 13

Prepared Loan Proposals
   SBA And Conventional................. August 19

Financial Planning For The
   Small Business Owner.................. August 15

How To Use Your Small
   Business Computer.......................August 22

- The Economic Development Financing Division administers various state economic development financing programs.

The DOD provides assistance to small and developing businesses through a Small Business Division and a Minority Business Development Division. The Small Business Division assists small businesses in the areas of licensing, business structure, taxes, and financing. It also serves as liaison between the small business community and state government agencies. The Minority Business Development Division provides services to aid the growth of the state's minority-owned businesses and monitors state-administered loan and funding programs for minority businesses.

Other divisions of a state DOD include an International Trade Division, a Community Development Division, a Division of Energy, a Marketing and Research Division, a Policy and Intergovernmental Relations Division, and an Administration Division. In addition, many state DOD's

Illus. 14-3   The Minority Business Development Division provides services to aid the growth of the state's minority-owned businesses.

Robert E. Daemmrich/Tony Stone Worldwide/Chicago Ltd.

have one department that is equipped to supply new business owners with all of the information, and sometimes applications, they need regarding licensing and permit requirements for their particular businesses.

OTHER STATE AGENCIES

Further assistance is available to small business owners through a variety of other state agencies. The following paragraphs identify five agencies that exist in most states in the United States.

All business owners who have employees are required to provide insurance that gives employees or their survivors benefits in the event of work-related injuries or deaths. The Workers' Compensation Board works with employers to provide this protection at a reasonable cost.

The State Department of Agriculture and Consumer Protection Division issue permits for businesses involved with the processing, handling, storage, or distribution of food products. These departments also issue permits for businesses that are of public interest, such as day care centers, schools, financial institutions, and employment agencies.

The State Sales and Use Tax Division issues identification numbers to retail businesses, which must collect and remit sales taxes. It also provides instructions for collecting, reporting, and remitting the sales taxes to the state.

The State Department of Labor provides information regarding employer responsibilities in relation to unemployment insurance. All employers must contribute a specified percent of wages to the state's fund for compensation for displaced workers.

The Office of the Secretary of State provides general business information as well as information and forms for incorporation. Forms for registering state trademarks and business names are also available.

COMMUNITY RESOURCES

Many communities offer their own assistance centers for small business owners. The principal community assistance center is often a chamber of commerce.

Chambers of Commerce

The purpose of a chamber of commerce, operated and funded by local municipalities and businesses, is to stimulate local economic growth.

Economic growth is important to all communities. It ensures that there will be enough jobs and income to attract and keep residents. The chamber of commerce office is usually staffed by people who are very familiar with the commercial activities of the community. They are an excellent source of information for owners of both new and established businesses.

Members of a chamber of commerce are local business owners and managers. Becoming a member of the chamber of commerce is an excellent way to make contact with other business owners.

Other Community Resources

Colleges, universities, and technical schools often offer community outreach services through educational training and research support. Entrepreneurs should take advantage of these resources, if they are available.

A trip to city hall or the county courthouse to determine what municipal and county government agencies exist in your community is worthwhile. Often included among municipal and county agencies are the following offices with which entrepreneurs may want to be familiar.

- Licensing and Permit Offices—business licenses
- County Health Department—local health and safety regulations
- County Extension Services—resources for agricultural businesses

PROFESSIONAL SERVICES

Small business owners can also obtain assistance from individuals who make their living providing information and assistance. These services seldom come without a cost. Entrepreneurs usually need to plan ahead and include such services in their budgets.

Attorneys

Many business owners seek help from attorneys to be sure that they follow the proper procedures in any legal aspects of their business operation, such as drafting and/or signing lease agreements. Attorneys provide valuable information about business owners' rights, the best legal structure for a business, protecting assets, preventing legal action, obtaining patents and trademarks, and tax and business legislation. Business owners should establish a relationship with an attorney even if legal services are not needed on a regular basis.

Accountants

In addition to designing and maintaining bookkeeping systems, accountants can often provide planning and management advice. In particular, they may be able to make valuable recommendations for minimizing tax liability.

Insurance Agents

Certified insurance agents have extensive training related to insurance requirements and regulations. Entrepreneurs should discuss their insurance needs with a qualified agent. Good agents will help small business owners determine how to obtain the coverage they need at the lowest possible cost. They will also provide suggestions for changes that can be made to reduce insurance cost, such as certain safety and security precautions.

Illus. 14-4   In addition to bookkeeping services, accountants can provide financial planning and management advice as well as recommendations for minimizing business tax liability.

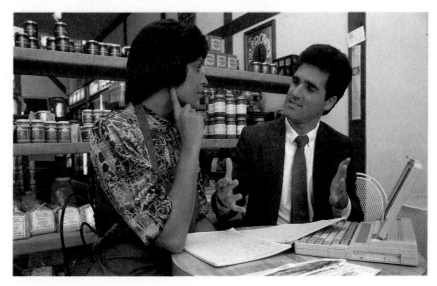

JEFF BURNETT—ENTREPRENEUR

Jeff was feeling quite pleased with his business plan after his meeting with Mrs. Contel. She commented that his plan looked complete, but that a return trip to the SBDC advisor for a full analysis might be a good idea. Jeff made an appointment to see Don Carson, his SBDC consultant, the next day.

Don reviewed Jeff's plan and was quite complimentary about the organization of the plan.

I.   Description of the Business
II.   The Market
III. The Competition
IV.   Location of the Business
V.   Management
VI.   Personnel
VII. Financial Data
VIII. Application and Expected Effect of Loan
IX.   Executive Summary

"It looks good, Jeff, but there is no detail about your insurance program. How did you arrive at the estimated insurance cost?"

"I asked a friend of my father's. He told me how much he thought it would cost to protect my inventory."

"You need to talk with a professional insurance agent, Jeff. There is a lot to learn about proper insurance coverage and you must make sure you are adequately protected. A good agent will be able to help you determine what your insurance needs are. If you put this off until the last minute you may be unpleasantly surprised about the cost. I don't believe your business is as complicated as some, but please be sure to investigate this thoroughly before proceeding. After that, you will be ready to start your business education."

"Education?"

"Yes. I recommend that you attend a few seminars or workshops to be sure you have all the information you need. The seminars provided by the SBDC are inexpensive, and they will be very helpful. Also, you will meet other business owners. Let's look at the current schedule and see which programs will meet your needs."

Don found four seminars he thought would help Jeff. He suggested that Susan also attend, since she would be involved in the business. Jeff signed up for the seminars and hurried home to tell Susan what he had learned.

SUMMARY

Entrepreneurs have a support system—they can obtain assistance from many outside sources. Various government agencies provide assistance, counseling, and information. These agencies function at federal, state, and local levels. Types of services include information packets and brochures, seminars and workshops, financial assistance, planning assistance, and one-on-one counseling. Professionals such as attorneys, accountants, and insurance agents also provide valuable services to business owners. It is important that entrepreneurs take advantage of the help available.

VOCABULARY BUILDER

On a separate sheet of paper, write a brief definition of each word or phrase based on your reading of the chapter.

1. Small Business Administration
2. Service Corps of Retired Executives
3. Small Business Development Center
4. Department of Development
5. Attorney
6. Insurance agent

REVIEW QUESTIONS

1. Why was the Small Business Administration created?
2. What services are available through the SBA?
3. What does the acronym SCORE stand for? What do SCORE volunteers do?
4. What agency should you contact for information regarding patents and U.S. trademarks?
5. What services are available through Small Business Development Centers?
6. What purpose do chambers of commerce serve?
7. What professional services might small businesses use?
8. How can attorneys help small businesses?

DISCUSSION QUESTIONS

1. What roles do the various federal agencies play in assisting small businesses?
2. Why should small business owners attend SBDC seminars?

3. What impact does your local chamber of commerce have on the business community?
4. Do any of the professional services appeal to you as a career? Why or why not?

CRITICAL THINKING

The SBA's existence has been threatened during times of government budget reduction. However, it has always continued to receive congressional support. What makes this agency so important? What would happen if it were eliminated?

SHORT CASE: READY OR NOT?

Janet Stolen had completed the preparations for opening her new candy and nut store. She was looking forward to her grand opening—it was only three days away.

Because she had enough capital to finance her business, Janet had decided that she did not need to write a business plan. She felt her background as an employee in a small retail store had given her enough knowledge about operating a business that she did not need to attend any of the business development workshops her friend Rollin had recommended.

Rollin had opened a sporting goods store two years ago. The classes he attended—and the business plan he had developed with the information he obtained—had been a big help to him. When he opened his door to the public for the first time, he felt confident that he was ready to serve his customers and that his business was likely to succeed.

Rollin decided to call Janet to wish her luck and to find out if she needed any help with her final preparations.

"Hello, Janet. This is Rollin. I just called to wish you the best of luck and to see if you need anything."

"Thank you, Rollin! I'm ready to open my store *now;* I'm really looking forward to Monday. The store opens at 10:00, and one of my employees will be in at 10:30. I don't think we'll have any problems at all."

"I'm glad to hear that, Janet. Did you have any trouble getting your identification numbers or the licenses and permits you need?"

"What identification numbers? What licenses and permits? I have my vendor's license—what else do I need?"

"Didn't you get a checklist of the requirements for your business when you attended the workshops I suggested?"

"Well, I didn't go, Rollin. I was awfully busy, and I felt like I knew everything I needed to know to get started. What do I do now? Can I still open my store on Monday?"

"Call the SBA right away, Janet. They can tell you who to get in touch with to find out what you need and how to get it as quickly as possible. Good luck!"

After checking with the SBA, Janet called her state's One-Stop Business Permit Center. The representative she talked with suggested that she stop by the center and pick up the necessary forms, then contact the agencies involved to determine if she would be able to open her store as planned.

Questions

1. What was Janet's big mistake?
2. Janet told Rollin she hadn't had time to attend the workshops he recommended. Were there other ways she could have found out what was required for her business?
3. What requirements had Janet failed to meet for her business?
4. Do you think Janet was able to open her store as planned? Why or why not? Contact the agencies that issue the permits you think she needed and verify your answer.

PROJECT CHALLENGE

Visit the nearest SBA office or SBDC sub-center for an informal review of your business plan. (If there is no SBA office or SBDC sub-center near you, take your business plan to the local chamber of commerce or the business education department of a college for review.) Review any changes or additions that are recommended and decide whether you will make these changes or additions. Give reasons for your decisions. Make a list of scheduled seminars and/or workshops that might be helpful to you.

UNIT 5

LEGAL REQUIREMENTS

15

Special Regulations

There is more to successfully operating a business than hanging a sign and opening the door. You have examined the importance of marketing, financing, and managing to the success of your entrepreneurial venture. Now it is time to take a look at some legal considerations.

As an entrepreneur, you will enjoy a considerable amount of freedom to operate your business as you see fit. This freedom may be somewhat restricted, however, by certain laws and regulations. To prevent costly lawsuits and other unpleasant encounters, you should understand certain basic laws that exist to regulate business activities. By becoming familiar with these regulations, you will have knowledge that will enable you to succeed.

FEDERAL TRADE COMMISSION

The Federal Trade Commission (FTC) is a federal administrative agency charged with the responsibility of ensuring fair, free, and open business. In general, it concerns itself with unfair business practices in interstate commerce. Its scope is very wide, affecting advertising, consumer credit, product safety, and business competition.

The FTC accomplishes its job in several ways. First, it interprets laws and creates regulations. It also advises businesses when requested to do so. If unfair business practices are suspected, the FTC will investigate. Its powers enable it to issue "cease and desist" orders to businesses who then voluntarily discontinue unfair, deceitful, or illegal business practices. If a business does not agree to stop such activities, the FTC may hold hearings to prosecute the firm. As you read about the FTC's four major areas of responsibility—advertising, consumer credit, product warranty, and competition—in the following paragraphs, think about which ones might apply to the business you would like to start.

Illus. 15-1 The FTC's role is to ensure that accurate information is presented in advertising.

Advertising

The FTC's role in advertising is to ensure that accurate information is presented in advertisements to the public. Being accurate is not enough, though. The information must also be presented in a way that is not untrue or misleading. Let's look at some circumstances in which the FTC might take an interest in the advertising methods of a small business.

false advertising, advertising that contains information that is not true or would cause the average consumer to reach a false conclusion about a particular product or service

False Advertising. **False advertising** is any advertising that contains information that is not true or would cause the average consumer to reach a false conclusion about the product or service concerned. For example, marketers of products containing oat bran had to drop their claims that oat bran lowered levels of cholesterol because it was a false claim. They were engaging in false advertising.

deceptive advertising, advertising that contains information that would cause the average consumer to be misled about a particular product or service

Deceptive Advertising. **Deceptive advertising** is any advertising that contains information that would cause the average consumer to be misled about a particular product or service. Marketers presently advertise many foods as "light" or "low fat" when they actually may contain high levels of fat and/or have high calorie counts. This is deceptive advertising.

Prior to the establishment of the FTC in 1914, false and deceptive advertising was fairly common. Since then it has become less common, but has not disappeared altogether.

There is a fine line between false advertising and deceptive advertising. For example, consider "Billie's Steppin' Out Shoes." Billie's sales have been lower than normal for the past month. She decided that a little advertising is what she needs to pump some life back into her business. In her newspaper ad is an illustration of a popular, national brand name sneaker (see Figure 15-1). The caption indicates that Billie carries those shoes at the lowest price in town. In reality, Billie has not checked prices outside her own shopping area. She has no idea what the sneakers cost at the mall across town. Billie has just engaged in false advertising. Her claim of offering the brand name sneaker at the lowest price in town is just a claim. She does not know whether it is true or not. Her reason for making the claim was to entice customers into the store.

Now consider Billie's competitor, the owner of "Frank's Fine Footwear." Seeing Billie's ad, Frank decides to fight back with an ad of his own. He places an ad in the newspaper with this statement: "BRAND NAME SNEAKERS FOR SALE. SNEAKERS PRICED AT $10." Frank thinks he is being smart. What he says is true. He does have brand name sneakers for sale and he does have some sneakers for $10. They are not

Figure 15-1

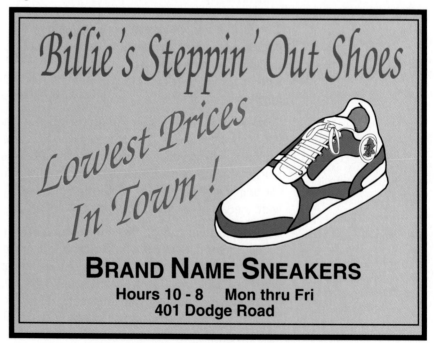

the same sneakers, however. Therefore, Frank has engaged in deceptive advertising. The average consumer would probably assume that the brand name sneakers were priced at $10. Both Billie and Frank have broken the law and are subject to penalties as prescribed by the FTC.

Bait and Switch Advertising. **Bait and switch advertising** is the practice of advertising a lower priced item as a means of luring customers into the store for the real purpose of selling them a different, higher priced item. With bait and switch, an actual attempt is made to convince the customer that the advertised product is inferior and should be ignored in favor of higher priced merchandise. As an example, recall Frank's advertisement for $10 shoes. His ad lures customers in. The "bait" is the inexpensive shoes. If Frank tries to "switch" the customer's preference from the lower priced sneakers to higher priced brand name sneakers, he has engaged in bait and switch advertising. Again, he has violated the law.

bait and switch advertising, the practice of advertising a low-priced item as a means of luring customers into the store for the real purpose of selling them a higher priced item

Sometimes salespeople claim that all of the advertised models have been sold when the fact is that the items were never in stock in the first place. This practice is often difficult to prove, especially if the store has the advertised product in stock.

Deceptive Pricing. You have probably noticed that many stores—especially some major chains—always seem to be having sales. These repeated occurrences have attracted the attention of the FTC. The reason for the attention is a concern that the advertised sale price is actually the true value of the merchandise and not the original retail price.

As an example, imagine that "Merchandise for America" is a large general merchandise company found in any mall across the country. Because it has so many stores, it can go directly to a factory and have clothing made exclusively for its stores. Recently, "Merchandise for America" had the factory make 20,000 swimsuits for the summer season. The swimsuits have a retail value of $20 each. The company had the factory put price tags on each suit listing the suggested retail price at $30.

In a memo to store managers, a store executive instructed them to put the swimsuits on sale after displaying them for only one week. If the FTC investigated this, they would probably conclude that the pricing was deceptive. The only reason the price was originally set at $30 was so that it could be marked at a sale price. The lower price would deceive customers into thinking that they were getting a bargain when, in fact, they were not.

Consumer Credit

The FTC regulates consumer credit through the enforcement of several pieces of federal legislation. All entrepreneurs who extend credit to customers should be aware of the requirements set forth in these laws.

Truth-in-Lending Act. This act was created because consumers were often not aware of the true cost of borrowing and credit terms. The law requires creditors to provide consumers with details about the complete costs of the credit they are seeking. Specifically, business owners extending credit to consumers must disclose the annual interest rate and any finance charges they request for the use of credit. The impact of this act is that it influences what businesses charge for credit; it has created competition among creditors.

Small businesses are often not financially able to deal with the high cost of extending credit to customers. With the common use of credit cards today, though, this is not as big a problem as it once was. When credit cards are used, the requirements of this law are shifted from the entrepreneur to the credit card company.

Offering credit card usage to customers is a marketing strategy. Consumers tend to spend more money on goods in a business where credit

Illus. 15-2   Entrepreneurs who extend credit should be aware of consumer credit legislation.

payments are allowed. If entrepreneurs permit payment with major credit cards, they are likely to see sales increase since it is easier for most customers to pay by credit than with cash.

Fair Credit Reporting Act. The **Fair Credit Reporting Act** allows consumers access to their personal credit information. Business owners use consumer credit agencies to determine whether or not to grant credit to particular consumers. If an individual is denied credit by a business owner, that business owner is required by law to provide the consumer with the name and address of the credit agency used. Business owners may also report delinquent credit customers to consumer credit agencies. For example, Mike Camp applied for a loan for a new car at a local car dealership. The car dealer ran a credit check on him. Mike failed the credit check and the dealer denied Mike the loan.

Under this act, Mike has a right to know what information is included in his credit history. If he feels that some of the information is incorrect, he may challenge it. If Mike challenges the information, the credit company must either provide documentation of the information or remove it from the record. This must be done in a reasonable time period.

In Mike's case, he contacted the credit company and requested a copy of his file. When he received and examined the file, he discovered the problem. Two years ago, Mike had joined a health club and signed a one-year contract. After six months, the club closed. Yet it continued to send Mike bills. He refused to pay. They then reported this to the credit company. Mike challenged the part of the credit report dealing with the health club. The credit company tried to document the information, but could not. It, therefore, had to remove the information from Mike's report. Mike later went back to the car dealer. This time he was successful in his attempt to buy and finance a new vehicle.

Equal Credit Opportunity Act. The **Equal Credit Opportunity Act** states that any business offering credit must make it available to all creditworthy customers regardless of race, national origin, marital status, religion, sex, age, or receipt of public assistance. If you, the entrepreneur, decide to extend credit as a service to your customers, you must make it available to everyone.

Product Warranty

Generally speaking, a warranty is a guarantee of the integrity of a product. Entrepreneurs need to be aware of two types of warranties—express and implied.

express warranty, a clearly stated fact about the quality or performance of a product

Express Warranties.

An **express warranty** is a clearly stated fact about the quality or performance of a product. The warranty often serves as an important factor in the buying decision. It may be either written or verbal. For example, a label on a sweater saying "100% cashmere" is an express warranty.

Entrepreneurs need to exercise caution when purchasing goods from suppliers. They need to judge whether or not products can deliver what their manufacturers or their labels state they can. Furthermore, entrepreneurs or salespeople working for the business need to be careful what they say about product performance or quality when talking to customers. If they are not careful, sales talk may become an enforceable warranty.

As an example, consider Jeanne Ellis. She works at Mountain Products Limited, a sporting goods store. A customer, Mary, enters the store and wants to look at sleeping bags. During the course of the sales pitch, Jeanne says, "I guarantee that this bag will keep you warm even if the temperature drops to 30 degrees below zero." Whether the bag was designed for that temperature or not does not matter. Jeanne has issued an express warranty. The store can now be held liable for failure of the product to protect the buyer at −30 degrees. This bit of sales talk can ultimately be costly to the store if what is stated is not true. The salesperson should never warranty a product in any way that is not supported by the manufacturer.

implied warranty, a warranty imposed by law ensuring that a product will perform under normal use and circumstances

Implied Warranties.

An **implied warranty** is an unwritten warranty ensuring that a product will perform under normal use and circumstances. In other words, the consumer is entitled to certain minimum levels of quality when purchasing products.

As an example, assume a customer purchased a radio designed for use in the shower from your retail store. The first time the buyer used the radio, it stopped playing as soon as it got wet. Since the radio was designed to be used in the shower, getting it wet would be considered normal use. Therefore, due to the implied warranty, the customer is legally able to return the radio to your store and get a replacement.

Magnuson-Moss Warranty Act, law that sets standards for companies that offer written express warranties on consumer products

FTC's Role in Warranties.

The FTC is charged with enforcement of the **Magnuson-Moss Warranty Act,** which provides standards for companies that choose to give written express warranties on consumer products. Specifically, the law requires the seller to disclose fully, in simple language and in a conspicuous fashion, the following information:

- the words "This warranty gives you specific legal rights and you may also have other rights which vary from state to state."

Illus. 15-3   Product warranties provide consumers with specific legal rights.

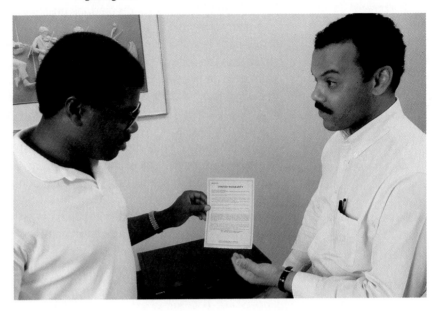

- which parts of the product are covered by the warranty
- a description of the product, including parts not included
- time limits of the warranty (such as 90 days or 2 years)
- instructions for obtaining repair or replacement
- manufacturer's responsibilities in case of warranty breach

Competition

The FTC guarantees fair competition among U.S. businesses through the enforcement of the Sherman Antitrust Act, the Clayton Act, and the Robinson-Patman Act (see Chapter 4). Sometimes, however, a business may do something that does not violate one of these acts, but still interferes with fair competition. The FTC can still step in if a valid complaint is filed. As an example of this kind of situation, consider a bank that wants to increase its deposits. As an incentive, it offers an interest rate that is a full percentage point higher than what other local banks are offering. For consumers to earn this higher rate, though, they must agree to do all of their banking business with this particular bank. The bank is not violating any antitrust laws, but it is still trying to interfere with fair competition. The FTC has the authority to step in and investigate the issue.

STATE AND LOCAL REGULATIONS

In addition to the federal regulations presented in this chapter, there are also many state and local regulations that restrict business activity. Many states have enacted their own versions of federal laws and some are more strict than the federal regulations. To learn about laws that affect you and your enterprise, talk to other small business owners in your particular industry or join a trade association. As mentioned in Chapter 14, the SBA and SCORE may have detailed information regarding regulations affecting your business.

In addition, if you want to engage in certain types of business such as real estate or car sales, most states require that you have a license. Some licenses require testing or certification as well as the payment of fees.

Knowledge of rules and regulations is essential during the planning stages of a business. It is also very important to keep that knowledge current throughout the life of the firm. The risks of simply not knowing— fines, negative public relations, legal hassles, and even imprisonment— are simply too great to ignore.

CONSUMER PROTECTION

When planning the opening of a new small business, entrepreneurs must be aware that there is considerable legal protection available for consumers. Several areas of this protection have already been discussed. There are three additional areas of consumer protection: product safety, environmental protection, and fair credit billing. These issues are important to both retailers and manufacturers. Lack of knowledge about these areas can seriously impede entrepreneurial success.

Product Safety

Consumer Product Safety Act, law that protects the public from dangerous products by providing for the evaluation of product safety hazards

With the growing realization that thousands of consumers were being injured and/or killed annually as a result of faulty products, Congress created the **Consumer Product Safety Act** in 1972. This law was passed to protect the public from dangerous products and to provide for the evaluation of product safety hazards.

In addition to passing the act, Congress created the Consumer Product Safety Commission (CPSC) to administer it. The CPSC administers the act in many ways. It establishes and enforces product safety standards

Illus. 15-4   Under the Hazardous Substances Labeling Act, labels must warn consumers of possible hazards in the use of a product.

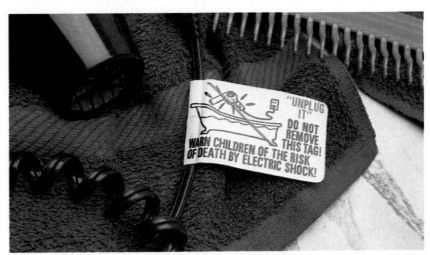

Hazardous Substances Labeling Act, law stating that labels must warn consumers of the hazards of using products that may cause illness or death if improperly used

such as design, manufacture, quality, and labeling. Regarding labeling, the CPSC administers the federal **Hazardous Substances Labeling Act,** which states that labels must warn consumers of the hazards of using products that may cause illness or death if improperly used. The CPSC may also ban, seize, and prevent the sale of hazardous products. In addition, it establishes industry product safety standards and collects, records, and analyzes product injury data.

As an entrepreneur, think about all the trouble that could arise for your company if you were not aware of the Hazardous Substances Labeling Act. Take Marty Schmidt as an example. Marty developed a new chemical formula for killing garden insects. After extensive testing to make sure that the new formula worked, Marty decided to start a small chemical plant to produce the product. After he produced 50,000 five-pound bags of the product, he sold and distributed it in eight states. Then the CPSC informed Marty that his initial production would have to be recalled and relabeled. Why? Marty had not been aware of the Hazardous Substances Labeling Act and had not properly labeled his product and revealed the hazards of using it. Marty had to recall all 50,000 bags because they were not labeled correctly. The profit he would have made from the first batch of chemical is lost because of the extra expense of the recall and relabeling process. Marty had not investigated all the legal requirements for starting his business.

Another federal act relating to safety is important to all employers. The Occupational Safety and Health Act (OSHA) requires that certain safety standards are maintained in the workplace. OSHA states that every worker in the United States should have a safe place to work. Entrepreneurs need to make sure that the physical place of work is free from hazards that may cause injuries to employees, customers, or clients.

Environmental Protection

In 1969 Congress passed the National Environmental Policy Act (NEPA). This act of Congress set the stage for a series of laws designed to prevent air and water pollution and to reduce noise.

NEPA, in turn, established the Environmental Protection Agency (EPA) in 1970 to pull together all of the federal government's efforts to protect the environment. In a nutshell, the EPA's primary role is to prevent pollution. It investigates violations dealing with air, water, pesticides, radiation, land, and noise.

During the business planning process, small business owners should determine if any part of the proposed business venture has environmental implications. If there are concerns, they should be examined carefully and provisions should be made for dealing with them. Entrepreneurs with EPA concerns are typically those planning to start manufacturing operations. Retail and service businesses, as a general rule, have few serious concerns in this area. There are exceptions to this rule, however, so be careful to look at your individual business.

Fair Credit Billing

Fair Credit Billing Act, law enacted in an attempt to protect consumers against unfair and incorrect billing activities

All entrepreneurs should be aware of the **Fair Credit Billing Act,** which was enacted in an attempt to protect consumers against unfair and incorrect billing activities. From an entrepreneurial perspective, the law has two kinds of application. First, it provides protection for consumers dealing with businesses. Second, it provides protection for businesses dealing with suppliers.

The Fair Credit Billing Act has several components. There are four areas of primary interest to entrepreneurs planning to extend credit to consumers. First, business owners must give consumers an address where billing questions can be sent. Second, business owners must observe certain billing timelines. Specifically, they must mail bills 14 days in advance of the due date. Consumers have 60 days to question billing. Businesses must acknowledge billing questions within 30 days, and settle billing questions within 90 days. The act also addresses the issue of billing harassment. If a bill is not paid by a credit customer, a creditor may pursue collection, but is prohibited from making threatening phone calls and sending threatening letters. The law also allows businesses to offer discounts to customers paying cash as opposed to paying by credit, and grants certain other rights to consumers who purchase defective merchandise using a credit card.

JEFF BURNETT—ENTREPRENEUR

Jeff didn't realize all the special regulations that would apply to his new business. As an employee of a big company, he never had to deal with those types of things. There was always somebody back in the home office to take care of it. Well, that wasn't the case any longer. Jeff would have to devote some time in his planning process to consider all the special regulations he had learned about.

Because he was planning a retail record business, Jeff didn't feel that the environmental protection legislation would have much impact on him. He decided to more or less ignore those regulations and concentrate on some of the other regulations.

The material on advertising had really gotten him to thinking. Now there was an area where a business owner could get into real trouble if he or she wasn't careful. He immediately made a commitment to try not to deceive his customers in any way. To accomplish this he would do several things. He would check and double-check all of his advertisements to ensure honesty and integrity. He would address the topic of bait and switch advertising during the training of his sales team. He planned to tell his salespeople to be very careful when dealing with customers to avoid the appearance of bait and switch practices. He also decided to use rain checks for advertised merchandise that wasn't available when a customer asked for it. With rain checks, customers would be able to purchase advertised but out-of-stock merchandise at a later date and for the advertised price. Finally, Jeff made a commitment to only have "real" sales, and to never run phony sales advertisements simply to lure customers into the store.

The whole subject of warranties also concerned Jeff. After what he had read, he decided that he had better investigate warranties a little further. He wanted to make sure that he had sufficient knowledge in this area to pass on to his sales team. He would need to make sure that each of his sales clerks understood the concept of express warranties and the potential liability to the store.

Since Jeff did not intend to offer credit other than major credit-card use to his customers, he was not overly concerned with credit regulations. He would, however, remember his rights under the law. Jeff decided that the time he devoted to special regulations in his planning process was probably well worth the effort. In the long run, it would probably save him time and money.

SUMMARY

The Federal Trade Commission is a federal administrative agency charged with responsibility for ensuring fair, free, and open business. It interprets laws and creates regulations; advises businesses when requested; and investigates if unfair practices are suspected. The FTC has several overall areas of responsibility, including advertising, consumer credit, product warranty, and competition.

In the area of advertising, entrepreneurs should be sensitive to false and deceptive advertising, bait and switch advertising, and deceptive pricing. In the area of consumer protection, several acts are important to remember: Truth-in-Lending Act, Fair Credit Reporting Act, and the Equal Credit Opportunity Act.

Two types of warranties are important to remember: express and implied. These are regulated by the FTC through enforcement of the Magnuson-Moss Warranty Act. Additionally, product safety is monitored through the Consumer Product Safety Act. Product safety is further supported by the Hazardous Substances Labeling Act. The Occupational Safety and Health Act monitors workplace safety.

The National Environmental Policy Act set the stage for a series of laws designed to prevent air, water, and noise pollution. It established the Environmental Protection Agency, which monitors all of the federal government's efforts to protect the environment.

All entrepreneurs should be aware of the Fair Credit Billing Act, enacted in an attempt to protect consumers against unfair and incorrect billing activities. It provides protection for consumers dealing with business owners as well as protection for business owners dealing with suppliers.

VOCABULARY BUILDER

On a separate sheet of paper, write a brief description of each word or phrase based on your reading of the chapter.

1. Federal Trade Commission
2. False and deceptive advertising
3. Bait and switch advertising
4. Fair Credit Reporting Act
5. Equal Credit Opportunity Act
6. Express warranty
7. Implied warranty
8. Magnuson-Moss Warranty Act
9. Consumer Product Safety Act
10. Hazardous Substances Labeling Act
11. National Environmental Policy Act
12. Environmental Protection Agency
13. Fair Credit Billing Act

REVIEW QUESTIONS

1. What are four areas of responsibility of the Federal Trade Commission?
2. What are the names of three acts that deal with consumer credit?
3. What is the difference between the two major types of warranties?
4. What is the name of the agency that monitors all of the federal government's efforts to protect the environment?

DISCUSSION QUESTIONS

1. What are false and deceptive advertising? Give examples of each.
2. What is deceptive pricing? Give an example.
3. Why is the Fair Credit Reporting Act important to consumers?
4. How could an express warranty hurt a business?

CRITICAL THINKING

Charles Spitz owns a small car rental agency. Recently, a customer came into the business inquiring about renting a car. The customer was considering a small economy model. When Charles' salesperson was asked about the car's gas mileage, she replied that the car in question averaged about 40 miles per gallon. The truth was that the car averaged only 25 miles per gallon. The salesperson was relatively new and did not know much about that particular model.

1. What type of warranty was issued on the car's gas mileage?
2. What recourse does the customer have if the car does not average 40 miles per gallon?
3. How could Charles avoid this type of problem in the future?

SHORT CASE: THE HABERDASHERY HOAX

Tom Flynn works for the Federal Trade Commission. His assignment is to investigate complaints about advertising in the Chicago metropolitan area. Recently, he has received several complaints concerning a clothing store located on Michigan Avenue.

The store, Wircenski's Haberdashery, has been in business for ten years at the same location and has a good reputation. If he had received a single complaint, Tom would ordinarily consider the reputation of the store and then decide what to do. A store such as Wircenski's would probably not be investigated further. The complaint would simply be attributed to a disgruntled customer.

This time, however, there have been several complaints from different people. Tom decides to investigate. To begin, he went to the newspaper office and requested a copy of the most recent ad run by the store. The advertisement is shown below:

WIRCENSKI'S HABERDASHERY

sale   SAVE   sale

DRESS SHIRTS $10—POPULAR BRAND NAMES AVAILABLE

MEN'S DESIGNER SUITS—LOWEST PRICES IN TOWN

SHOES ON SALE—TRUCKLOAD JUST ARRIVED—SAVE $$$

sale   sale

Assume that Tom has asked for your help. Evaluate the advertisement and answer the following questions as they apply to the complaint against Wircenski's Haberdashery.

Questions

1. Do you think there are areas of concern? If so, what are they?
2. What questions should Tom ask Mr. Wircenski about the advertisement?

Now rewrite Wircenski's advertisement for shirts, suits, and shoes. Word the advertisement so that there is no question as to what the products are and the prices at which they are being offered.

PROJECT CHALLENGE

As you continue to plan your new business, consider any special regulations that might apply to you. In your business plan notebook, record the following information.

1. List any special regulations that may apply to your hypothetical business.
2. Rank the regulations in your list in order from the one that has the greatest impact on your business to the one that has the least.
3. Next to each item on your list, write at least one step that you can take to comply with that regulation.

16

Contracts and Agreements

After mastering the information contained in this chapter, you should be able to:

16-1 List and explain the components of a legally enforceable contract.
16-2 List and explain six types of contracts.
16-3 Explain breach of contract.
16-4 Understand assignment of contract.

contract, a promise or set of promises creating a legal duty of performance

Entrepreneurs encounter contracts and agreements—both formal and informal—on a daily basis. These contracts take many forms and occur under many different circumstances. Each contract or agreement an entrepreneur establishes may be different from his or her other contracts. Because of the variety—and the potential complexity—of contracts, it is important for entrepreneurs to understand the basic principles by which contracts and agreements operate.

CONTRACTUAL REQUIREMENTS

A **contract** is a legally enforceable agreement negotiated between two or more "persons." A "person" may be either a juristic person or a human being. A juristic person is an entity, such as a corporation, created by law. A legally enforceable contract fulfills requirements in five areas:

- agreement (offer and acceptance)
- legality
- consideration
- contractual capacity
- contractual form

Agreement (Offer and Acceptance)

A contract must provide for an offer by one party and an acceptance by another. This is not as simple as it sounds, however; certain requirements must be met for the offer and for the acceptance.

offer, communication of a proposal

Offer. A contractual **offer** must be an offer that is intended to be legally binding. The intent is judged to be legally binding if a reasonable person would consider it binding.

Illus. 16-1 Entrepreneurs should understand the basic principles of contracts and agreements.

> Marty, a salesperson, is taking a client to lunch and her car won't start. She says, "I'd sell this thing for two cents. It's no good." Marty is angry; she wouldn't really sell her car for two cents.

This is not an offer in the legal sense.

> Marty calls her friend Bill and says, "I'm buying a new car; would you like to buy my old one for fifteen hundred dollars?" Marty really wants to sell her car.

An offer has been made in the legal sense.

The offer must also be in definite terms and communicated in some ordinary fashion. In the second example above, Marty made a definite offer—sale of her car. Marty also communicated the offer to Bill in some ordinary fashion—verbally.

Once communicated, the offer does not remain open forever. It may be ended in several ways, as listed here.

1. The party making the offer retracts it prior to acceptance.
2. The party receiving the offer rejects it. NOTE: Once the offer is rejected, the party that rejected it cannot later demand that the offer be honored.

3. The party receiving the offer makes a counter offer—the original offer is ended and a new offer exists. In the second example above, Bill might tell Marty that he will give her $1,000 instead of $1,500. At that point, the original offer is ended and replaced by the second.
4. An offer ends after the passage of a reasonable length of time.
5. The death or mental incapacity of either party ends an offer.
6. Any change in a law, making an offer illegal, ends an offer.

Hector offers to sell a three-wheeled recreational vehicle to Tom for his customers at the hotel to use. After the offer has been made, a law is passed that makes it illegal to drive a recreational vehicle with less than four wheels. The offer is now illegal and, therefore, ended.

acceptance, an offer is agreed to by the receiving party

Acceptance. An **acceptance** must be clear and positive. The party accepting an offer must agree to all of the terms of the offer unconditionally. The acceptance may be communicated to the party making the offer in any fashion unless a specific method of acceptance is designated. If, however, the acceptance is not communicated in a manner equal to or better than that of the communication of the offer, the acceptance is not effective until thus received.

Illus. 16-2 An acceptance must be clear and positive.

> Suppose Marty wrote Bill a letter to offer the sale of her car. If Bill writes a letter back accepting the offer, his acceptance is effective when he mails the letter. Marty cannot change her mind, even if she has not yet received the letter.

Legality.   A legally enforceable contract must have a lawful objective. If the satisfaction of a contract requires breaking the law or violating a statute or policy, it does not have a lawful objective.

> Jo told Ben she would use her retail computer store employee discount to buy a computer for his new clothing store if he would sell her two new outfits at cost. Since the discount is for Jo's personal use and is not transferable, the contract does not have a lawful objective and is not enforceable.

Consideration

consideration, value given and value received as a result of contractual agreement

Each of the parties involved in a contract must receive value. The legal term for that value is **consideration.**

> If Bill accepts Marty's offer, the consideration (value) to Marty is Bill's $1,500 and the consideration to Bill is Marty's car.

Contract law does not require that the considerations be equal. Marty's car may be worth $2,000; that does not matter. As long as consideration is involved, the contract is binding.

Something that has already been done or something that a person has a legal duty to do is not consideration.

> If Mario comes back from his vacation and discovers that two of his employees were responsible for the apprehension of a would-be thief, he may be so happy that he promises to give each of them $100.

This is not a legal contract. Consideration is current or future value. Past actions are not part of a legally enforceable contract.

> Gloria agrees to purchase a certain percentage of the remote-controlled airplanes she sells from her competitor, the only other company that sells the planes, in exchange for the competitor's promise not to sell planes to consumers at prices below a certain level.

This is not consideration on the competitor's part—the competitor already has a legal obligation not to undersell Gloria because of the laws that prohibit monopoly. These laws also prohibit pricing policies that present price reductions to some customers and not others, unless justified by quantity discounts. NOTE: There are exceptions to the consideration requirement.

Contractual Capacity

capacity, ability to fully understand and comprehend the requirements of a contract as specified by law

All parties to a legally enforceable contract must meet the legal requirements for **capacity.** Among those who do not meet the legal requirements for capacity are minors (persons under age 21), persons who are under the influence of alcohol or drugs when the agreement is made, or persons who are mentally deficient.

Minors can choose to fulfill the terms of a contract, but since they do not meet the requirements for legal capacity, are not *required* to do so. The parties who enter into contracts with minors, however, are obligated to fulfill the terms of the contracts. Business owners take great risks if they enter into contracts with minors. A minor may void or enforce the contract. The business owner has no choice—the wishes of the minor must be honored.

If a minor chooses not to honor a contract, the other parties involved may try to recover any goods given to the minor as a part of the contractual agreement, but they cannot legally enforce any other aspects of the contract.

Billie Marcus, a 16-year-old high school junior, is an avid reader. She reads an average of three novels a week. With the price of books increasing steadily, Billie's reading is getting very expensive.

Last month an offer to join a book club came to Billie's house in the mail. Billie could get 10 novels for 99 cents by joining the club. Billie would then have to purchase 10 novels at regular prices in 12 months. The offer stated that regular prices on the novels would be at least 25 percent less than the prices at a bookstore and that future selections would be made from a list of hundreds of books.

Billie decided the offer was great. After all, the required 10 novels represented less than one month's purchases. What could go wrong if the purchase requirement was 10 in one year? Billie signed the form and returned it with the 99 cents. The 10 novels would soon be on their way.

A few days later, Billie's mother noticed the book club information and asked what it was. Billie explained why accepting the club's offer had been a good decision. Billie's mother sat down and read the book club information very carefully.

After reading the information, Billie's mother said, "Buying 10 hardcover novels may be very expensive." Billie had not read the statement that said all novels except the first 10 would be in hardcover! Billie intended to pay for the books with earnings from a part-time job. Instead of being obligated to spend about $40, Billie was obligated to much more. Even with a 25 percent discount, the total would be more than $300.

Sending the signed form to the publisher meant that Billie had entered into a contract. Is there any help for Billie? Is there a way out of this mess?

Billie may either honor the contract and purchase at least 10 more novels, or she may return the 10 paperback novels as soon as they are received and void the contract.

A person under the influence of alcohol when a contract is negotiated may void the contract, but only if the other party can be restored to precontract condition.

Illus. 16-3   Mail solicitations should be carefully studied to avoid unwanted agreements.

Lu-Yin was intoxicated at the time she told Carla she would buy 50 books of the coupons that Carla was selling in her store. Lu-Yin took the coupons and promised to pay Carla $150 the following week. Later that day, the coupons were stolen from Lu-Yin's car. She sought to void the contract on the grounds that she was intoxicated at the time the contract was made, but since she cannot restore Carla to her precontract condition (return her coupons), she must honor the contract and pay the $150.

A person who claims mental deficiency as a reason for voiding a contract must prove that the mental deficiency existed at the time the contract was made. The condition does not, however, have to be permanent. Lack of knowledge is not considered mental deficiency.

Jamie is a business owner who never had any formal education. He can sign his name and read a little, but that's about it. Jamie signed a lengthy contract to purchase some very expensive equipment from Walt. Later, he explained the deal to his attorney and showed him the contract. After reading the contract, the attorney told Jamie that, according to the contract, Jamie's cost for the equipment would be about ten percent higher than the price Walt had quoted.

Jamie sought to void the contract on the grounds that he could not read the contract and thus did not fully understand what was involved. Jamie must honor the terms of the contract, however, because ignorance is not lack of legal capacity.

Contractual Form Contracts may be verbal or written; both are legally enforceable. Some contracts, however, *must* be written, such as contracts that are regulated by the Statute of Frauds. This is a law that requires certain contracts to be written and signed. The Statute of Frauds monitors several types of contracts.

Sale of Land. Any contract for transferring an interest in real property must be written. Real property includes land, buildings, or other things permanently attached to land.

Sale of Goods Exceeding $500. Most contracts for the sale of goods for $500 or more must be written. This will be discussed in detail in Chapter 17.

Contract for Services That Cannot Be Performed within One Year. According to the Statute of Frauds, the expiration of the time limit for satisfaction of a contract is determined by the date of the contract. Performance of the duties of the contract must be completed within one year from the date of the contract, not the date the performance begins. A contract for services that cannot be completed within one year from the date of the contract must be written.

> On January 1, Antonia hires Candy to paint a mural on the wall of the restaurant she is building. The wall will not be available to Candy until November. Candy knows she will need at least three months to complete the job.

Since the job will not be completed within one year from the date the agreement was made, a written contract that specifies the date of completion is required.

Promise to Assume the Debt or Legal Responsibility of Another. Any agreement to assume the debt or legal responsibility of another person must be written.

> Jon wants to buy a building for his new business. Because he has no credit history, either in his personal name or the business's name, the bank refuses to lend him the money he needs. Jon's father decides to help, and accompanies him back to the bank. Jon's father tells the banker that if the loan is made and Jon is not able to repay it, he will pay it himself. The contract for this loan must be written.

Promise by the Administrator or Executor of an Estate to Assume Responsibility. An administrator or executor is a person charged with the responsibility of handling the final distribution of a person's possessions and funds after death. The law does not require this person to assume personal responsibility for repayment of the debts of the deceased. If the administrator or executor chooses to assume this responsibility, a written contract must be drafted and signed.

> Luisa's business partner passed away, naming her as executor of his estate. He had cash and assets of $63,000 when he died, and his personal debts totalled $68,000. To protect the business, Luisa promised her partner's creditors that she would pay the debts personally. This agreement must be written.

CONTRACT CLASSIFICATIONS

There are many different types of contracts. The most common contract classifications are unilateral or bilateral, express or implied, and formal or simple.

Unilateral or Bilateral

In a unilateral contract, an offer is accepted through performance of the requested act.

> Brian initiated a new program for his employees. He set up a suggestion box and posted a notice on the bulletin board stating that he would give a $10 "reward" to the employee who contributed the best suggestion for improving client relations or business operations each month. Brian is contractually obligated to pay one of the participating employees the reward.

In this unilateral contract, acceptance takes place when Brian actually chooses the monthly winner.

In a bilateral contract, two parties exchange promises.

> Phyllis asks Jennifer, "I'll complete all of the cash reports if you will finish stocking the shelves. Will you?" Jennifer says, "Yes."

They have established a bilateral contract.

Express or Implied

In an express contract, the terms of the agreement are stated, either verbally or in writing. In an implied contract, intent is shown by a party's conduct; the contract is established when a person performs a certain action.

> Yoriko and her date go to a restaurant and order dinner. By their conduct (ordering dinner), they have entered into an implied contract: They have a contractual obligation to pay for their dinner.

Formal or Simple

A formal contract must be prepared in a specific manner and must contain certain components. For example, a personal check is a formal contract. It is negotiable only if it meets certain requirements. The check must be made out to a specific person or company, the amount must be written in figures as well as spelled out, and the check writer's signature must be included in a certain place.

A simple contract can be structured in any manner; there are no specific requirements as long as all components are included. All contracts are either formal or simple; most are simple.

BREACH OF CONTRACT

breach of contract, failure of a party to a contract to perform its obligation(s) as specified in the agreement

When a **breach of contract** occurs, the injured (nonbreaching) party has certain rights. Commonly referred to as remedies, these rights include rescission or cancellation, suit for monetary damages, demand for specific performance, and restitution.

Illus. 16-4   An injured party has certain rights, including filing a lawsuit for monetary damages.

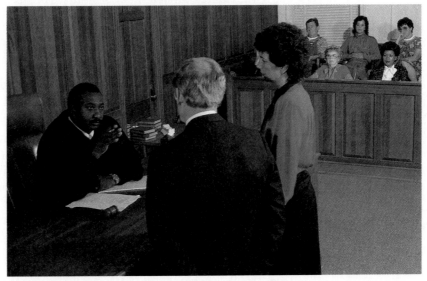

Billy E. Barnes/Tony Stone Worldwide/Click Chicago, Ltd.

Rescission or Cancellation

The injured party in a breach of contract has a right to rescind or cancel the contract. If the contract is rescinded, all parties are returned to their precontract condition and no damages are claimed. If the contract is cancelled, the contract is voided but the injured party may seek damages.

The question of whether rescission or cancellation is appropriate is usually decided by determining what sort of damage the injured party suffered as a result of the breach. If the injured party suffered inconvenience but no monetary loss, the contract would be rescinded. If the injured party suffered monetary loss, the contract would be cancelled.

Suit for Monetary Damages

The injured party in a breach of contract may sue the noninjured party for monetary damages. The amount of money awarded to the injured party is usually the amount required for restoration to nonbreach position.

> The dance committee at West Wilson High School agreed to pay the Live Wires, a rock and roll band, $5,000 for five hours' worth of music at a school dance. The band members later reconsidered and decided they did not want to play for the dance. The dance committee then located another band at the rate of $6,500. The committee could sue the Live Wires for the difference—$1,500—to restore the dance fund to nonbreach condition.

Demand for Specific Performance

In a demand for specific performance, the injured party forces the breaching party to comply with the original terms of the contract.

> Alternatively, the West Wilson dance committee could sue the Live Wires for specific performance. Instead of hiring the other band for $6,500, the committee could ask that a court force the Live Wires to honor their agreement because the school cannot obtain the same services elsewhere for $5,000. The only way the committee will be restored to nonbreach condition is if the Live Wires play for the dance.

Restitution

Restitution is required when the injured party has a right to request that something that was delivered as part of the contract be returned.

Lois, a retired administrative assistant, started a small word processing pool to provide services to local businesses when they had overflow clerical work and word processing. She designated the den in her home as a working room. She purchased computer equipment, workstations, and comfortable chairs for the word processors who worked for her. Lois accepted delivery of the equipment and arranged to pay in five equal installments. After paying the first two installments, Lois stopped paying. Since Lois breached the contract by not paying, the equipment company could sue her for restitution. Lois would probably be required to return the equipment.

ASSIGNMENT OF CONTRACT

Assignment of a contract is transfer of contractual rights to a party that was not part of the original agreement.

Dennis bought a car from Gina and agreed to pay it off in monthly installments. Gina ran into some other expenses and needed cash immediately. She assigned her rights under the contract with Dennis to an acquaintance of hers, Karl, for a set amount of cash. Dennis must now pay Karl each month. If Dennis breaches the contract by not paying, Karl may sue for damages.

Any party to a contract can usually assign the rights of the contract unless the assignment is specifically prohibited by law. Circumstances where rights may *not* be assignable include the following:

1. The contract specifically states that rights are nonassignable.
2. Risk is increased for the nonassigning party.

Marla has a small fleet of freezer trucks, which she hires out to various frozen food vendors. Jackie agrees to pay Marla to transport frozen meat from Jackie's meat processing plant to a frozen food distribution center. Marla overbooks her trucks and hires Ben Harada to transport a load of Jackie's frozen meat. Mr. Harada does not have a freezer truck, but the trip is quite short and Marla feels it won't be a problem. This, however, increases the risk to Jackie—her product may be spoiled during transport.

3. Terms are personal in nature and cannot be delivered in the same fashion by another party.

Illus. 16-5   Terms of a contract are personal in nature.

W. Bertsch/H. Armstrong Roberts

Jerry is an interior designer. Sharon has agreed to pay Jerry a specific sum in exchange for his services in redecorating her store. Jerry cannot assign the contract to another designer—Sharon contracted for a personal service that can only be delivered by Jerry.

NOTE: Legal restrictions concerning assignment vary. You should verify local laws before making a decision concerning assignment of rights.

JEFF BURNETT—ENTREPRENEUR

Jeff has learned that contracts are more complicated than he thought. He had never thought about what might be required to make a contract legally enforceable. Now that he knows what is required, he will be sure to verify that all of his business contracts meet the requirements and can be enforced.

Jeff was especially intrigued by what he learned about his rights in contracting with minors. He knows that a substantial portion of his business will involve teenagers, and he knows that it will be best to avoid making contractual agreements with this segment of his clientele.

Jeff has considered offering some of his customers a credit plan. He now makes a mental note to stipulate that potential credit customers be at least 21 years old. Charge accounts are contracts and are subject to the same requirements as other contracts. He now knows that if he extends credit to teenagers and they refuse to pay he cannot legally collect the debts.

With the knowledge he has now, Jeff will be sure that all of his contractual agreements are properly structured, and he will know what to do if the terms of a contract are not satisfied.

SUMMARY

A contract is a legally enforceable agreement that is negotiated between two or more "persons." A contract must fulfill requirements in five areas:

- agreement
  (offer and acceptance)
- legality
- consideration
- contractual capacity
- contractual form

Contract classifications include unilateral or bilateral, express or implied, and formal or simple. In a unilateral contract, an offer is accepted through performance of the requested act. In a bilateral contract, two parties exchange promises. In an express contact, the terms of the agreement are stated, either verbally or in writing. In an implied contract, intent is shown by a party's conduct. A formal contract must be in a specific form. A simple contract can be structured in any manner, provided all components are included.

When a breach of contract occurs, the injured (nonbreaching) party has certain rights. Commonly referred to as remedies, these rights include rescission or cancellation, suit for damages, demand for specific performance, and restitution. Any party to a contract can usually assign the rights specified unless assignment is specifically prohibited by law.

VOCABULARY BUILDER

Write a brief description of each word or phrase based on your reading of the chapter.

1. Contract
2. Offer
3. Acceptance
4. Consideration
5. Legal capacity
6. Statute of Frauds
7. Unilateral contract
8. Bilateral contract

9. Express contract
10. Implied contract
11. Formal contract
12. Simple contract
13. Breach of contract
14. Rescission
15. Cancellation
16. Suit for damages
17. Demand for specific performance
18. Restitution
19. Assignment

REVIEW QUESTIONS

1. What five requirements must a legally enforceable contract fulfill?
2. What five types of contracts must be written?
3. What are the most common contract classifications?
4. What are four remedies for breach of contract?

DISCUSSION QUESTIONS

1. What are the differences between unilateral contracts and bilateral contracts? Give an example of each.
2. What are the differences between formal contracts and simple contracts?
3. What is the concept of "demand for specific performance" as it applies to breach of contract?
4. What two conditions dictate that a contract cannot be assigned?

CRITICAL THINKING

Marsha Lynch owns a small record store. Her store is very close to the local high school, so a large portion of her clientele is high school students. Many of the students are repeat customers—they buy from her on a regular basis. She lets several of the regulars take records home and pay for them later. She asks these students to sign agreements. Recently, a student refused to pay her. She told this student that a contract had been signed and she could require him to pay.

1. Does Marsha have a legally enforceable contract with the student? Why or why not?
2. What would you advise Marsha to do?
3. What is the student's responsibility in this situation?

SHORT CASE: ASSIGN AND BREACH— ARE THEY THE SAME?

Jim Arnold owns an unusual auto body shop in Pueblo, Colorado. He specializes in rebuilding antique automobiles. When Jim started his business 10 years ago, he had very few customers. However, the last five years have been very busy and very profitable.

Five years ago Jim rebuilt a classic Model A Ford for a customer from Detroit. Shortly after Jim delivered the car, a story featuring the car's owner was printed in a national magazine. The story included a description of the car and mentioned that the car had been rebuilt by a man named Jim Arnold in Pueblo, Colorado. As a result, Jim has been getting business from all over the country. Sometimes he has more than he can handle.

Jim recently agreed to rebuild a 1965 Corvair for a man from Florida. Although he was busy, he thought he could complete the car by the time the man wanted it. They signed an agreement specifying the charges and the delivery date, and Jim scheduled his time so that he could start the Corvair job on June 3.

Jim encountered an unusual problem while working on another project and had to spend a lot of time taking care of it. He knew he was taking more time than he had planned, and there was no way he could get to the Corvair on time. That meant he would never finish it on schedule.

Jim called his cousin Blaine, who was also in the auto body business, and asked him to do the work on the Corvair. Blaine agreed and started immediately. When he finished, Jim checked the work. He was a bit disappointed. Blaine had done a good job on the car, but not as good as he might have done. It would have to do.

When the man from Florida came for his car, Jim told him what he had done and gave him the bill. The man was very angry and refused to pay. He claimed that Jim had breached the contract.

Questions

1. Did Jim have the right to assign this contract to his cousin? Why or why not?
2. Did Jim breach the contract? Why or why not?
3. If Jim did breach the contract, what remedy or remedies can the car owner seek?

PROJECT CHALLENGE

Make a list of the contracts you think you will require for your hypothetical business. Consider any particular specifications the contracts should include and what form they should take. Make sure that all of the contracts meet the requirements covered in this chapter.

17
Buying and Selling

After mastering the information contained in this chapter, you should be able to:

17-1 Understand the sale of goods.

17-2 Describe sales contracts as related to other contracts.

17-3 Explain the nature of sales contracts.

17-4 Explain transfer of ownership and risk of loss.

17-5 Understand the rights and responsibilities of vendors and purchasers in sales contracts.

At the heart of any entrepreneur's dream business is buying and selling. It does not really matter if the entrepreneur sells a product or a service. Regardless of what entrepreneurs sell, they must buy products to support the business and sell products or services to ensure business success.

The skill and knowledge with which entrepreneurs approach buying and selling is a key element to business success. Entrepreneurs can learn the hard way or the easy way. The hard way consists of learning it on the job through considerable trial and error. The easy way consists of a fair amount of reading and study and/or consultation with an attorney *before* the business opens.

Aside from the entrepreneurial aspects of buying and selling, these concepts are also important in every person's daily life. Hardly a day passes

Illus. 17-1   A mastery of the principles of buying and selling is essential for the entrepreneur.

when the average American does not buy something. Whether it is a can of pop or a new car, the laws of sales apply. Mastery of the principles contained within this chapter will make the reader not only a better entrepreneur but a better consumer as well.

SALE OF GOODS

sale, the immediate transfer of ownership of goods for a price

goods, items of tangible personal property other than money

Uniform Commercial Code, a group of uniform business rules adopted by most states

A **sale** is defined as the immediate transfer of ownership of goods for a price. **Goods** are defined as items of tangible personal property other than money.

Laws about the sale of goods are included under Article 2 of the **Uniform Commercial Code** (UCC). The UCC unifies state laws pertaining to the sale of goods and makes them simpler to understand. In a sales transaction, the seller is known as the vendor and the buyer is known as the purchaser (also called vendee). Entrepreneurs should be familiar with the legal aspects of buying and selling so that the rights of their business are protected.

SALES CONTRACTS

In Chapter 16, you learned about contracts and the components needed to form them. Generally speaking, when a contract is *not* for the sale of goods, common-law principles of contracts apply. And, from a general perspective, what you learned in the last chapter holds true for the sale of goods as well. The UCC simply takes those same components and applies them in a less strict fashion to the sale of goods.

Just as other contracts have certain requirements for legality, so do sales contracts. Sales contracts depend upon the types of sellers involved. In addition, an offer must be made and accepted, and there must be consideration in the sale. There are certain required terms for the sale as well as optional, or permissible, terms. Certain legal restrictions are placed on sales. Also, there are requirements concerning written sales contracts as well as exceptions to those requirements.

seller, a person who offers a good or goods for sale

casual seller, a person who offers a good or goods for sale but is not in the business of selling

Types of Sellers

For any type of sale, there are two types of **sellers.** The first, a merchant, sells a particular good or goods on a regular basis and claims special knowledge. The second, a **casual seller,** only sells occasionally and claims no special knowledge. The UCC makes a distinction between the two types of sellers. Since merchants are supposedly knowledgeable about the products or services they sell, they are usually held to a higher standard and may have to be licensed or meet other special regulations. As examples, let's see the distinction between Mark and Kay.

> Mark has a shotgun with which he shoots skeet. Because he has given up the hobby, he wants to sell the gun. Mark sells the gun to Susie for $200. Mark, according to the UCC, is a casual seller. He does not have to meet any special regulations.
>
> Kay sells shotguns for shooting skeet at the store she owns. These shotguns are the store's main product line; Kay sells guns on a daily basis. The UCC considers Kay a merchant. She must meet special regulations, such as possession of a Federal Firearms License, and she must keep very detailed sales records.

Consideration in Sales Contracts

In a sales contract, consideration is required. It usually takes one of two forms. The first is price. Price is the amount of money agreed to by the parties to the sale. Once agreed upon, price becomes the consideration. The second form of consideration is that of **barter,** the term used to describe a sale involving only the exchange of goods, when no money changes hands. In the case of barter, the UCC considers both parties to the sale as vendors of the goods they have transferred. Once agreed upon, the bartered goods become the consideration.

barter, a sale involving only the exchange of goods; no money changes hands

Offer and Acceptance

There are some exceptions to common law when dealing with the offer and acceptance of sales contracts. Entrepreneurs should know and understand these exceptions.

The Offer.   The first exception has to do with the offer. Remember that in a contract, an offer can be revoked. That is also true of sales contracts, unless the offer is a firm offer. A **firm offer** is a written, signed sales offer in which the merchant expresses the intention that it cannot be revoked. The merchant may also express a time period of up to three months for the contract to be irrevocable. In addition, no consideration is required for a firm offer. In other words, the merchant is held to the sales contract for the period of irrevocability even though no consideration has been received.

firm offer, a written, signed sales offer in which the merchant expresses the intention that it cannot be revoked

Ricardo owns a small manufacturing plant. He makes an offer to Gerald to sell him a machine made in the plant. The written offer includes a price for the machine, indicates that the offer will not be revoked for 60 days, and has Ricardo's signature on it. This is a firm offer and cannot be revoked by Ricardo. Note that Gerald has not given Ricardo any consideration to hold the offer open. Gerald may accept the offer or not. He has up to 60 days to decide.

Acceptance.   The second exception in acceptance of a sales contract deals with the counteroffer. According to common law, if an offer is not accepted as is, the counteroffer becomes a rejection of the original offer. In relation to a sales contract, this is not true. The counteroffer may become part of the original offer unless specifically forbidden in the original offer.

Marcie, a merchant, made a firm offer to Roger of a new Ford Bronco with a six-cylinder engine for $20,000. Roger responded that he would accept if Marcie would substitute the regular radio with a CD player. Since the offer does not alter the original offer significantly, it can become part of the contract if Marcie does not object.

Illus. 17-2   Once an offer is accepted, consideration must be present for a legally binding sales contract to exist.

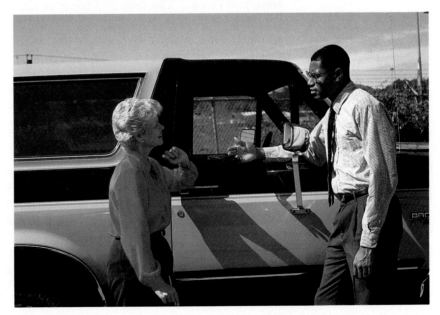

Once the offer is accepted, however, consideration must be present for a legally binding sales contract to exist. The exact amount of that consideration does not have to be included in the sales contract, however.

Required Terms

In relation to the actual required terms of the sales contract, the UCC is much less strict than common law. Basically, three things are required by law in a sales contract. First, the contract must include the names of the people involved in the contract. Second, the contract must specify the monetary amount of the goods involved. Third, the signature of the person responsible for breach or nonperformance must be included.

Permissible Terms

In addition to the required terms of a sales contract, certain other terms are permissible. They include price, time and place, the purchaser's right to inspection, risk of loss terms, and transfer of ownership.

Price. The price may be included in the contract but is not required. If the price is not included, it will be assumed to be a reasonable and customary price that is charged in the industry.

Time and Place. The time and place for the performance of the contract may or may not be included in the contract. If the time and place for things, such as delivery of goods, are not specified, it is assumed that such performance will be reasonable.

Purchaser's Right of Inspection. The sales contract may include the purchaser's right of inspection prior to payment. If this term is included in the contract, the purchaser may check goods for damages before accepting and paying for them.

risk of loss, the financial responsibility assumed by a party in a sales contract for damaged or destroyed goods

Risk of Loss. The sales contract may also include terms dealing with **risk of loss.** In other words, the contract may specify which party—the vendor or the purchaser—will assume the financial responsibility if the goods are damaged while being shipped or transported.

Transfer of Ownership. Terms in a contract that deal with the actual transfer of title of the goods may also be included. This, along with risk of loss, will be discussed in more detail later in the chapter.

Legal Restrictions

Just as a regular contract is not enforceable if it pertains to an illegal product or service, neither is a sales contract. Parties involved in illegal sales activities are subject to be prosecuted. Also, there is no legal recourse for persons involved in illegal sales contracts.

> Joel wanted to buy some fireworks to sell to a few of his best customers who had been inquiring about them. Fireworks are illegal in the state in which Joel lives. He paid Charlie $200 to buy some for him out of state. What he has asked Charlie to do is illegal. Charlie never bought or delivered the fireworks, but kept the money instead. Joel cannot go to court to get his $200 back from Charlie since he was party to an illegal sales contract.

Exceptions to Written Contract Requirements

As with common-law contracts, sales contracts may be either verbal, written, or implied. If the amount of goods involved in the sale is $500 or more, then the contract must be in writing. There are exceptions to this requirement, however. The exceptions are discussed in the following sections.

1. If an oral contract for $500 or more is confirmed in writing and signed by one party, it is then enforceable. The receiving party must have knowledge of the confirmation and not object to it within ten days. If the receiving party does object within ten days, the contract is void.

> Sumio agreed verbally to buy $800 worth of fresh fish from Chris. Chris later wrote to Sumio to confirm the verbal contract, and Chris signed the confirmation. If Sumio knows of the confirmation and does not object within ten days, the verbal agreement becomes enforceable.

2. If a person admits, in writing, to a verbal contract for $500 or more, the verbal contract becomes enforceable. Using the previous example, let us see how this works.

> Sumio changes his mind about buying the fish. He writes to Chris saying that the verbal contract to purchase the $800 worth of fresh fish

is not enforceable because it is for goods totalling $500 or more. By admitting the contract in writing, it is now enforceable.

3. When the goods in question have been received and accepted by the buyer, the verbal contract becomes enforceable.

Millie enters into a verbal contract with Regina to sell her $600 worth of lawn furniture. Millie delivers it and Regina accepts possession of the furniture. Because Regina accepted delivery, she is bound by the verbal contract.

4. When the goods have been paid for in full and the seller has accepted payment, the verbal contract becomes enforceable.

Suppose that Regina paid Millie the $600 for the lawn furniture before it was delivered, and Millie accepted the payment. Once Millie accepted the payment, the verbal contract became enforceable.

Illus. 17-3   When the goods in question have been received and accepted by the buyer, the verbal contract becomes enforceable.

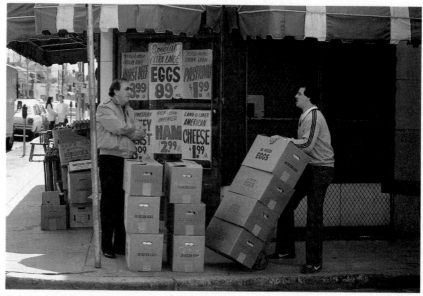

Eric Neurath/Stock Boston

5. When the goods involved are of special manufacture and not suitable for other uses, a verbal contract is enforceable if the manufacturer has made a substantial beginning in either the manufacture or purchase of goods.

> Leah owns a specialty advertising company. Chou contracts verbally for $1,000 worth of matchbooks bearing the name and logo of his Chinese restaurant. One month later Chou changes his mind and tries to get out of the contract by claiming that it was not in writing. Leah has already contracted with a printing company to have the work done. Since a substantial beginning has been made by Leah, Chou is bound by the verbal contract.

TRANSFER OF OWNERSHIP AND RISK OF LOSS

Entrepreneurs should be aware of when the transfer of ownership occurs and when risk of loss shifts from the vendor to the purchaser.

> James, who owns a video arcade, enters into a sales contract with Gene, who manufactures video game machines. Gene agrees to sell James five new machines for a total of $10,000. Gene ships the machines by train to James. While in transit, the machines are destroyed in a train accident. Who is responsible for the loss?

Usually, the risk of loss is associated with the holding of title. Knowing the law pertaining to these issues can be very important in future business situations that involve damaged or lost goods.

Ownership

It is best if the transfer of ownership/title is specifically addressed in the sales contract. If it is not, then a court must decide to which party merchandise belonged at the time of damage. To have goods or the title to goods tied up in court proceedings can become a very expensive venture for entrepreneurs. It is also possible to lose good customers or honest suppliers if you enter into legal proceedings. Avoid this type of situation, if possible. The cost of collecting damages may be greater than the compensation from the other party.

Remember, the concern over transfer of ownership usually has to do with risk of loss. The following are examples of common situations involving such transfer between vendors and purchasers.

When Vendors Deliver Merchandise. Generally speaking, when the vendor is to deliver the merchandise to the purchaser, ownership/title passes upon agreed to delivery and notification.

> Jennifer, the vendor, agrees to deliver to Julio, the purchaser, ten dozen dresses for the fall season. Julio's receiving department takes delivery from Jennifer's truck driver. Ownership transfers at that point. Jennifer's driver could not just unload the cartons of dresses on Julio's receiving dock, however, and drive off. The driver needs to notify Julio or one of his employees of the delivery.

When Vendors Ship Merchandise. The sales contract may authorize the vendor to ship the merchandise by a third party, such as a trucking or railroad company, to the purchaser. If it does, then ownership transfers once the merchandise is delivered to the third-party shipper.

> In the previous example, Julio authorizes Jennifer to ship the dresses via ABC Trucking, Inc. Jennifer then delivers the dresses to the trucking company. Once the goods are delivered to the trucking company, ownership passes to Julio. If the goods are damaged while in ABC's possession, Jennifer has no responsibility.

When Purchasers Pick Up Merchandise. If the purchaser picks up the merchandise at the vendor's location, ownership passes at the time of the pick-up.

> Continuing with the same example, Jennifer might offer Julio a ten percent discount if he will pick up the dresses. Julio agrees and sends one of his trucks to Jennifer's manufacturing plant. Once Julio's driver takes possession of the dresses, ownership passes to Julio. Jennifer has no further responsibility for the goods.

Ownership in Retail Sales

The following sales terms pertaining to transfer of ownership are common to retail sales and those handled over the phone or through the mail.

Cash and Carry. When a buyer goes into a store and purchases merchandise with cash, ownership passes when the transaction is complete—that is, with payment to the store.

> Jackie goes into an auto parts store and purchases windshield-wiper blades. Once Jackie pays the clerk and the transaction is complete, ownership of the wiper blades passes from the auto parts store to Jackie.

Credit. Ownership passes in a credit sale in the same way as in a cash sale. The only difference is that payment is mutually agreed upon at a later date.

> If, in the above example, Jackie went to the auto parts store and purchased the wiper blades on credit, ownership would pass once the sales transaction was complete—in this case, when the purchaser signs the charge slip.

C.O.D. Ownership in a C.O.D. transaction passes once the cash is paid to the delivering party. This is different from other cash transactions, however, because the buyer is not permitted to inspect the merchandise prior to acceptance.

Illus. 17-4   In a credit sale, payment at a later date is mutually agreed upon.

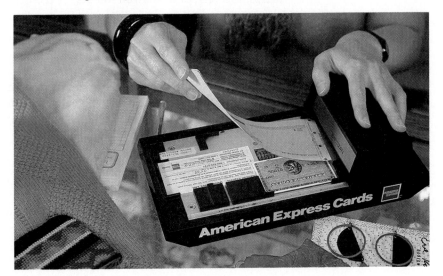

sale on approval, a sales transaction in which the buyer has a right to approve the merchandise prior to the transfer of ownership

Sale on Approval. Sometimes goods are sold to a customer as a **sale on approval.** Even though the buyer has actual possession of the merchandise, ownership does not transfer until the buyer approves the merchandise.

> Sandi received an offer in the mail for a new type of windshield-wiper blade with three sides. The offer said that the blades would be sent to the buyer for a ten-day trial without obligation. At the end of ten days, either payment or the blades must be sent to the manufacturer. If after ten days, Sandi returns the blades, ownership remains with the manufacturer. If Sandi sends payment, ownership transfers to her.

OBLIGATIONS AND PERFORMANCE

Sales contracts, like all other contracts, can be breached. If there is a sales contract breach or nonperformance, the injured party has certain rights. The obligations and performance agreed to in the contract can be enforced in certain circumstances, which are described in the following paragraphs.

Vendor Rights when the Vendor Is at Fault

Even though a vendor is at fault in a contract nonperformance, he or she still has certain rights. If sufficient time (according to the agreement) remains, the vendor is allowed to correct the error and fulfill the contract.

> Woody owns a small sporting goods store. He orders 25 Brand X fishing reels from Reels, Inc. Reels, Inc. substitutes brand Y by mistake in Woody's order. Woody informs Reels, Inc. that the contract has been violated because he received the wrong merchandise. If time remains according to the original agreement, Reels, Inc. can still honor the contract by sending the correct merchandise. If they are able to do this, Woody is still obligated to the contract.

Vendor Rights when the Purchaser Is at Fault

The purchaser may be at fault by doing such things as refusing to accept merchandise or refusing to pay. If such is the case, the vendor has certain rights, including the right to sue the purchaser for payment or damages, or to cancel the contract.

315

Chapter 17 Buying And Selling

Purchaser Rights when the Vendor Is at Fault

The vendor may be at fault for such things as failing to deliver goods or delivering incorrect merchandise. If such is the case, the purchaser has certain rights. These include the right to sue for specific performance, such as requiring the vendor to deliver the contracted merchandise; to sue for recovery of any money paid to the vendor; to sue for damages due to lost profit or due to excess cost in obtaining substitute merchandise; and to cancel the contract.

JEFF BURNETT — ENTREPRENEUR

Jeff was familiar with some of the laws concerning the sale of goods and sales contracts from his exposure to them in his last job in the wholesale music business. Some of them, however, scared him a bit. There were so many rules and exceptions! It all seemed more complicated than other aspects of entrepreneurship that he had learned. He wasn't sure he could remember everything he needed to know.

Since it would take a lawyer to remember all the details about buying and selling, Jeff decided that the best thing he could do was to develop some buying and selling policies for Rock 'n' Soul Music. If he did that and wrote the policies down as part of his business planning process, he wouldn't have to memorize specific aspects of the law. His policies would cover the law. After using the policies for a while, Jeff knew he would have them memorized.

Jeff made the following preliminary list to start the process. As you read through the list, try to determine which areas Jeff missed. Remember, this is very important to the success of Rock 'n' Soul Music.

1. All sales contracts must be in writing.
2. No offers will be accepted unless they are firm.
3. Price must always be a written part of the sales contract.
4. Contracts must include the right of inspection.
5. Transfer of ownership information will be included in the sales contract.
6. No C.O.D. orders will be made by Rock 'n' Soul Music.
7. No merchandise will be sold on approval to customers of the store.

Would you add any policies to Jeff's initial list? Did he forget any important points? If so, name them.

SUMMARY

A sale is defined as the immediate transfer of ownership of goods for a price. Goods are defined as items of tangible personal property other than money. The sale of goods is covered under Article 2 of the Uniform Commercial Code. In a sales transaction, the seller is known as the vendor and the buyer is known as the purchaser (also called vendee).

Sales contracts have required components for legality. Sales contracts are affected by types of sellers. They require an offer and acceptance, consideration, and three required terms for the sale. Sales contracts permit some other terms as well. Legal sales contracts must pertain to legal goods and legal transactions. Entrepreneurs should also be aware of the requirement that contracts worth more than $500 must be written, and the exceptions to that requirement.

Entrepreneurs should be aware of when the transfer of ownership occurs and risk of loss shifts from the vendor to the purchaser. Risk of loss refers to the financial responsibility assumed by a party to a sales contract if something happens to damage or destroy the goods or merchandise in question. Usually, the risk of loss is associated with the holder of title. It is best if the transfer of ownership/title is specifically addressed in the sales contract.

Sales contracts, like all other contracts, can be breached. If there is a sales contract breach or nonperformance, the injured party has certain rights. The obligations and performance agreed to in the contract can be enforced in certain circumstances.

VOCABULARY BUILDER

Write a brief description of each word or phrase based on your reading of the chapter.

1. Sale
2. Goods
3. Uniform Commercial Code
4. Vendor
5. Purchaser
6. Vendee
7. Seller
8. Merchant
9. Casual seller
10. Price
11. Barter
12. Firm offer
13. Risk of loss
14. Sale on approval

REVIEW QUESTIONS

1. What set of rules governs the sale of goods in most states?
2. What are the two types of sellers in day-to-day sales?
3. What are the two common types of consideration used in sales contracts?
4. What are the three required terms in sales contracts?

DISCUSSION QUESTIONS

1. What terms are permissible, but not required, in a sales contract?
2. What are two exceptions to the requirement that a written contract is necessary for the sale of goods totalling $500 or more?
3. Why is it important for entrepreneurs to know when the transfer of ownership of merchandise takes place?
4. When does transfer of ownership occur in a credit sale?

CRITICAL THINKING

Marla Grubbs owns a plant that manufactures office furniture. Recently she received an order from Clarksdale High School for 25 red office chairs. The purchaser specified in the contract that the chairs should be delivered by September 1. On June 30, Marla shipped the chairs. Since she had no red chairs in inventory, she sent black ones. Upon receipt of the chairs on July 20, the principal of the school called Marla and informed her that she had breached the written contract by sending the wrong color of chairs.

1. Did Marla violate the sales contract?
2. What are Marla's rights in this situation?
3. Can Marla still enforce the terms of the contract against Clarksdale High School?

SHORT CASE: MINI-GOLF, ANYONE?

Gabe DeGabrial lives in Key West, Florida. After working for other people around town for several years, Gabe decided to open his own business. After much thought and research, he decided to open a miniature golf course. That was about a year ago. Since then he has been developing his business plan and moving forward with the project.

One of the first things Gabe did was to design the various holes for his miniature golf course. Using an Everglades theme, he designed what he considered to be 18 challenging and fun holes. After he completed the design, Gabe contacted a local contractor and discussed the fixtures he would need for each golf hole. Upon reaching a verbal agreement concerning what was needed, the two shook hands and parted.

The contractor agreed to deliver the fixtures five weeks before the scheduled opening, so that there would be ample time to install them. With the scheduled opening six months away, the contractor felt that he had enough time to complete the $12,000 job.

Three months later, Gabe was visiting with a friend about the new miniature golf course. When the friend, who was a carpenter, heard how much the fixtures were going to cost, he told Gabe that $12,000 was entirely too much for the work. He told Gabe that he could build the whole thing for $8,000.

After thinking about it for a couple of days, Gabe decided to let his friend do the work. After all, he had no written sales contract with the contractor. Gabe then entered into a written contract with his friend to do the work. Upon calling the contractor, Gabe was told that he was breaching the sales contract. Gabe told the contractor that since the contract was not in writing, it was not enforceable.

Questions

1. Is Gabe correct about the contract not being enforceable? Why?
2. What rights does the contractor have?
3. If the contract is enforceable, how does that affect the new contract with the carpenter? What are the carpenter's rights?

PROJECT CHALLENGE

As you continue your business planning process, it is time to develop a set of policies regarding sales contracts. Develop policies in the following areas:

1. Sales contracts for which your business is the purchaser.
2. Sales contracts for which your business is the vendor.

18

Real Property and Insurance

property, something that is owned or can be owned

PROPERTY OWNERSHIP

Entrepreneurs choose their life-style because they want the independence of being the boss. Their ultimate goal is freedom. To have this freedom requires properly managing a business in an independent fashion, and making the decisions that guide the business.

One of the primary goals of many entrepreneurs is property ownership. Without this ownership, a small part of the freedom they may want is missing. Entrepreneurs should give property ownership serious consideration during the business planning process to determine if it is a realistic expectation. It may be something that occurs later—lease or rental may make more sense during the start-up phase. Property ownership is not required, and leasing or renting may give the entrepreneur adequate control of the property at a lower cost.

A certain level of knowledge is required whether the entrepreneur chooses to buy property or rent it. Real property is an expensive part of any entrepreneur's dream, and its acquisition must be carefully planned.

Property Classification

Property is usually classified as either real property or personal property. The distinction is made for legal purposes.

Real Property. Real property includes land, buildings, and fixtures. Land usually consists of the earth's surface, a reasonable airspace above the land, and anything that is located below ground. Growing things, such as trees and crops, are usually considered real property until they are removed (that is, harvested). They then become personal property. In certain circumstances, however, things that are below ground may be a

Illus. 18-1   *Real property includes land, buildings, and fixtures; personal property is unattached.*

separate concern. Entrepreneurs who are planning to purchase land should be sure to verify their rights and responsibilities for what cannot be seen.

Buildings, as they relate to real property, are structures that are permanently attached to land. Movable structures, such as sheds, that are on skids or other foundations are usually not considered buildings.

Fixtures are items of personal property that are permanently attached to real property. As a rule, once it is attached, a fixture becomes a part of the real property.

> Phyllis is planning to open a store that sells antique dolls. To protect the dolls, Phyllis hires Misty, a carpenter, to build several display units with glass doors. Misty delivers the units and Phyllis has them permanently attached to the walls of the store she is renting.

When Misty delivers the units to Phyllis, they become Phyllis' personal property. Once Phyllis attaches the units permanently to the walls, they become fixtures and may become the landlord's property. When Phyllis moves or closes her business, the provisions concerning leasehold improvements as stated in the lease contract determine the disposition of the fixtures—that is, whether they will remain or be removed.

Personal Property.   The distinction between real and personal property is important—personal property is any property that is unattached and, therefore, not classified as real property. Personal property includes items such as clothing, furniture, jewelry, and automobiles.

Acquiring Real Property

Entrepreneurs may acquire real property in one of the following three ways:

- through purchase or receipt as a gift
- by inheritance
- by adverse possession

Purchase or Gift.   Most owners of real property purchase their property. A written contract is required for the purchase of real property, and the contract must detail all terms of the transfer.

Real property may also be gifted. A gift is the transfer of property without charge. The gift is valid only if the person who gives does so unconditionally. The gift must take place in the present, not at some future time (such as after the giver's death), and the gift must be accepted.

The actual transfer of title, after purchase or receipt by gift, is accomplished through the use of a **deed.** There are two main types of deeds—warranty deeds and quitclaim deeds.

deed, a written document by which an individual conveys title and other rights of ownership of real property to another individual

A warranty deed is a deed that transfers a seller's interest in real property with certain warranties. These warranties ensure that the item to be transferred is free from defects and from any claims. The following provisions are usually warranted.

1. The seller owns the property or has authority to transfer it.
2. No undisclosed claims, such as unpaid taxes, exist against the property.
3. The purchaser's right to possession will not be disturbed. This means no person or company will, at a later date, make a claim against the property based on circumstances that existed at the time of purchase.
4. The seller will do whatever is necessary to ensure that the title to the property is valid.

A quitclaim deed transfers whatever ownership interest the seller has, including liabilities, to the buyer. There are no warranties made concerning validity of the title. Accepting a quitclaim deed to real property is generally *not* a good idea.

The deed for the property should be recorded, or legally documented, as soon as it is received. This is usually done in the courthouse of the county in which the property is located. Once recorded, the deed provides a public record of ownership, which protects the new owner. Recording the deed will prevent possible loss in any dispute over ownership of the property.

Inheritance. Real property may be inherited. In this situation, title does not pass by deed but by distribution from an estate. This transaction must also be recorded at the county courthouse.

Adverse Possession. An individual can take real property from the legal owner without paying for it through **adverse possession.** If a property is to be taken in this manner, however, several requirements must be met. They are as follows:

adverse possession, acquisition of another's land by occupation, without the owner's permission and without payment

1. The adverse possessor (person trying to take the property) must be occupying and using the property.
2. The adverse possessor's use of the property must be clearly evident.
3. The adverse possessor must be using the property without permission.
4. The adverse possessor must openly claim ownership to the property.
5. The adverse possessor's occupation and use of the property must meet the duration requirement established by the laws of the state in which the property is located (usually 5 to 20 years).

Mary Sherman purchased a 35-acre parcel of land in a mountain resort area as an investment. She visited the undeveloped land prior to purchase, then returned home. Since the land was undeveloped, Mary did not feel it would be necessary to visit the property on a regular basis. Six years after purchasing the property, Mary decided to visit it while in the area on vacation. Much to her surprise, the land was fenced and had cattle grazing on it. A sign identified the property as part of the Lazy S Ranch. Mary learned that the fence and sign had been in place for more than five years and that the owner of the Lazy S Ranch had been using the land for cattle grazing continually. The adverse possession period for the state in which the property was located was five years. As unfair as it seemed, Mary had lost her land.

If all of the requirements for adverse possession are met, the original owner will probably lose title. However, the circumstances are not usually as extreme as those in Mary's situation.

Illus. 18-2   A survey can help determine property rights.

Robert Rathe/Stock Boston

Jim and Katie own adjacent pieces of property in the downtown section of their city. Katie recently built a restaurant on her property. The construction company erroneously extended Katie's parking lot five feet onto Jim's property. Neither Jim nor Katie is aware of the error. If Jim does not discover the error before the lapse of the adverse possession period in his state, Katie will gain title to the portion of his property she is using.

Owning Real Property

If an entrepreneur decides that purchasing, rather than leasing, property is the best course, then the form of ownership becomes an issue. Joint tenancy, tenancy by entirety, or tenancy in common are the forms of real property ownership to consider. Entrepreneurs should weigh these choices carefully; a decision made now will determine the future disposition of the property.

Joint Tenancy.   Entrepreneurs who are co-owners of a business may choose **joint tenancy** as the form of ownership to ensure that the other owner or owners will acquire ownership interests upon their deaths.

joint tenancy, ownership by more than one person, with rights of survivorship

> Bill and his friend Charles started a business together, and they bought a building to house the business. They chose to own the building in joint tenancy. If Bill dies, the building becomes Charles' property—Bill's heirs have no claim on the property. The same is true for Charles' heirs if he dies.

A joint tenancy may be dissolved if one of the parties to the agreement sells his or her interest. The buyer does not automatically become a joint tenant.

tenancy by entirety, ownership by husband and wife, with rights of survivorship

Tenancy by Entirety. The **tenancy by entirety** form of ownership is available only to entrepreneurs who are married to each other at the time the property is acquired.

> Susie and Jon are husband and wife. They purchase a building for their business and choose tenancy by entirety as the form of ownership. If one of them dies, the other becomes the sole owner of the property.

A tenancy by entirety can be dissolved only if both parties agree to sell the property.

tenancy in common, ownership by more than one person, without rights of survivorship

Tenancy in Common. In the **tenancy in common** form of ownership, if one of the parties to the agreement dies, that person's interest in the property passes to his or her heirs.

> Maria, Chin, and Shaun started a small business together. They purchased a building as tenants in common. One year after the business opened, Shaun died. His interest in the building passed to his heirs.

In this example, any of the three parties is free to sell his or her interest in the building. This type of ownership is the most common when the entrepreneurs involved are not related.

community property, property acquired during marriage

Community Property. Several states have **community property** laws. Under these laws, all property acquired during marriage automatically becomes community property and is owned jointly by the husband and wife. If either spouse dies, his or her interest is distributed as dictated by the will, or if no will exists, as dictated by state law.

> Christi, a wealthy movie star, married Jerry who did not work. During the first five years of their marriage, Christi used her earnings to buy

Illus. 18-3   Under community property laws, all property acquired during a marriage automatically is owned jointly by the husband and wife.

Fred McKinney/The Stock Market

real estate around California where she and Jerry lived. After the fifth year, the two got a divorce. Jerry claimed that he owned half of all the real estate purchased during the marriage. Christi claimed that, since Jerry did not work during that time or pay a share of the costs, she owned the real estate. She claimed Jerry had no interest.

In the example above, the property is covered under community property laws since California is one of the states that recognizes such laws. As a result, Jerry does indeed own one-half of all the real estate purchased during the five year marriage.

Easements

easement, a nonpossessory right to use land owned by another party

An **easement** allows one person to cross another person's property to gain access to his or her own property. The party that is granted the easement must maintain the property involved in the easement. The other party may not interfere with the easement.

Figure 18-1   Map of Jabar's Property

Jabar bought 50 acres of land that is completely surrounded by land owned by Gene (see Figure 18-1). An easement must be granted if Jabar is to have access to his property.

LEASING REAL PROPERTY

Many entrepreneurs find that leasing a facility is more sensible than buying. This is especially true during business start-up when entrepreneurs have so many expenses to cover.

Types of Leases

Leases for business properties usually fall into one of four categories—tenancy for years, periodic tenancy, tenancy at sufferance, or tenancy at will. The terms of a lease are what determine which type of lease it is.

tenancy for years, lease for a fixed period of time

Tenancy for Years.   The fixed term for a **tenancy for years** lease may be any specified period of weeks, months, or years. This type of lease often includes an option for renewal or an option for purchase. Entrepreneurs may choose this type of lease, with an option to purchase, if the facility is a good candidate for a permanent place of business.

periodic tenancy, lease for a set period of time, which will continue for similar periods of time until terminated

Periodic Tenancy.   The most common type of **periodic tenancy** lease is a month-to-month lease. A designated period of notice is usually required for cancellation of a lease of this type.

tenancy at sufferance, lease in which a tenant may remain in the facility after termination of the lease

Tenancy at Sufferance.   When a **tenancy at sufferance** lease expires, the landlord can choose to evict the tenant or allow the tenant to remain by continuing to accept lease payments. If payment is accepted, a new periodic tenancy is created. The length of the new lease will be tied to the length of the old one. If the old lease was for one year, the new one will also be a one-year lease.

tenancy at will, possession of real property without benefit of an agreement that documents terms

Tenancy at Will.   If the lease is a **tenancy at will** lease, neither the duration of the tenancy nor the amount of the rent is documented. This type of lease allows change or termination at any time, by either party.

Rights and Duties

Both landlords and tenants have certain rights and duties under ordinary lease agreements. Tenants are given the right to possess and use property in return for the duties of paying rent and taking care of the property. In some leases, the tenant is also given the right to sublet (lease all or part of the leased property to a third party) or assign (transfer the entire interest in the property to a third party) the property. In a sublet, the person with the original lease remains responsible to the landlord. In an assignment, the third party becomes primarily responsible to the landlord.

The right to sublet or assign is governed by the lease agreement. It is very important to be sure these rights are included in a business lease. Their absence could be very costly in the event that a business is dissolved.

> Millie signed a two-year lease on a small building in which she opened a manufacturing business. After six months she had to close the business because of poor health. A clause in the lease allowed her to assign her tenancy, so she was able to transfer the lease to a competitor who needed additional space.

If Millie's lease had prohibited assignment, she would have had to pay rent on the facility for 18 months after she closed the business. This would have been a financial disaster.

Landlords have the right to receive rent and, in some cases, to keep any fixtures that are added to the property in return for the duties of maintaining the facility and paying taxes on the property. If rent is not paid, landlords may sue for the amount due and/or evict (remove) tenants from the property.

INSURANCE

There are many risks involved in operating a business in modern-day America. Successful entrepreneurs are aware of probable risks and plan for them. The most important form of protection against the hazards of operating a business is insurance. Entrepreneurs must procure several types of business insurance if they are to be properly protected.

Obtaining the proper insurance coverage for a business begins with determining what the business's insurance needs are. Entrepreneurs must be sure that they provide for coverage of all aspects of the business. The types of coverage most commonly needed to ensure proper protection include the following:

1. Property insurance—provides protection against loss or damage for any property that would need to be replaced (e.g., business facility, equipment, inventory).
2. Liability insurance—provides protection against losses that result from customer claims of bodily or monetary injury. These claims often result in lawsuits and usually in a legal responsibility for payment of damages. The liability can be a result of an injury that is incurred while the customer is at the place of business or an injury that results from use of the product or service purchased.

Illus. 18-4 Property insurance provides protection against loss or damage for any real property that might need to be replaced.

Norris Klesman/Picture Group

3. Business interruption insurance—provides protection against loss of revenue that results from an unexpected temporary shutdown.
4. Key person insurance—provides protection against potential loss of revenue that results from loss of personnel whose services are critical to the successful operation of the business.
5. Life insurance—provides owner(s) with sufficient capital to purchase a deceased owner's interest in the business

Certain relationships must exist if insurance on people or property is purchased. Those relationships are referred to as insurable interest. The concept of insurable interest was established by law to prevent profit from a situation in which there was no real involvement.

> Abby knows that Viana likes to drive her car very fast and take risks. Abby buys a one million dollar life insurance policy on Viana. She figures she will be a million dollars richer if Viana happens to get killed.

Under the concept of insurable interest, situations such as the one in this example are illegal. NOTE: Insurable interest must exist at the time personal or property insurance is purchased.

Insurable Interest in People

Entrepreneurs may discover that other people—partners or employees—are critical to the success of a business. Without them, the business might suffer tremendous financial loss. If this is the case, an entrepreneur has an insurable interest in them and may purchase insurance, called key person insurance, to protect against such a loss.

> Blain, an electrical engineer, and Wylie, a chemical engineer, form a partnership to manufacture small electronic components for the defense industry. The skills of both men are essential to the success of the business. To protect themselves against potential loss, Blain and Wylie each take out a life insurance policy on each other.

Blain and Wylie have a legitimate insurable interest in each other's lives.

Insurable Interest in Property

Generally speaking, a person with a legitimate insurable interest in property is one who owns, rents, or holds the property as security for another debt. It is essential to insure any property associated with the business that is critical to its success. Do not overlook rental property—it can be as essential to success as owned property. Its destruction or damage could hinder or even prevent the continuation of business.

JEFF BURNETT—ENTREPRENEUR

Jeff had not given much thought to real property. After all, he did not intend to purchase any for his business. He has already signed a three-year lease for a 2,000-square-foot facility in Lakeside Mall (see Chapter 5). He thought that the decisions about his facility had all been made. However, after reading information about leases, Jeff became concerned about the terms of the lease he had signed. He could not remember if the lease addressed sublet or assignment. He had not known how important that information could be.

Jeff decided to get the lease from his files and read it again as soon as possible. Maybe it was not too late to get it changed if it did not allow him to sublet or assign his mall space. He hoped he had not made a critical error. If he had and he was forced to close Rock 'n' Soul before the three-year lease expired, it could cost him a lot of money.

Jeff also plans to investigate the cost of insuring the mall space he had rented. He had never thought about what might happen if his rental space or its contents were destroyed. Jeff's original plan had been to insure his inventory. Now he knew that even if his inventory could be replaced, the cost of replacing equipment, relocating, or being closed for an extended period of time would be very expensive. It might be so expensive that he would lose his business.

SUMMARY

One of the primary goals of many entrepreneurs is property ownership. Entrepreneurs must consider carefully whether to buy property or rent it. Real property is an expensive part of any entrepreneur's dream, and its acquisition must be carefully planned.

Property is usually classified as real property or personal property. Real property includes land, buildings, and fixtures. Personal property is any property that is unattached and therefore not classified as real property. Personal property includes such items as clothing, furniture, jewelry, and automobiles.

Real property is usually acquired in one of three ways: purchase or gift, inheritance, or adverse possession. The actual transfer of title, after purchase or receipt by gift, is accomplished through the use of a deed. There are two major types of deeds—warranty and quitclaim.

When the decision to purchase property is made, a form of ownership must be selected—joint tenancy, tenancy by entirety, or tenancy in common. Property ownership may involve an easement. The nonpossessory right provided by an easement allows a person to cross another person's property.

Many entrepreneurs find that leasing a facility is more sensible than buying. A lease for business property is usually one of four types—tenancy for years, periodic tenancy, tenancy at sufferance, or tenancy at will. The terms of the lease determine which type of lease it is.

Both tenants and landlords have certain rights and duties under ordinary lease agreements. Tenants have the right to possess, use, and possibly sublet or assign the property. Landlords have the right to receive rent and to keep any fixtures added to the property.

Insurance is very important to entrepreneurs. They should purchase insurance to protect against potential losses. To purchase personal or property insurance, certain relationships must exist. Those relationships are referred to as insurable interest. The concept of insurable interest was established by law to prevent profit from a situation in which there was no real involvement.

VOCABULARY BUILDER

Write a brief description of each word or phrase based on your reading of the chapter.

1. Property
2. Real property
3. Land
4. Buildings
5. Fixtures
6. Personal property
7. Deed
8. Warranty deed
9. Quitclaim deed
10. Adverse possession
11. Joint tenancy
12. Tenancy by entirety
13. Tenancy in common
14. Community property

15. Easement
16. Tenancy for years
17. Periodic tenancy

18. Tenancy at sufferance
19. Tenancy at will

REVIEW QUESTIONS

1. What items are classified as real property?
2. What are some examples of personal property?
3. What are the three ways in which real property is usually acquired?
4. What are the two main types of deeds?

DISCUSSION QUESTIONS

1. What is adverse possession? What five conditions must be met to claim adverse possession?
2. What are the characteristics of two types of real property ownership?
3. What is an easement? Why are easements sometimes necessary?
4. What does *insurable interest* mean?

CRITICAL THINKING

Trip's apartment is owned by a friend of his father's. He has lived there for two years and pays $250 per month in rent. He has no written lease that documents the terms of the lease. When he moved in, the friend told him he could stay in the apartment and pay what he could afford. Last week the friend told him that he would have to move at the end of the month.

1. What type of lease does Trip have?
2. Does Trip have to move? Why?

SHORT CASE: INSURANCE INFORMATION WANTED

Sheila is planning to start a new business with three friends—Barry, Ruth, and Charlton. They are currently finalizing their business plan.

Sheila has five years of experience as a licensed and certified architect. She specializes in custom designing private homes. Barry is a real estate agent. He specializes in new home sales. Ruth is an interior designer and is considered the best in the business by many of the builders in town. The majority of her work is in new home interior design. Charlton's specialty is residential construction. He has been running his own business successfully for three years.

Sheila, Barry, Ruth, and Charlton are planning to start a real estate development company. Their dream is to purchase land, design and build houses, and market the houses. All functions would be performed by their company—no subcontractors would be involved.

The four are currently planning for their insurance needs. They are considering their life and property insurance needs, including coverage for the small office space they plan to lease.

Questions

1. Which of the four people involved should be insured? Why?
2. Should the partners purchase insurance for the new office space? Why?

PROJECT CHALLENGE

It is now time to make your final decision about your facility. In your business plan notebook, answer the following questions.

1. Are you going to lease or purchase? Why?
2. If you lease, what type of lease will you choose? Why?
3. If you purchase, what type of ownership will you choose? Why?
4. What insurance will you need for the new business?

UNIT 6

CAREER OPPORTUNITIES IN ENTREPRENEURSHIP

19

Purchasing an Existing Business

After mastering the information in this chapter, you should be able to:

19-1 List sources of business for sale opportunities.

19-2 Describe the advantages and disadvantages of buying an existing business.

19-3 Describe how to identify a good business opportunity.

19-4 Explain how to evaluate a business for sale opportunity.

19-5 Know what information to acquire before deciding to buy a business.

market value, the value of similar goods, homes, properties, businesses, etc., in similar markets

PURCHASING AN EXISTING BUSINESS

For many aspiring business owners, the best way to enter the world of entrepreneurship is through the purchase of an existing business. Before deciding to open a new business, it is wise to investigate the business for sale market. Why? Talking to someone who has a business for sale is an excellent way to learn about the market conditions of the community in which you wish to operate. The potential buyer will be able to see the sales revenues of an industry member and a possible future competitor firsthand. In addition, it provides the opportunity to find out the potential **market value** of the particular type of business *after* it is established and any start-up problems have been worked out. Furthermore, it might lead to an opportunity to enter the market at a lower cost than originally anticipated. For these reasons it is wise for potential small business owners to inquire about businesses for sale, even if it was not the original intention.

How to Find Businesses for Sale

Business owners wishing to sell their businesses commonly advertise their intentions to sell by advertising in the classified section of newspapers, by listing their businesses with business brokers, or by getting the word out through industry and community sources.

Classified advertising. Potential buyers should check first in the business opportunities pages of the classified section of local newspapers. There they will find numerous advertisements similar to the one shown in Figure 19-1.

Information provided in such advertisements is often very general. However, a telephone call or mail inquiry should provide enough basic

Figure 19-1   Business for sale advertisement

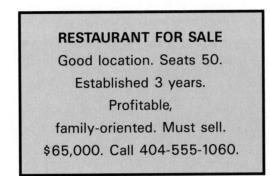

RESTAURANT FOR SALE
Good location. Seats 50.
Established 3 years.
Profitable,
family-oriented. Must sell.
$65,000. Call 404-555-1060.

information to determine whether it is worth investigating. If the idea shows promise, you should arrange a time to meet with the seller to discuss the opportunity. Since buying a business requires very intensive research, the first meeting is normally a general discussion of why the business is for sale and how the seller foresees the future performance of the business. If you are still interested after this meeting, you and the seller should schedule meetings to discuss the opportunity further and for you to observe business operations during working hours.

business broker, agent who brings business buyers and sellers together

Business brokers.   Business brokers act as selling agents for business sellers, just as real estate brokers do for people selling homes. Brokers represent sellers and assist them by bringing potential buyers and sellers together. As part of handling a business sale, brokers advise sellers to have specific information available that will be needed to answer potential buyers' questions. Brokers also handle advertising businesses for sale. Many sellers use brokers to keep their intention to sell confidential. Brokers advertise without giving the name of the business and provide their own business phone number and address for interested parties to contact. Only when they have screened the prospects and identified qualified buyers do they tell the prospects how to contact the seller. Business brokers may also assist in drawing up sales contracts and arranging financing. Brokers are paid for their services by receiving an agreed-upon percentage of the selling price. The percentage is normally 10 to 15 percent.

Industry sources.   Many businesses are sold by announcing to industry members that a business is for sale. This works either through referral from salespeople or by advertising in industry publications. Since potential new business owners frequently ask industry suppliers about business

Illus. 19-1   Owners wishing to sell their businesses commonly make their intentions known by advertising in the classified section of newspapers.

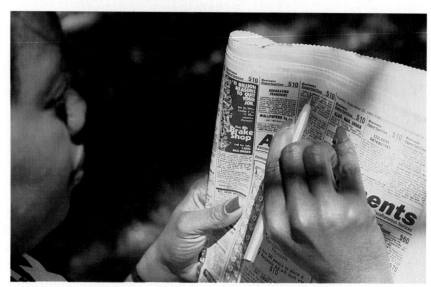

opportunities, both are effective ways to learn about businesses that are for sale. Many companies have referral systems in place to put individuals making inquiries in touch with those who wish to sell. They will normally only get involved with the selling process as a referral.

Entrepreneurs may also find businesses for sale through other sources, such as the following:

- landlords/leasing agents
- attorneys
- bankers
- SBA
- Small Business Development Centers
- management consultants
- shopping center management offices
- venture capitalists
- chamber of commerce offices
- acquaintances
- bankruptcy announcements

Often the best business opportunities will come from businesses that are not for sale. If there is an existing business that meets all of the requirements a potential business buyer is looking for, the buyer can make the owner an offer. The owner may, of course, refuse. However, if the offer is attractive enough, he or she might consider the opportunity to sell.

Advantages of Buying an Existing Business

There are many advantages to buying an existing business, particularly for entrepreneurs with little experience. It is an ideal way to "learn the ropes" because, in many cases, the previous owner will stay on for a period of time to train the new owner and/or be available for consultation.

It is also a less risky way to become self-employed. The existing business has a track record—procedures are in place, suppliers are lined up, and a customer base is established. New owners will have an idea about what they can expect of revenues, expenses, and profits. These figures are easier to forecast for an established business than for a start-up. If new business owners have some of the security anchor characteristics described in Chapter 1, buying a business will certainly alleviate some of the anxiety of getting started in owning and operating a business.

Purchasing an established business may also be financially advantageous. Sellers often assist with financing arrangements to sell their businesses. It is not uncommon for sellers to accept an initial partial payment with the agreement that the balance will be paid off in monthly installments in the form of a promissory note. This arrangement may reduce or eliminate the need for bank financing and is often negotiated at a lower interest rate. If the seller does not wish to help finance the purchase of the business, buyers are still (in most cases) more likely to receive financing from a bank or other financial institution for an *established* business than for a *start-up*. Why? It is less risky for the lender.

Entrepreneurs sometimes purchase businesses because it is the only way to successfully enter the market. If a particular business dominates the market because of its superior location and reputation, buying that business might be the best way to ensure success. Other advantages of buying an existing business may include the following:

- No business start-up is required.
- Suppliers have already been tried and tested.
- The company has survived the start-up phase (the first year or two) and has a better chance of succeeding.
- Experienced employees will already be functioning and probably will not require much, if any, training.

Disadvantages of Buying an Existing Business

Many businesses are for sale due to internal problems. It is not a good idea for aspiring business owners to assume someone else's problems. If a business has a poor reputation with customers, has trouble with suppliers, or is poorly located, it is unlikely that new ownership will automatically change customers' negative opinions about the business. Too many business buyers have learned the hard way that it takes a long time to restore customer confidence in a business.

Another disadvantage is that buying a profitable business will initially cost more. The seller has built a business, poured time and energy into it, and will usually expect to be rewarded with a selling price that reflects his or her efforts. Capital limitations on the part of the buyer, however, might prevent the purchase of an existing business. It might be more economically feasible to take the risk of creating a new business with a smaller capital investment.

Some entrepreneurs might consider purchasing part of, or investing in, a business. The risk is that there might be a lack of compatibility between the parties that have been more or less forced together for economic reasons. A bad partnership arrangement prevents a business from building the comraderie described in Chapter 12 that is so essential for small business success.

Another drawback to purchasing an existing business is that the employees currently working in the business may have to be replaced. Poor training by the former owner or unacceptable work habits may not be tolerated by the new owner. It may also be necessary to invest money to modernize the operation.

Reasons Why Businesses Are Sold

In considering the purchase of a business, the potential buyer should determine why the business is for sale. This will help the buyer determine the price he or she feels is fair for the business. If sellers are under great pressure to sell, they may be more flexible about the selling price. The following is a list of some of the many reasons businesses are sold.

- Insufficient profits
- Owner's retirement
- Death or illness of a working partner
- Business heirs are disinterested
- Partner or shareholder dispute

Illus. 19-2 An owner's plan to retire is one of the many reasons a business is offered for sale.

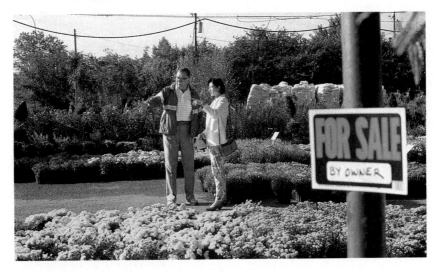

- Management "burnout"
- Business is growing too fast or too slowly
- Forced liquidation or sale
- Fear of new competition
- Fear of current or predicted economic conditions
- Lack of desire or capital to do necessary remodeling
- Owner's desire for a change of career
- Owner's desire to take advantage of another opportunity requiring the liquidation of business assets

HOW TO BUY A BUSINESS

Buying a business is an intricate process that requires the same thoroughness as creating a business plan for starting a business from scratch. As a potential business buyer, you should follow these steps.

1. Write clear, specific personal and financial objectives about what kind of business you want to buy. Whatever the type of business for sale, it must match these statements before you consider it for purchase.
2. Locate business opportunities that offer growth and provide an attractive return on investment. Read classified advertisements, discuss opportunities with business brokers, and check industry sources as you formulate a list of potential opportunities.

3. Meet with business sellers or brokers for an introduction to specific business opportunities. The initial information provided by the seller should include a brief financial report, the history of the business, selling price, and the reason for sale.

4. Request a second meeting to probe for more information if the seller's material fits the objectives you stated in Step 1.

5. Inspect the facility closely to determine how well it has been maintained.

6. Prepare a checklist of information needed. The checklist should include the following:

   • A complete financial accounting of operations—the income statements and balance sheets—for at least the past three years, or from the beginning of operation if the business is less than three years old—federal income tax returns, and state sales tax forms should be included

   • A list of all assets to be transferred to the new owner—this should include an itemized list of all inventory as of the last accounting period

   • A statement about any past or pending legal action against the business

   • A copy of the business lease or mortgage

   • A list of all of the business's suppliers

7. Once you examine all of the information you receive, you should then meet with several key individuals to receive their professional recommendations or approvals before going any further.

   First, consult an accountant and a lawyer. They should be able to provide you with any further interpretation of the financial and legal information you received. Your accountant will review all of the financial information regarding the business. He or she may uncover flaws or inaccuracies that may provide a more accurate financial picture than what the seller presented. Your lawyer will need to check, among other things, to see if the lease or title may be transferred to you. You need to conduct an on-site meeting with the landlord or mortgage holder to ensure the facility is in satisfactory condition. In the case of a lease, you should discuss the expiration date and, if possible, negotiate the terms and price to fit your needs.

   Potential buyers are wise to consult the chamber of commerce and other local assistance centers to discuss the future of the market and the location. It would be in your best interest to contact industry representatives presently selling to the business to validate the sales reported and to obtain their assessment of the likelihood of the business's future growth.

8. It is essential that potential buyers arrange a convenient time with the seller to observe operations. Look for employee and customer satisfaction and/or dissatisfaction, as well as pros and cons of the operation in general. All of these considerations enter into the final sales price.

9. Determine a fair purchase price to offer the business owner. In some cases, the owner will have already stated a price; you now must make a counteroffer based on your research. Determine what financing arrangements are available through a lending institution or with the seller. Present the offer in writing to the seller. You should present a letter of intent which, in essence, says, "I will purchase the business at the stated price and under the stated terms provided that an audit shows that the inventory, work in process, accounts payable, and accounts receivable are as shown to be."

   At this point, there will normally be some negotiation. You will have to use your best persuasion techniques to point out the validity of the offer and the advantages to the seller for accepting the offer. Either party may bring his or her attorney, or another agent, to assist in negotiations.

10. If an agreement is reached, an attorney should draw up a suitable sales contract. Usually, there are many terms included in a business sale contract. Many details need to be clarified, and questions answered, such as whether the seller is permitted to open a competing business within the buyer's market area. Which party will be responsible for paying any unreported claims, liens, or unpaid taxes on the business following its sale? What should be done about customers' long-standing debts? What about union contracts for unionized employees? Employee benefits and pensions? How will costs for insurance coverage, taxes, and utilities be divided? As you can see, a lawyer can be very helpful at a business closing and can protect you from costly, unforeseen entanglements. The contract should be contingent upon examinations of all assets to validate that what is represented is true.

11. Before signing a sales contract, the buyer should be present when the seller takes final inventory of assets.

EVALUATING BUSINESS FOR SALE OPPORTUNITIES

Normally an investigation of businesses for sale produces a range of opportunities from bad to promising to good. Categorizing a business opportunity as bad, promising, or good helps prospective buyers determine the value of the business and, therefore, the price they are willing to offer.

Types of Opportunities

The first sign of a bad business opportunity is poor bookkeeping. If a business owner has been negligent in maintaining proper financial records, it is more than likely that the business has suffered because of it. Failure to present adequate validation of sales revenues and expenditures is often a sign that the seller is attempting to hide information. It is wise to avoid this type of situation.

Many business opportunities are not easy to distinguish or measure. For example, a business's recordkeeping may be adequate, but not entirely complete; a solid, but unspectacular, customer base may have been established; or relationships with suppliers may be satisfactory, but not as efficient as they could be. Many times these are the best business opportunities because their greatest need is better management. Proper management might generate greater sales and better customer reception. Since previous management has not been able to reach all of its objectives, the selling price of the business should not include goodwill. Therefore, it might be a bargain for the right buyer.

An example of a promising business opportunity is a store that has leveled off in sales at a certain point and cannot seem to increase sales even though the market is good. Management is evidently not doing some things right or else does not have the capital available to aggressively pursue the market. If a new owner can make some changes, such as remodeling, adding new inventory, or increasing advertising expenditures, he or she could quite possibly increase profits and receive a healthy return on investment. Potential buyers should look for this type of opportunity.

Good businesses keep good records and maintain a good customer image. Buying a business that has been properly managed is an asset to the new owner. He or she will not have to spend time convincing customers that they will be given better service, quality, and/or prices under the new management. However, if a business has been profitable and managed well, it will be more costly to purchase. In cases of successful

Illus. 19-3   Remodeling an existing business is often enough to increase profits.

Roy Morsch/The Stock Market

goodwill, the value of a business's image and community relations

businesses for sale, it is customary for the seller to specify a dollar amount for **goodwill.** Goodwill is the value of the efforts of building a successful business and a good reputation with customers and with the community.

Evaluation Considerations

Unfortunately, there is no easy, standard formula to use to compute the value of a business. Many deals are based on how motivated both the seller and the buyer are to close the deal. Sometimes the terms are more important than the price. However, the following evaluation methods will help to generate a price at which you can begin negotiating.

Prospective buyers must evaluate opportunities for buying businesses in terms of profit earnings and return on investment. The most important factor to look for is the business's potential to make money. Unfortunately, this is not always easy to determine because the buyer is dealing with what he or she *thinks* might happen. To help, buyers use a method called the **earnings approach.** Using this approach, buyers determine whether the business will be able to pay them for their time. Potential buyers should identify their proposed changes and develop pro forma financial statements to examine the impact of the changes on the business. If this forecast looks positive, they then need to examine their return on investment.

earnings approach, the method of determining the value of a business by calculating its potential profit and return on investment

Entrepreneurs should expect earnings to provide a return on investment over a period of time. Usually that period of time is five years, or 20 percent per year. Too often, businesses are bought with the assumption that as soon as the new management takes over, business will improve dramatically. However, it takes time to change operations procedures, employee performance, and customer buying habits. Therefore, opportunities must be evaluated considering the long-term potential.

Potential buyers must also research the market value of the business for sale. This requires learning the selling prices of similar businesses and comparing them to the price of the business being considered. It is a good way to get a general idea of the market, but since no two businesses are exactly alike, this is not always accurate. Buyers would be wise to hire an appraiser to appraise the building and other assets.

replacement value, the cost of purchasing new assets at current market value

Buyers must determine the **replacement value** of the assets they are considering purchasing. Since the value of assets listed on a balance sheet is based on the previous purchase price of assets such as equipment, furniture, fixtures, and inventory, the buyer should determine the *current* replacement value of assets listed. The replacement value is usually higher than the asset value.

liquidation value, the value of assets if liquidated or sold immediately

A final measure should be the **liquidation value** of a business's assets. Using a worst-case scenario, the prospective buyer should

Illus. 19-4   The prospective buyer should determine the immediate cash value of all assets in case the business must be sold.

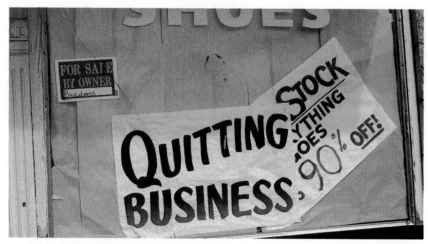

H. Abernathy/H. Armstrong Roberts

determine the immediate cash value of all assets (including the present value of future income) in the event a problem arises that requires immediate sale of the business.

It is a good idea for prospective buyers to review the current income statement of a business for sale and indicate any foreseeable adjustments to that financial statement due to the new ownership. Table 19-1 is an example of such a list of adjustments.

Inadequate review and investigation in buying a business can lead to problems like those experienced by Bailey Robinson, as recounted in the following paragraph.

Table 19-1

INCOME STATEMENT FOR YEAR ENDING DECEMBER 31, 19____		
ACTUAL		**COMMENTS FOR NEW OWNER FOR FIRST YEAR**
Sales and revenues	$180,000	Should increase 10 percent
Less cost of goods	93,000	add $25,000—new inventory
Gross profit	87,000	minus approximately $7,000
Operating expenses		
Payroll	26,000	− $5,000, cut one employee
Rent	19,500	no change
Utilities	2,200	no change
Maintenance	1,600	+ $500 for new lights
Insurance	2,400	+ $200, cover added inventory
Accounting	2,000	− $1,000, keep own books
Advertising	2,800	+ $550, announce new owners
Supplies	4,100	+ $600, new bags, boxes
Miscellaneous	4,000	+ $1,000, other changes
Total operating expense	$ 64,600	minus approximately $3,150
Net operating profit	$22,400	approximately $18,550

Bailey Robinson bought a retail clothing business believing she could increase profits as soon as she took over. The business financial statement looked like this:

Sales	$ 250,000
Cost of goods	– 130,000
Gross profit	120,000
Operating expenses	– 95,000
Net profit	25,000

To buy the business, Bailey borrowed from the bank with a promise to pay back $20,000 per year. She knew that this would only leave $5,000 per year for her salary, but she was sure that she could immediately increase sales by $50,000. This would allow her a salary of $25,000. One year later she was forced to sell the business. Although she had increased sales by $10,000, it was not enough and she ran out of time.

JEFF BURNETT—ENTREPRENEUR

Jeff was advised to investigate business for sale opportunities before definitely deciding to open his business. In doing so he discovered that one of his future competitors, located in a discount shopping center, wanted to sell his business. Although Jeff didn't end up buying the business, he learned quite a bit of important information from his investigation. He discovered that his competitors had sales of $150,000, a profit of $15,000, and an inventory of $22,000. He learned about the pricing strategy used by that store and that it suffered because it was usually undersold by the record department of a nearby discount store. He also found out what suppliers they bought their inventory from, at what price, and with what terms. It was very useful information which he later used in setting up his own business.

He decided the asking price of $75,000 was too high for a store with marginal profits, an inventory of only $22,000, and equipment and fixtures valued at $18,000. He realized that to make it successful he would have to increase sales by 50 percent, which would require investing in more inventory and advertising, thereby making his total purchase cost close to $100,000. Looking back, he was glad he had decided to open his own store.

SUMMARY

Many entrepreneurs choose to buy an existing business rather than create a business. To find business for sale opportunities, prospective buyers research the classified sections of the newspaper, make inquiries to business brokers, discuss their interest with industry representatives, and inquire throughout the community.

The advantages to buying a business, as opposed to starting one from scratch, includes owning a business with a history, which reduces risk by knowing what to expect. In addition, the new business owner will inherit an immediate customer and supplier base, and often will receive preferable financial arrangements through seller financing. However, many businesses that are for sale have poor customer relations and/or negative images that take a long time for new owners to improve.

Buying an existing business requires detailed research and planning, just as when starting a new business. Buyers must make sure that all documents presented are accurate and that the final price is fair. If the opportunity does not appear to be a good investment, it should be avoided. The buyer should realistically project what impact the change of ownership will have on the business. Business buyers should not expect immediate turn-around of profits and growth.

VOCABULARY BUILDER

On a separate sheet of paper, write a brief description of each word or phrase based on your reading of the chapter.

1. Market value
2. Business broker
3. Bad business opportunity
4. Promising business opportunity
5. Good business opportunity
6. Goodwill
7. Earnings approach
8. Replacement value
9. Liquidation value

REVIEW QUESTIONS

1. Why is it a good idea to investigate business for sale opportunities before deciding to start a new business?
2. What are three sources of finding business for sale opportunities?
3. What are three advantages to buying an existing business?

4. What are three disadvantages to buying an existing business?
5. Why is it important to determine why a business is for sale?
6. What information should a prospective buyer collect to properly evaluate a business opportunity?
7. What is a sign of a bad business opportunity?
8. What does an earnings approach determine when used to evaluate a business for sale?
9. What is determined when calculating liquidation value?
10. Why is it wise to make a pro forma income statement before purchasing a business?

DISCUSSION QUESTIONS

1. What are some characteristics of a promising business opportunity?
2. What is the advantage of using seller financing as opposed to conventional financing?
3. What steps should an entrepreneur take to investigate a business for sale opportunity?
4. A business is advertised for sale for $100,000. The stated profit is $25,000 after all salaries, including the owner's, are paid. Is this opportunity worth investigating? Why?
5. How does replacement value differ from the asset value listed on a balance sheet? Why should prospective buyers determine the replacement cost?

CRITICAL THINKING

Some business sellers are hesitant about disclosing all of their business's financial information to potential buyers. They believe they should only have to show sales results and asset totals, not tax returns or confidential payroll information. As a prospective buyer, how would you react to this attitude? How would this affect your purchase decisions? Explain your answers.

SHORT CASE: A BUSINESS FOR SALE OPPORTUNITY

Henry Murphy studied the two business propositions before him, trying to judge which was the best opportunity. Both restaurants were offered for sale for $50,000. The income statements reveal the following profits before the owner's salary is deducted.

	Restaurant #1	Restaurant #2
Sales	$135,000	$160,000
Food purchases	45,000	68,000
Gross profit	90,000	92,000
Operating expenses	65,000	73,000
Net profit	$ 25,000	$ 19,000

Restaurant #1 showed greater profits, however Restaurant #2 had more assets — $35,000 compared to Restaurant #1's assets of $24,000. Restaurant #1 is 10 years old and has experienced a slight downturn of sales during the past year. Restaurant #2 is only three years old and has had a 22 percent sales increase during the past year. Restaurant #1 underwent a recent remodeling and appears to be operating under better management than Restaurant #2. Both are located on main thoroughfares in the same growing community. Henry is looking for a business that can afford to pay him a $14,000 salary with a good return on investment. He is confused about which restaurant offers the best opportunity.

Questions

1. Based on this initial information, what restaurant would you recommend that Henry purchase? What are your reasons for recommending that particular restaurant?
2. Describe a strategy to increase profits for the restaurant you chose.

PROJECT CHALLENGE

Review the classified section of the newspaper to find a business for sale opportunity for a business similar to the hypothetical one you are planning. Also, contact business brokers and inquire if they have any current listing of similar businesses. How do the newspaper or brokers' descriptions compare with what you have learned about your business project? Write a report that analyzes the existing business opportunities and compares them with your planned new business.

20

Purchasing a Franchise

After mastering the information contained in this chapter, you should be able to:

20-1 Define the terms associated with business franchises.

20-2 List some of the classifications of franchises that are available in the United States.

20-3 List some advantages and disadvantages of franchising.

20-4 Understand and explain some of the legal aspects and requirements of franchising.

20-5 List questions to ask before purchasing a franchise.

franchise, a right or privilege to conduct a particular business using a specified trade name

franchising, method of doing business by which a franchisee is granted the right to engage in offering, selling, or distributing products or services under a specified marketing format

A person who has a burning desire to become an entrepreneur and own a small business may have no real idea of what particular business to choose or how to run a business. This aspiring entrepreneur may want to consider a **franchise.** There are thousands of franchises in the United States from which entrepreneurs can choose. These businesses currently account for about one third of the U.S. retail economy—more than $600 billion of business per year. Well-known franchises include Computerland®, McDonald's®, Kentucky Fried Chicken®, Coca-Cola®, Midas®, Wendy's®, Century 21®, Dunkin' Donuts®, Dairy Queen®, Video Connection®, and Ramada Inn®.

There are numerous benefits—as well as some drawbacks—to **franchising.** One of the benefits of franchising is business experience. When

Illus. 20-1A, 20-1B, 20-1C   Well-known franchises.

someone purchases a franchise, the past experiences of other entrepreneurs who have chosen that franchise are included in the purchase. In other words, practical business advice, based on the experiences of all other owners of the same franchise, comes with the franchise. This advice is a valuable asset.

Purchasing a franchise is certainly a desirable option for some entrepreneurs. For others, it is not. Read the following information carefully and decide if a franchise may be the right decision for you.

DEFINITION

franchisee, the person who buys a franchise from a franchisor

franchisor, the person or company that offers the franchise to others

The U.S. Department of Commerce defines franchising as a method of doing business in which a **franchisee** is granted the right to engage in offering, selling, or distributing goods or services under a marketing format that is designed by the **franchisor.** The International Franchise Association defines a franchise as a continuing relationship between franchisor and franchisee in which the sum total of the franchisor's knowledge, image, success, manufacturing, and marketing techniques are supplied to the franchisee for a consideration.

Franchising is described in the following terms[1]:

1. Franchising is a business opportunity. An owner (producer or distributor) of a service or trademarked product grants rights to an individual for distribution and/or sale of goods or services and receives a payment or **royalty** in return.

royalty, an ongoing fee paid to a franchisor at specific intervals—usually a percent of gross revenue or net sales

2. Franchising is a pattern or method of doing business. A franchisee is granted a right to offer, sell, or distribute goods or services under the marketing format designated by the franchisor.
3. Franchising is a licensing relationship. A franchisor of a product, service, or business grants distribution rights to affiliated dealers (franchisees). These rights often include exclusive access to a defined geographic area.
4. A franchise is a continuing relationship. Franchisors provide a licensed privilege to do business. They also provide management and technical assistance and training.

---

[1]Robert T. Justis and Richard J. Judd, *Franchising* (Cincinnati: South-Western Publishing Co., 1989)

CLASSIFICATIONS

Franchising opportunities are available in many types of business in all areas of the United States. A publication that is offered by the U.S. Department of Commerce, the *Franchise Opportunities Handbook,* lists, by category, the franchise opportunities that are available. Entrepreneurs have more than three dozen categories from which to choose. The publication includes information about costs, capital required, number of franchises already operating, etc. A current copy can be obtained by contacting the U.S. Government Printing Office in Washington, D.C.

Some of the categories in the *Franchise Opportunities Handbook* are the following:

- automotive products/services
- business aids/services
- campgrounds
- clothing/shoes
- cosmetics/toiletries
- dental centers
- educational products/services
- employment services
- foods
- motels/hotels
- printing
- real estate
- security systems
- vending

Other sources for finding franchise opportunities include the *Wall Street Journal, Forbes* magazine, *Barron's* magazine, the *Info Franchise Newsletter,* "The Franchise Annual" (published by Info Press, Lewiston, NY), "Franchise Yearbook" (published in Los Angeles, CA), "Franchising for Free" (published by John Wiley & Sons, New York, NY), *Venture* magazine, and *Entrepreneur* magazine.

ADVANTAGES

There are many advantages and disadvantages to purchasing a franchise. The entrepreneur should evaluate these carefully before deciding to purchase.

A franchise provides an established product or service. One of the most challenging problems any entrepreneur faces when starting a new business is that of product/service acceptance by the consumer. The process of becoming established can take years. With a franchise, the process has already been underway for some time and is usually reinforced with large-scale advertising.

Many, but not all, franchisors offer management and/or technical assistance. Management assistance usually includes provision of the

Illus. 20-2 Franchisors provide management, technical assistance, and training.

McDonald's Corporation.

knowledge needed to start the new business and handle daily operations as well as crisis management. This assistance is available through on-site training or classes at the franchisor's base. Technical assistance can include anything from site selection and building design to equipment purchase and food recipes.

For consumers, one of the main attractions of franchised businesses is consistency. A franchise contract mandates a certain level of quality. That level of quality is determined by past business experience. Most franchisees realize that they must match or exceed the quality available in related franchises if they are to be successful. The consumer knows that a franchised business in New Jersey will offer the same basic range of products or services as the same franchised business in California. It is unlikely that there will be any major surprises.

The operating capital required for a new business can be considerable. Association with a franchise may reduce some of these expenses. General supply purchases are a good example. Franchisors may be able to negotiate low prices because of the large volume they purchase. Independent entrepreneurs usually do not have that advantage. The same holds true for equipment, insurance, and many other expenses.

A franchise contract may provide for the franchisee's professional growth. If the contract guarantees a certain geographic territory to the franchisee, future competition within that territory cannot come from within the same franchise. Any growth in the territory is limited to the purchase or sale of additional locations by the original franchisee. For example, if you purchased a franchise for a certain service station and, as part of the contract, were given an exclusive geographic territory, you may be able to purchase franchises for additional locations or sell franchises to others.

DISADVANTAGES

Entrepreneurs who purchase franchises may have certain expectations as to services that they receive from the franchisor. If these services are not clearly included in the contract, they may not be provided. The franchisor's only legal responsibilities are those included in the contract.

A franchisee is required to pay the franchisor on an ongoing basis. If the value of the services the franchisee receives does not at least offset the payment, the payment becomes a financial drain on the new business.

Franchisees may depend heavily on the advice of the franchisor at first, but should be careful not to become overdependent. Overdependence often clouds common sense and interferes with sound business practices. The level of dependence should decrease as time passes.

The franchise package will usually carry restrictions that involve products or services to be offered, types of customers to be served, geographic territory, and pricing. Many entrepreneurs object to this type of control because it inhibits the freedom they sought as business owners.

Franchise contracts usually control the terms of a sale or closure to a degree. This means that a franchisee may have little or no say about the terms of a termination of the franchise agreement.

For franchises that are part of a chain, the performance of existing locations may influence the success of new businesses. If service and quality slip at one location, customers may associate that slip with the other locations as well.

LEGAL ASPECTS OF FRANCHISING

An entrepreneur should not sign a franchise contract without the advice of a competent attorney. Only an attorney can properly analyze the legal documents that are required for a franchise arrangement. Two of these

Illus. 20-3   An entrepreneur should seek the advice of a competent attorney before signing a franchise contract.

Frank Siteman/Stock Boston

documents are the disclosure document, or the Uniform Franchise Offering Circular (UFOC), and the Franchise Agreement.

The Disclosure Document

The Federal Trade Commission (FTC) requires that a franchisor disclose certain information to a prospective franchisee, in writing, at least ten business days prior to any legal commitment to purchase.

The franchisor can meet the disclosure requirements of the FTC by following the format of the UFOC, developed by the North American Securities Administrators Association.[2] This format requires including information under the following headings:

1. The Franchisor and Any Predecessor—description and background of the company, owners' prior business experience, and details about any business that preceded the one being offered.
2. Prior Business Experience of Persons Affiliated with Franchisor: Franchise Brokers—identity and business experience of the franchisor's directors, executive officers, and **franchise brokers.**

franchise broker, a person who obtains the right from a franchisor to sell franchises within a certain territory—the franchisee pays royalties to the franchise broker, who pays royalties to the franchisor

---

[2]Justis and Judd, *Franchising.*

3. Litigation—details of any involvement in criminal, civil, or administrative law complaints. If none, so stated.
4. Bankruptcy—details of any bankruptcies. If none, so stated.
5. Franchisee's Initial Franchise Fee or Other Payment—a detail of the franchisee's purchase cost and terms of payment.
6. Other Fees—a detail of fees that must be paid by the franchisee on an ongoing basis (such as royalties) and the terms of payment.
7. Franchisee's Initial Investment—a detail of the franchisee's estimated initial investment cost, how the funds are to be distributed, franchisor's policies regarding financing, and detail of any other costs to the franchisee, either direct or indirect. If none, so stated. NOTE: These costs are separate from the franchise fee.
8. Obligations of Franchisee to Purchase or Lease from Designated Suppliers—a detail of franchisee's obligations to purchase only from franchisor-designated suppliers. If none, so stated.
9. Obligations of Franchisee to Purchase or Lease in Accordance with Specifications or from Approved Suppliers—a detail of franchisee's obligations to purchase or lease certain items, such as equipment, advertising materials, and insurance, and details concerning restrictions in sources for purchases or leases. If none, so stated.
10. Financing Arrangements—information about what financing assistance (partial or full financing, assistance with application for third-party financing) is offered and the terms of such assistance. If none, so stated.
11. Obligations of Franchisor; Other Supervision, Assistance or Services—details of the provision, supervision, service, and assistance obligations of the franchisor and when those obligations must be met. If none, so stated.
12. Exclusive Area or Territory—information about territorial (geographical area) and sales restrictions, including details about any option for sub-franchise.
13. Trademarks, Service Marks, Trade Names, Logotypes, and Commercial Symbols—a detail of any particular formats that must be used in business operations. If none, so stated.
14. Patents and Copyrights—details of patents and copyrights that pertain to the offering and are owned by the company, and how they affect the franchisee. If none, so stated.
15. Obligation of the Franchisee to Participate in the Actual Operation of the Franchise Business—details about the personal participation obligations and staffing obligations of the franchisee.

16. Restrictions on Goods and Services Offered by Franchisee—details of limitations on the products or services the franchisee may offer, either within the offered franchise or in outside business transactions (e.g., a second business).

17. Renewal, Termination, Repurchase, Modification, and Assignment of the Franchise Agreement and Related Information—details about rights, obligations, or restrictions in renewal, termination, repurchase, modification, or assignment of the franchise agreement.

18. Arrangements with Public Figures—details about current involvement of any public figure in the franchise system—whether a famous person's name or image is used in conjunction with the franchise, what that person's true involvement is, what benefits that person receives, and what, if any, investment that person has made in the business; details of any restrictions on the franchisee's right to use a public figure. If none, so stated.

19. Actual, Average, Projected, or Forecasted Franchise Sales, Profits, or Earnings—details about the franchise's actual or projected revenues. If not available, so stated.

20. Information Regarding Franchises of the Franchisor—a detail of the operational franchises that the franchisor has sold, including franchisee names and franchise locations; history of cancellations, terminations, refused renewals, or re-acquisitions; details about additional franchises to be offered, including location and number of offerings in each location. If none, so stated.

21. Franchisor's Financial Statements—audited financial statements, usually for the prior three fiscal years, should be attached. Statement of attachment is to be included in the UFOC.

22. Agreements—a detail of the documents that are included in the franchise, i.e., the franchise agreement and all related contracts and agreements.

The Franchise Agreement

The franchise agreement (contract), with all accompanying documents, must be delivered at least five business days before signature is required. It is the legal document that details the terms of the franchise purchase. This document, along with the accompanying documents, specifies the relationship between the franchisee and the franchisor. The entrepreneur should not sign such documents without

Illus. 20-4 A franchise agreement may include a list of tasks that must be completed prior to opening.

having an attorney review them. A typical franchise agreement may include the following[3]:

1. Grant of Franchise—general information about the nature of the franchise, a list of parties to the agreement, and details about any copyrights, patents, trademarks, etc., that are involved.
2. Exclusive Territory—statement regarding franchisor's right to operate or sell similar franchises within a specific territory. If none, so stated.
3. Term—specification of contract duration and renewal/termination requirements.
4. Development and Opening—list of tasks that must be completed prior to opening and time limits for completion; details regarding site selection and territory designation, site preparation, and, if the site is to be owned by the franchisor and leased to the franchisee, terms of the lease.
5. Payments—specific information about payments to be made to the franchisor, including franchise fees, continuing royalties, advertising fees, and interest penalties.

---

[3]Justis and Judd, *Franchising.*

6. Advertising—a detail of obligations, both franchisee's and franchisor's, related to advertising.
7. Trademarks—specifications regarding franchisee's use of symbols, logos, etc., and description of the process for franchisor's possible discontinuance of the use of any such marks.
8. Products, Supplies, and Equipment—specifications for franchisee's purchase and use of products, supplies, and equipment.
9. Standards and Procedures—detail of requirements that franchisee must meet in relation to management, personnel, personal participation, and insurance.
10. Training and Assistance—detail of obligations, both franchisee's and franchisor's, in relation to training required for successful operation of the business.
11. Business Conduct—detail of franchisee's responsibilities in business communications.
12. Reports and Inspections—a detail of the accounting documents and reports that the franchisee must provide to the franchisor, and at what intervals; details about the franchisee's and franchisor's rights concerning inspection.
13. Relationship of the Parties—specifics concerning the franchisee's relationship with the franchisor, limitations, and rights in transactions concerning the franchisor.
14. Assignment of Franchise—specifications for franchisee's right to transfer ownership of the franchise, and any obligations that must be met prior to such transfer.
15. Termination—detail of reasons for franchisor's termination of contract.
16. Rights and Obligations of the Parties Upon Termination or Expiration—detail of franchisee's responsibilities at termination of the contract.
17. Enforcement and Construction—specific information about enforcement and construction of the franchise agreement.

As you can see, the franchise agreement can be very long and complicated. All of the items must be included so that there is no misunderstanding between the franchisor and the franchisee.

QUESTIONS TO ASK

Entrepreneurs should ask several pertinent questions before they purchase a franchise. The final decision to purchase should not be made until these questions have been answered satisfactorily. These questions involve the franchise, the franchisor, the franchisee (entrepreneur), and the franchisee's market.

The Franchise

The following are questions that prospective franchisees should ask about the franchise in general.

1. Was the franchise agreement approved by a lawyer?
2. Are any of the requirements of the contract illegal in the area where business is to be conducted?
3. Will the franchisee receive an exclusive territory for the duration of the franchise term or can the franchisor sell additional franchises in the territory?
4. Is there a connection between the franchisor and any other franchise company dealing in similar merchandise or services?
5. If there is a connection between the franchisor and another franchise company, is the franchisee protected against competition from the second franchise company?
6. What is required if the franchisee wishes to cancel the contract?
7. Will the franchisee receive any payment for goodwill (customer loyalty) if the franchise is sold?[4]

The Franchisor

Prospective franchisees should ask these questions about the specific franchisor with which they are dealing.

1. How long has the company existed, and how long has the franchisor been in business?
2. Do other franchisees consider the franchisor honest and fair?
3. Has the franchisor shown the franchisee profit statements for several franchise locations? Have they been verified by the franchisee at each location?
4. Does the franchisor provide the following services?

   - credit
   - capital
   - management training
   - employee training
   - marketing and/or marketing assistance
   - merchandising assistance
   - site selection assistance

---

[4]*Franchise Opportunities Handbook,* U.S. Department of Commerce, Washington, D.C., 1982.

5. Is the franchisor on firm financial ground?
6. Is there an experienced management team from which the franchisee can seek advice?
7. What services or opportunities can the franchisor provide that the franchisee cannot obtain?
8. In what kind of detail has the franchisor investigated the franchisee and the franchisee's ability to run a profitable business?
9. Has the franchisor followed all state, federal, and local laws that govern the sale of franchises?

The Franchisee

Each prospective franchisee must determine the answers to these questions before he or she can make a decision about investing in a franchise.

1. How much money is required to open and run the business until it becomes profitable?
2. Does the value (monetary and/or psychological) of the franchise balance the loss of the freedom of being an independent business owner?
3. Does the franchisee have what it takes to open the franchise and turn it into a profitable business?
4. What kind of commitment is the franchisee willing to make to the franchise? Is the franchisee willing to devote years to its success?

The Franchisee's Market

And, finally, prospective franchisees should consider these questions about the market and location of the franchise.

1. Has the franchisee conducted in-depth marketing research to determine that the franchise will be successful in the intended location?
2. What does marketing research indicate about potential future changes in the intended location?
3. What is the projected demand for the franchised product or service in the area surrounding the intended location?
4. What is the competitive environment for the franchised product or service?[5]

---

[5]*Franchise Opportunities Handbook,* U.S. Department of Commerce, Washington, D.C., 1982.

Illus. 20-5   The entrepreneur must analyze the competition for the franchised product or service.

JEFF BURNETT—ENTREPRENEUR

Very early in his planning process, Jeff had toyed with the idea of purchasing a franchise. He knew that there were several franchising opportunities in the retail music business. If he chose one, much of the business planning process he had gone through would have been done for him. Merchandise selection, pricing, interior decorating, and many other areas of planning would have been affected. He would still have had to plan, but not from scratch. The franchisor would have provided him with much of the needed information.

In deciding not to purchase a franchise, Jeff had asked himself several questions:

1. What could the franchisor do for Jeff that he couldn't do for himself? *Answer:* Nothing. Sure, the franchisor could make the business planning process easier, but Jeff could do it himself and probably learn a lot in the process.
2. Was he willing to give up some of the freedom of being an independent business owner? *Answer:* No. Freedom was one of the main reasons that Jeff had decided to start a business. He wasn't about to lose any part of that freedom.

3. Was the name recognition of a franchise important? *Answer:* Possibly, but Jeff felt that effective advertising and good customer service could do the same thing for Rock 'n' Soul.

No, franchising was not for Jeff Burnett. He figured the cost would be far too high for the benefits received. Besides, he liked his freedom; he wanted to run the new business in the manner that he chose.

Who knows? Someday Rock 'n' Soul might be so successful that he could start his own franchising operation. Wouldn't *that* be something?

SUMMARY

A person who wants to become an entrepreneur and own a small business may not know what particular business to choose or how to run a business. This person may want to consider a franchise. There are thousands of franchises from which entrepreneurs in the United States can choose. These businesses currently account for about one third of the U.S. retail economy.

The U.S. Department of Commerce defines franchising as a method of doing business in which a franchisee is granted the right to engage in offering, selling, or distributing goods or services under a marketing format that is designed by the franchisor. Franchising opportunities are available in many types of business.

Advantages and disadvantages of purchasing a franchise should be evaluated carefully before a decision to purchase is made. An entrepreneur should not sign a franchise agreement without the advice of a competent attorney. Only an attorney can properly analyze the legal documents that are required for a franchise arrangement, such as the disclosure document and the franchise agreement.

The Federal Trade Commission requires that a franchisor disclose certain specified information to a prospective franchisee, in writing, at least ten business days prior to any legal commitment to purchase. The franchise agreement, with all accompanying documents, must be delivered at least five business days before signature is required. Several pertinent questions should be asked and answered before the entrepreneur purchases a franchise. These questions involve the franchise, the franchisor, the franchisee (entrepreneur), and the franchisee's market.

VOCABULARY BUILDER

Write a brief description of each word or phrase based on your reading of the chapter.

1. Franchise
2. Franchising
3. Franchisee
4. Franchisor
5. Royalty
6. Franchise broker

REVIEW QUESTIONS

1. What are two descriptive phrases for franchising? What information do they provide?
2. What U.S. Department of Commerce publication contains information about franchise opportunities, costs, capital requirements, and number of franchises already operating?
3. What are four advantages of franchising?
4. What are four disadvantages of franchising?

DISCUSSION QUESTIONS

1. What are royalties? What effect do they have on business profits?
2. What is the Uniform Franchise Offering Circular? Why is it important?
3. What is the purpose of the franchise agreement?
4. What are three of the questions entrepreneurs should ask about a franchisor before purchasing a franchise?
5. What are three of the questions you should ask yourself—a prospective franchisee—before purchasing a franchise?

CRITICAL THINKING

Chris, a 28-year-old, has worked as a clerical assistant at city hall for the past nine years. She recently inherited a considerable amount of money from her grandmother and is thinking about using the money to start her own business. She is considering the purchase of a motel franchise.

1. Is a franchise purchase a reasonable consideration for Chris?
2. Are there any special attributes Chris needs to look for in selecting a franchise?

SHORT CASE: CAREER DECISION

Joe Ramos is a third-generation Mexican-American who lives in a suburb of Chicago. He has worked for his uncle Paco in the restaurant business for 20 years. Uncle Paco's restaurant, "Casa del Mexico," is very successful.

When Joe began working for Uncle Paco, he bussed tables. Over the years he has successfully performed every job in the restaurant, including chef. Since Uncle Paco went into semi-retirement five years ago, Joe has managed the restaurant.

Joe has always been very happy working at Casa del Mexico. He figured that he would stay there until he retired. All that changed recently, however. Uncle Paco's oldest son, Luis, moved back from the West Coast and began working at the restaurant.

During the six months that Luis has been working with Joe in the restaurant, things have been changing. Joe is sure that it is just a matter of time before Uncle Paco makes his son manager of Casa del Mexico. Joe sees his career experiencing a serious setback when that happens.

Because of what is happening, Joe has decided that going into business for himself might be a good idea. Joe has always invested a portion of his earnings and he now has quite a nice nest egg. He plans to either purchase a franchise or open a small restaurant on his own.

Questions

1. Would you advise Joe to purchase a franchise or open a restaurant on his own? Why?
2. What should Joe consider as he decides which option is best for him? What questions should he ask?

PROJECT CHALLENGE

Choose a franchise, gather as much information as you can, and answer the questions that were presented in this chapter to decide if this franchise would be a viable option for you. Then answer the following questions.

1. What are the advantages and disadvantages of purchasing a franchise in your particular situation?
2. Is purchase of the franchise you chose a suitable option for you? Why or why not?
3. If purchase of this franchise is not a suitable option for you, might you consider the purchase of a different franchise? Why or why not?
4. Prepare a UFOC for an imaginary franchise. Be sure that it details provisions that you would want in a franchise contract.

The Future for Entrepreneurs

After mastering the information contained in this chapter, you should be able to:

21-1 Describe current trends in opportunities for entrepreneurs.

21-2 Explain ways of investigating international trade opportunities.

21-3 Describe the government agencies that assist small international businesses.

21-4 Describe ways that entrepreneurs are helping to conserve the environment through entrepreneurial pursuits.

balance of trade, the difference between the amount of goods and services a country imports and how much it exports

One thing that is for certain is that the world of entrepreneurship is constantly changing. As we learned in Chapter 1, part of the definition of an entrepreneur is an individual who senses the needs of the marketplace. The marketplace is constantly changing because the needs of our society are always changing. Entrepreneurs thrive on opportunities created through change. New technology creates opportunities, as do changes in economic conditions, politics, and people's life-styles. As the twenty-first century approaches, two areas of great opportunity for entrepreneurs have surfaced—international trade and environmental conservation.

INTERNATIONAL ENTREPRENEURS

Until recently, only large companies engaged in international trade. However, with the development of technology in the computer, communications, and transportation industries, opportunities have mushroomed for small businesses to engage in international trade. No longer are small businesses confined by our country's borders—they are now able to compete in the global market. Exciting opportunities exist for you if you are willing to take the time to learn the intricacies of trading goods and services with consumers or businesses from other countries.

Presently, only a small percentage of the more than 300,000 manufacturers in the United States export their products. The number is growing, however, particularly among small businesses. Of the companies that export, 37 percent have fewer than 500 employees, and 25 percent have fewer than 100. Due to the increasing internationalization of our economy and the slowdown of the growth of our population, exporting will continue to grow in the new century.

For too long the United States has endured a deficit, or shortage, in its **balance of trade** with other countries. When a country imports more goods than it exports, a trade deficit results. When a country has a trade deficit, its economy suffers. It does not have new employment opportunities for its citizens. Manufacturers in other countries hire their own citizens to manufacture goods and, thus, create jobs. In addition, the United States' trade deficit makes us more dependent on other countries for goods and services. To help balance the trade deficit, the United States government encourages small businesses to export goods by offering business assistance through the International Trade Administration (ITA) of the U.S. Department of Commerce.

International Trade Administration

The ITA acts as an information source for people interested in exploring international trade possibilities. There are 47 district offices and 21 branch offices throughout the United States. These offices receive information from U.S. Foreign Commercial Service offices that are located in 125 foreign countries. The types of information available through the ITA include the following:

- Growing and changing foreign markets
- Policies and product standards of various countries

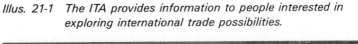

Illus. 21-1 The ITA provides information to people interested in exploring international trade possibilities.

Port of Tacoma

tariff, a fee imposed by a government on imported goods to protect the country's domestic industries from being undersold

- **Tariff** and non-tariff trade barrier laws and import regulations— As an example, to protect its automobile industry, the United States has increased tariffs and placed restrictions on the number of Japanese automobiles permitted to enter our country.
- Domestic and foreign competition
- Products and services that foreign markets are buying and what they seek that is in short supply
- Advertising media available in various foreign markets
- Distribution possibilities in foreign countries—This includes lists of possible wholesalers and retailers for particular industries and how to contact them.
- Sales trends and pricing information for specific products
- Assistance in providing credit checks and ratings on overseas companies, and opinions about their reliability and dependability
- Assistance in contacting foreign customers through seminars and trade shows—The ITA also helps arrange company visits for foreign visitors interested in exploring trade possibilities in the United States.

The Department of Commerce also publishes and distributes a number of publications to assist in the investigation of foreign market distribution. These publications are designed to inform market members of economic trends of foreign markets, foreign government procurement procedures, statistical data on various commodities traded throughout the world, and current trade regulations.

The Export-Import Bank of the United States

Another valuable resource to international entrepreneurs is the Export-Import Bank (Eximbank) of the United States. Eximbank is a government agency responsible for assisting the export of United States goods and services. Its primary role is to provide guaranteed loans to banks that, in turn, extend loans to United States exporters. It is particularly helpful to those who need short-term loans to complete a specific export order. Eximbank loans allow small businesses to obtain additional inventory, carry accounts receivable, and meet essential operating expenses. The agency is not a source, however, for start-up funds for new businesses. Small exporters can also seek financial assistance from foreign government banking agencies.

Tips for Getting Started As An Exporter

Entrepreneurs interested in exporting goods to foreign markets should consider the following steps. These steps apply whether an entrepreneur already owns a business or is interested in acquiring one.

1. Research the export potential of the company. Analyze the financial capabilities of the business, the industry trends, and the effect the decision to export will have on the domestic operations of the business.
2. Get professional advice. Contact the Department of Commerce, state development agencies, and any other expert resources to ask questions and obtain factual answers or sound advice from professionals with export experience.
3. Conduct thorough market research to find the one or two best markets for the company's products. Use the expert resources for assistance.
4. Develop an export strategy that is workable for the particular business. Set the objectives, plan marketing activities, and allocate the financial resources. Visit trade fairs and make contacts with foreign agents and representatives.
5. Decide how to sell the product or service. Will you sell directly or indirectly to your markets? If you choose a direct sales method, the company will sell its products or services through sales representatives, distributors, foreign retail outlets, or, in some cases, through government-controlled trading companies. If you choose the indirect sales method, the company will use commission agents, export management companies, or, perhaps, government-controlled buying agents.
6. Arrange financing through Eximbank or international banks.
7. Learn how payments are to be made from foreign buyers. The U.S. SBA publishes a booklet, "Market Overseas with U.S. Government Help," which will help with this step.

New Developments in International Trade

New markets are developing due to the tremendous political changes in Eastern Europe. The easing of trade barriers and restrictions in the states that were once the Soviet Union and the unification of Germany have resulted in a boom of sales to these countries, particularly in computers, telecommunications, energy-related equipment, chemicals, and medical equipment. Trade experts forecast continued growth of sales opportunities to these markets.

Sales to western European countries, already the biggest market in the world for American-made products, are also expected to continue to grow as restrictions decrease on the movement of goods and services due to the formation of the new Common Market in 1992.

Opportunities have developed in the Middle East due to the Gulf War in Iraq. Construction materials to rebuild from war damage are in great demand.

Japanese businesses will continue to be highly competitive with American exporters. American manufacturers will have to continue to emphasize higher quality to their workers and their customers to compete with efficient Japanese manufacturers.

International entrepreneurs must stay current with events in the global marketplace. They must expect the unexpected and be ready to adapt to change. The failed Russian coup in August 1991 is an example of how the political and economic climate of a country can change quickly. If the coup had been successful, the economic gains and trading conditions would have had a dramatic reversal. On one hand, the volatility of the market increases the risk factor. On the other hand, the unlimited growth potential increases the profit potential. The decision to enter the international market is one to make only after thorough analysis of all factors.

Illus. 21-2   Japanese business owners will continue to be highly competitive with American exporters.

Ben Simmons/The Stock Market

ENVIRONMENTAL ENTREPRENEURS

The past decade has brought great attention to the environmental dangers the world is facing. Earth Day celebrations, environmental awareness organizations, and the media have helped educate us about the plight of our planet.

The desire to do something about improving the world in which we live has also brought opportunities to entrepreneurs. The public will continue to be concerned with environmental issues, and many entrepreneurs are finding ways to help the environment *and* develop promising business opportunities. **Recycling** has become a household word and small businesses are leading the way in the recycling industry. The goal is to reduce the volume of trash we produce by, first, reducing the amount we use and, second, reusing whatever we can.

recycling, process of transforming used and obsolete goods into useable and saleable products

The product taking up the most space in our overloaded landfills is paper. Paper accounts for more than 40 percent of landfill waste. It is imperative that programs be put in place to collect and sort wastepaper for recycling at paper mills. The same is true for glass, aluminum cans, and plastic containers. Entrepreneurs are finding profitable ways to collect these waste products and get them to the proper locations for recycling.

You might consider starting a recycling business. Check with people in your neighborhood to find out what current method is being used to discard recyclable trash. If there is no program—or an inadequate one—in place, contact local households and offer to pick up their recyclables on a regular basis. Also, check with municipal and county agencies for assistance in getting started. Ask the residents to divide their recyclable items—paper, glass, aluminum, and plastics—into separate containers. Don't forget to contact businesses located nearby, such as laundromats, travel agencies, restaurants, insurance companies, gas stations, etc. Be creative! Think about what types of businesses generate a lot of pop cans, excess paper, or glass bottles. Often they are willing to pay a nominal fee for this pick-up service.

After you determine a method to do the pick up, return all recyclables to a central point, possibly your garage. When you have accumulated a sufficient amount of recyclables, call a recycling cartage service to arrange a pick-up or drop-off plan. The recycling cartage company will pay you by the pound for the items you collect. Whether your success is modest or great, you will be earning money and, at the same time, helping to save our environment!

Illus. 21-3   Paper takes up the most space in our overloaded landfills.

Peter Morgan/Picture Group

Many entrepreneurs are acting as the resources that convert waste into marketable products. For example, paper shredders can be used to convert trash paper into saleable confetti. The same shredded paper can also be used as packaging materials for shipping purposes. Another idea is recycling used furniture by refinishing it into like-new furniture. Many printers are printing on recycled paper. Other examples include entrepreneurs who assist in the removal of hazardous waste, and retail stores and franchises that sell recyclable paper products, furniture made of recycled materials, and wildlife-protection products.

Entering the recycling market requires researching subject matter through periodicals and government publications. You might pick up copies of *Inc.* or *Venture* magazines at a public library, or contact the Environmental Protection Agency. Other environmental groups support environmental efforts also. Groups such as the Sierra Club or the Nature Conservancy can provide information on many topics. These groups may have local chapters near you. Because many consumers are actively searching for companies that are environmentally sensitive and are refusing to deal with businesses that are not, there are a great many opportunities available to entrepreneurs.

OTHER SMALL BUSINESS TRENDS

Our increasingly fast-paced life-styles have opened up more opportunities for entrepreneurs in service areas than ever before. Although the retailing sector offers opportunities, particularly in specialized areas, service industries have out-performed retailing for small businesses in recent years. A recent survey by *Entrepreneur* magazine (see Table 21-1)

Table 21-1

The 25 Fastest Growing Franchises	
Name of Franchise	**Type of Product or Service**
1. Subway	submarine sandwiches
2. Jani-King	commercial cleaning
3. Coverall North America, Inc.	commercial cleaning
4. Intelligent Electronics Inc.	computer-related products and services
5. Chem-Dry	carpet, upholstery, and drapery cleaning and dyeing
6. Little Caesars Pizza	pizza
7. Mail Boxes Etc. USA	packing, mailing, and shipping services
8. Jazzercise Inc.	fitness centers
9. Choice Hotels & Motels International	hotels and motels
10. Hardee's	miscellaneous fast foods
11. Electronic Realty Associates	real estate services
12. Heel/Sew Quick	shoe repair
13. Sport It	sports equipment
14. Nutri-System	diet and weight control centers
15. Worldwide Refinishing Systems, Inc.	porcelain and marble restoration
16. Arby's, Inc.	miscellaneous fast foods
17. ServiceMaster	commercial cleaning
18. Decorating Den	miscellaneous decorative products and services
19. Days Inns of America Franchising, Inc.	hotels and motels
20. ABC Seamless, Inc.	siding
21. Help U-Sell Real Estate	real estate services
22. Handle with Care Packaging Store	packing, mailing, and shipping services
23. Jackson Hewitt Tax Service	income tax services
24. I Can't Believe It's Yogurt	frozen yogurt
25. Floor Coverings International	floor and wall coverings

Source: Based on a survey conducted by *Entrepreneur,* as printed in January 1991, page 202.

points out the dramatic growth of service-related franchises. This growth parallels trends in the rest of the retail economy.

As the survey shows, seventeen of the twenty-five fastest growing franchises are service companies. Service companies are very dependent on the abilities and talents of the owner, therefore they often appeal to very ambitious entrepreneurs. They are talent driven as opposed to investment driven. The service industries will continue to grow as our population becomes older, and as two-income families continue to be the norm. Many people do not have the time they once had to do activities unrelated to work. As a result, there are more fast-food restaurants, child care centers, and other services to assist us than ever before.

YOU AS AN ENTREPRENEUR

Do you think that someday you might wish to be an entrepreneur? Certainly the opportunities will always be there, if you so choose. As you have learned, it is important to thoroughly analyze your goals and determine a business environment that is right for you. Entrepreneurship starts with the desire and proceeds to the writing of a plan. The plan addresses market needs, competition, marketing strategy, and the financial plan. Important decisions must be made about the organization structure, management methods, and legal considerations. Successful entrepreneurs are risk-takers, but only after carefully researching and collecting information. It can be an exciting life-style and is always filled with challenges. Many entrepreneurs come from corporate employment and use what they have learned from their jobs to create successful enterprises. These business creators make an important contribution to the economy of our society. We are fortunate to live in a country that allows us to reach for our dreams.

JEFF BURNETT—ENTREPRENEUR

Rock 'n' Soul opened to great success. Jeff had followed his plan carefully and was enjoying his new business immensely. However, being responsible for a business was not always easy, and he *always* faced challenges of one sort or another. However, he certainly enjoys his work and feels proud of his store. He is providing jobs for the people in his community and his products are in demand. Jeff knows that if he works hard, someday he will be able to make great profits.

He still seeks advice from assistance services because he knows the importance of staying on top of the needs of the market-place. In the future he would like to expand his business and maybe open up additional stores. When he does, he will go back to the drawing board and write a new business plan and do additional market research. Owning a business is a never-ending job, but he feels a great sense of accomplishment with each goal that he achieves.

Jeff is helping others get started in business by volunteering, on a part-time basis, as a small business counselor for the local SBDC. It is exciting to see others explore available opportunities. He points out to his SBDC clients the importance of studying the needs of America's changing markets. Many of the clients are interested in opening service businesses. Some want to learn more about international trade opportunities; they are aware of the many emerging opportunities in the global marketplace. Others seek to learn ways that they can help conserve natural resources and at the same time operate a business. Jeff instructs his clients, "Don't be afraid to ask questions. Take the time to learn before starting a business."

SUMMARY

Entrepreneurs have found exciting opportunities to pursue in international trade and environmental businesses. The international marketplace is now open to small business owners who take the time to learn its intricacies. There are government agencies such as the International Trade Administration and the Export-Import Bank that assist small manufacturers in learning to export products. Recent changes, such as those in the eastern European and Soviet political systems, along with communication technology, offer exciting opportunities for the small business exporter or importer.

The rising consciousness of America in regard to our threatened environment has created opportunities for entrepreneurs, particularly in the recycling industry. Many opportunities have also been created by consumers' increasing demand for services of all types. It is quite evident that the future holds exciting prospects for entrepreneurs who take the time to learn the markets and properly plan their business activities.

VOCABULARY BUILDER

On a separate sheet of paper, write a description of each word or phrase based on your reading of the chapter.

1. Balance of trade
2. International Trade Administration
3. Tariffs
4. Export-Import Bank
5. Recycling

REVIEW QUESTIONS

1. What four factors keep the marketplace constantly changing?
2. Why are small businesses now able to compete in the international market?
3. What is happening when a country has a trade deficit?
4. What information is available from the International Trade Administration?
5. How do tariffs protect a country's domestic industries?
6. What is the primary role of the Export-Import Bank?
7. What is the leading environmental industry for entrepreneurs?
8. What product accounts for more than 40 percent of landfill waste?
9. What is an example of an occupation an entrepreneur might develop to convert waste into a marketable product?
10. What commercial sector currently holds the most opportunities for entrepreneurs?

DISCUSSION QUESTIONS

1. Why should entrepreneurs investigate international trade opportunities?

2. What is the danger to a country's economy if it maintains a trade deficit?
3. What steps would you follow if you wanted to export a product?
4. What opportunities are available for entrepreneurs who have a growing concern for the environment?
5. Do you believe that service businesses will continue to be more in demand? Why?

CRITICAL THINKING

In the mid-1980s, the U.S. government imposed quotas and raised tariffs on Japanese automobile manufacturers who exported to the United States. Was this fair to the Japanese? Why was it necessary? Did it accomplish its purpose?

SHORT CASE: PICK UP AND RECYCLE

Linda Cowan was upset after watching a television documentary about America's dangerously full landfills. She decided it was time to get serious about recycling. She called city hall to inquire about recycling services available in the area. She learned that although there were some suggested methods for residents to follow, there was not a regular recycling pick-up service available, and only one recycling drop-off center existed in her city.

"Someone has to do a pick-up service," Linda thought, "and it might as well be me." This set her off on a series of activities that included getting referral support from municipal and county agencies, arranging a method of and schedule for residential pick-up service, and establishing a suitable financial agreement with the recycling process center. The center would pay her by the pound for aluminum, glass (clear, brown, and green), PETE and HDPE plastic, and newspaper.

Two months later, Linda was operating a thriving business. She had bought a used pick-up truck and was doing pick-up service for more than 200 homes. The customers were responsible for sorting glass, plastics, aluminum cans, and newspaper into separate containers. Linda would pick up the container and take them to a small warehouse space she had rented. She would further sort items and when sufficient weight had been collected, she would arrange for the recycling process center to pick up the bundles and pay her. She charged a small annual fee to her customers for her service. Business was so good she was considering adding another truck and hiring an employee to help. Someday maybe she would have her own processing center.

Questions

1. How was Linda acting as an entrepreneur?
2. Should Linda consider expanding her operation?

PROJECT CHALLENGE

The plans for your hypothetical business should be nearly complete. Consider the options listed below as you finalize your plan.

- How can you and the hypothetical business you are planning become involved with international trade, either as an exporter or an importer? Explain the considerations you must take into account.
- Consider and describe any environmental concerns that might relate to your business.
- Examine the future market for your product or service.

Complete your Project Challenge by writing down your personal conclusions about the possibility of someday starting your own business. Do you believe you are a future entrepreneur? What are your strengths and weaknesses?

GLOSSARY

absentee management   when a business owner oversees the business but is not present at the location

acceptance   an offer is agreed to by the receiving party

accountant   an individual trained in the methods and procedures used in assimilating and maintaining financial records

adverse possession   acquisition of another's land by occupation, without the owner's permission and without payment

advertising   paid nonpersonal public notice

anchor store   a store large and strong enough to attract customers by itself

Articles of Incorporation   an application asking the state for permission to form a corporation

autonomy anchor   trait that allows individuals to be satisfied by being free thinkers and individualists

bait and switch advertising   the practice of advertising a low-priced item as a means of luring customers into the store for the real purpose of selling them a higher priced item

balance of trade   the difference between the amount of goods and services a country imports and how much it exports

balance sheet   a financial statement that shows the worth or value of a business

barter   a sale involving only the exchange of goods; no money changes hands

bond   certificate that verifies a debt owed to an individual by a corporation or government agency

breach of contract   failure of a party to a contract to perform its obligation(s) as specified in the agreement

break-even point   the price at which the costs of producing and/or selling a product or service are covered

business broker   agent who brings business buyers and sellers together

business plan a written description of all steps necessary to ensure success in opening and operating a business

capacity ability to fully understand and comprehend the requirements of a contract as specified by law

capitalization obtaining the necessary capital assets needed to operate a business

career anchors essential satisfiers we wish to achieve from our work

cash flow how money comes in and goes out of a business operation in a specific period of time

casual seller a person who offers a good or goods for sale but is not in the business of selling

certificate of deposit certificate that shows evidence of money being held by a financial institution for a specified period of time bearing a specified interest rate

chain of command the reporting relationship of positions depicted on the organization chart

charter document that allows a new corporation to do business in that state

Clayton Act a follow-up to the Sherman Antitrust Act that further prohibits monopolies from forming and makes tying agreements illegal

commercial lease a signed legal agreement that specifies the terms (length of time, cost, conditions to be met) for use of a business property by someone other than its owner

community property property acquired during marriage

community shopping center shopping center large enough to provide convenience goods and shopping goods to several neighborhoods

competition a rivalry between companies that sell similar products or services

competitive analysis identifying and examining the characteristics of a competing firm

competitive impact competing effectively with other businesses

competitor an individual or business that sells the same products or services as another business and appeals to the same types of customers

consideration value given and value received as a result of contractual agreement

Consumer Product Safety Act law that protects the public from dangerous products by providing for the evaluation of product safety hazards

contract a promise or set of promises creating a legal duty of performance

convenience goods products that people purchase regularly

corporation a legal entity created by law

creativity anchor trait that allows individuals to derive satisfaction from coming up with unique ideas

current asset asset that is easily converted into cash

current liability liability that is to be paid within 12 months

customer an individual who has the means to satisfy his or her needs

customer profile a recorded and complete description of the ideal customer for a business

debt capital money loaned to a business with the stipulation that the original amount borrowed, plus interest, will be paid to the lender within a certain time period

deceptive advertising advertising that contains information that would cause the average consumer to be misled about a particular product or service

deed a written document by which an individual conveys title and other rights of ownership of real property to another individual

demographic study a study of the statistics for the population in the proposed market

Department of Development a state agency that works to advance economic growth and to encourage new and existing businesses to operate within the state

direct competition competition by businesses that derive the majority of their profits from the sale of products or services that are the same or similar to those sold by another business

earnings approach the method of determining the value of a business by calculating its potential profit and return on investment

easement a nonpossessory right to use land owned by another party

economic stability an economy's ability to withstand changes

economics the study of how the resources of a society are allocated

entrepreneurship the act of managing an individual's enterprise

entrepreneur an individual who is willing to take the risk of investing time and money in a business that has the potential to make a profit or incur a loss

Equal Credit Opportunity Act law that requires any business offering credit to make it available to all creditworthy customers regardless of race, national origin, marital status, religion, sex, age, or receipt of public assistance

equity capital   money invested in a business in return for a share in ownership and, therefore, in the profits of the business

ethnic ratio   the proportion of a particular ethnic group to total population

express warranty   a clearly stated fact about the quality or performance of a product

Fair Credit Billing Act   law enacted in an attempt to protect consumers against unfair and incorrect billing activities

Fair Credit Reporting Act   law that allows consumers access to their personal credit information

false advertising   advertising that contains information that is not true or would cause the average consumer to reach a false conclusion about a particular product or service

Federal Trade Commission   a regulatory agency that enforces and monitors fair competition and other business practices

financial plan   portion of the business plan that projects start-up costs, income, operating expenses, and cash flow

firm offer   a written, signed sales offer in which the merchant expresses the intention that it cannot be revoked

fixed asset   asset that normally takes a longer time to convert into cash

fixed cost   a cost that does not vary even though there are changes in production and/or sales volume

franchise   a right or privilege to conduct a particular business using a specified trade name

franchise broker   a person who obtains the right from a franchisor to sell franchises within a certain territory—the franchisee pays royalties to the franchise broker, who pays royalties to the franchisor

franchisee   the person who buys a franchise from a franchisor

franchising   method of doing business by which a franchisee is granted the right to engage in offering, selling, or distributing products or services under a specified marketing format

franchisor   the person or company that offers the franchise to others

gender ratio   the proportion of each gender to total population

general partner   a partner who actively engages in the day-to-day management of the business and is fully liable for any actions for, by, and against the business

goods   items of tangible personal property other than money

goodwill   the value of a business's image and community relations

government security certificate that bears evidence of money on deposit with a government agency

Hazardous Substances Labeling Act law stating that labels must warn consumers of the hazards of using products that may cause illness or death if improperly used

home-based business a business conducted from the owner's residence

home equity the difference between the appraised value of a house and the amount owed on it

hygiene factor a work environment characteristic needed to ensure job satisfaction

implied warranty a warranty imposed by law ensuring that a product will perform under normal use and circumstances

income statement financial report that shows a business's revenues collected and expenses paid out over a specified period of time

incubator a facility that houses a number of small businesses, usually fewer than ten, which share certain operating expenses

indirect competition by businesses that derive only a small percentage of their profits from the sale of products or services that are the same or similar to those sold by another business

industrial park a section of land allocated for use by industrial businesses

inventory the number of units and the value of the units a business has available for sale or manufacture

inventory turnover the number of times a business sells the amount of its base inventory in a year

investor a financial source that provides capital in return for partial ownership of the business

joint tenancy ownership by more than one person, with rights of survivorship

leasehold improvement the fix-up performed on a store or business to appeal to its customers

lessee the person who promises to pay a specified sum of money for the use of space

lessor the person who allows someone to use his or her property under certain terms

limited partner a partner who does not actively engage in the day-to-day management of the business and has liability limited to the extent of his or her investment in the business

line and staff organization an organization that has staff positions to assist the line functions

line organization an organization in which all members are involved in performing duties directly related to creating and/or selling products or services

liquidation value the value of assets if liquidated or sold immediately

long-term liability debt that becomes due after 12 months, usually associated with the purchase of fixed assets

Magnuson-Moss Warranty Act law that sets standards for companies that offer written express warranties on consumer products

mall an enclosed shopping center with a controlled climate

management by objectives a management technique that clearly states the goals of the business and meshes them with the goals of the employees

managerial anchor trait that allows individuals to be satisfied by working with and through people and by assuming many duties and responsibilities

markdown the difference between the original selling price and the price at which an item is actually sold

market a group of consumers who have an unsatisfied need for a particular product or service

market potential total potential sales dollars for a particular market

market research systematic gathering, recording, and analyzing of information concerning the market for goods and services

market segmentation process of dividing the market into groups of similar consumers

market share the portion of a particular market that uses a particular product or service

market value the value of similar goods, homes, properties, businesses, etc., in similar markets

marketing concept the belief that consumer wants and needs are the driving force behind any product development or marketing effort

marketing mix four variables—product, place, price, and promotion—that must be manipulated to ensure success in marketing

marketing plan defines and quantifies consumers, demand, competition, geographic market, and pricing policy for a specific small business

marketing research the systematic gathering, recording, and analyzing of data relating to the marketing of goods or services

marketing strategy planned activity designed to increase the sale of a business's products or services

markup amount added to the cost of an item to arrive at a selling price

maturity date the predetermined time that a bond becomes payable to the bondholder

merchant association an organization of merchants who work together to promote shopping at their shopping area

monopoly a business agreement whereby a single company controls a specific supply of products or services

motivator a work environment factor that provides workers with satisfaction and motivation

neighborhood shopping center small shopping centers, usually with fewer than 20 stores, that serve their immediate neighborhoods

offer communication of a proposal

open to buy money that is available for the purchase of inventory

organization chart illustration of an organization's distribution of its human resources

partners individuals who voluntarily agree to conduct a partnership

partnership a voluntary association of two or more persons to carry on as co-owners of a business for profit

partnership agreement the official document forming the contract between partners

per capita income average amount of money made or received, per person, on an annual basis

periodic tenancy lease for a set period of time, which will continue for similar periods of time until terminated

perpetual inventory an approximate written record of the amount of inventory available

personal selling face-to-face communication between the buyer and the seller

physical inventory an actual count of all inventory on hand

price discrimination charging different prices to different customers for the same goods

price fixing the agreement between competitors to establish and maintain prices of their goods and services

primary data   information collected for the first time for a specific project

prime rate of interest   the publicly stated rate that major commercial banks charge their most creditworthy business customers for short-term loans

pro forma financial statement   projected statistical report used to illustrate the expected financial status of a business at a future date

profit margin   the difference between what the seller and the consumer pay for a product

promoter   a person who starts the process to create a corporation

property   something that is owned or can be owned

psychographics   psychological variables (personality, attitude, beliefs, self-concept) and life-style values

publicity   advertising that does not incur cost to a seller

recycling   process of transforming used and obsolete goods into useable and saleable products

regional shopping center   shopping center that usually has three or four anchor stores and more than 40 other stores

replacement value   the cost of purchasing new assets at current market value

retained earnings   profits that remain in a business for future use

return on investment   the payback of the money invested in a business operation

risk of loss   the financial responsibility assumed by a party in a sales contract for damaged or destroyed goods

Robinson-Patman Act   adds to the Clayton Act by outlawing price discrimination

royalty   an ongoing fee paid to a franchisor at specific intervals—usually a percent of gross revenue or net sales

sale   the immediate transfer of ownership of goods for a price

sale on approval   a sales transaction in which the buyer has a right to approve the merchandise prior to the transfer of ownership

sales approach   the part of the selling process that is intended to attract the potential buyer's attention and stimulate interest

sales close   the part of the selling process that requests an action, such as an order or purchase

sales plan   any planned attempt to stimulate a potential customer's attention, interest, and desire

sales presentation   the part of the selling process that emphasizes the features, advantages, and benefits of a product or service

sales promotion   increasing consumer interest in or awareness of the business by advertising and/or offering incentives

secondary data   information already published and available

security anchor   trait that allows individuals to be satisfied by working in a large organization with the assurance of long-term employment

seller   a person who offers a good or goods for sale

Service Corps of Retired Executives   a counseling service—staffed by volunteers who have business experience—for new and established small business owners

Sherman Antitrust Act   makes any business deal illegal that unreasonably restricts trade or commerce among states, and outlaws price fixing

shopping goods   products that people purchase occasionally

Small Business Administration   a federal agency created to assist the development of the country's small business sector

Small Business Development Center   an agency funded by both the federal government and state governments to provide counseling and training for small business owners

sole proprietorship   a business established, owned, and controlled by a single person

specialty goods   products that people purchase infrequently

staffing   the recruitment and selection of employees

stand-alone store   a store that is not located in a shopping area

stock   certificate representing ownership in a corporation

super regional shopping center   a colossal shopping mall made up of many anchor stores and sometimes hundreds of smaller stores

target marketing   marketing to a selected group of consumers

tariff   a fee imposed by a government on imported goods to protect the country's domestic industries from being undersold

technical anchor   trait that allows individuals to derive satisfaction from doing a specific job correctly

tenancy at sufferance   lease in which a tenant may remain in the facility after termination of the lease

tenancy at will   possession of real property without benefit of an agreement that documents terms

tenancy by entirety   ownership by husband and wife, with rights of survivorship

tenancy for years   lease for a fixed period of time

tenancy in common   ownership by more than one person, without rights of survivorship

Theory X manager   a manager who directs with little consideration for human relations

Theory Y manager   a manager who is very concerned with human relations

total pricing concept   prices are set to compete successfully, build good customer relations, and ensure the long-term success of a business

trade credit   a type of financing that allows delayed payment for merchandise

tying agreements   the practice of a seller requiring a customer to buy one type of product in order to be permitted to buy another type

undercapitalize   failure of a business owner to obtain the needed resources to meet operating expenses in early stages of business

Uniform Commercial Code   a group of uniform business rules adopted by most states

utility satisfaction   using one's money (utility) for the product or service that will bring the greatest need satisfaction

VANE   acronym for values, attitudes, needs, expectations

variable cost   a cost that fluctuates with changes in production and/or sales volume

venture capitalist   an investor who specializes in funding business proposals that are not acceptable by banks

visual merchandising   creative display of merchandise for attracting customer's attention and creating a desire to purchase

whole life insurance   an investment that yields cash value from premium payments that are invested

INDEX